THE SONS OF SUMMER

MICHAEL DAULT

Christopher
Matthews
Publishing

The Sons of Summer

© 2018 by Michael Dault

Editor: Jeremy Soldevilla
Cover design: MJC Imageworks
Typeface: Georgia

ISBN 978-1-945146-30-5
ebook ISBN 978-1-945146-31-2

Published by
CHRISTOPHER MATTHEWS PUBLISHING
http://christophermatthewspub.com
Oregon

Printed in the United States of America

Acknowledgments

For all the struggle trying to tell this story on a public platform, I have never lost sight of the people who have supported me through this rigorous and humbling process.

First and foremost, my grandmother, Margaret Thiem. She was there in the beginning when I woke up in the wee hours of the morning with an idea for a story that I couldn't get out of my head. She always believed in me and two weeks before she passed she expressed how she couldn't wait to see it. At the time I was trying to make it into a feature film. Regardless of the platform, she was and always will be my biggest fan.

Second, and maybe most important to the process of things, I'd like to thank one of my closest friends, Kenyon Kemnitz. When this story was just a screenplay, he was my proofreader and script doctor. We'd stay up all hours of the night going over every word, every detail. The moment I decided to turn it into a book, Kenyon never batted an eyelash and went right to work helping me edit, as he always did. He knew how much I wanted to tell this story and stuck by my side during the journey. The kind of loyalty he has is hard to find these days.

Of course, I'd like to acknowledge my sister and my two younger brothers, but also my parents. Thank you, Dad. Long ago, when I was just a child, he told me, "You don't come from privilege, so you have to fight for every opportunity. You have to want it more than anyone. The best work the hardest." Now, he was referring to baseball at the time, as I had dreams of becoming a professional like many kids do, but I'd like to think his words had a broader meaning somehow.

Every lesson that man taught his children, I think I took it most to heart. Growing up my father's word was God, and to this day that has never changed. The central father character in this book is based on him. He is the soul of him. My father is the epitome of a man's man. He's strong in so many ways and has a heart of gold. His passion for everything in life is contagious. And though he won't admit it, I believe my creative side came from him.

My mother—the silent leader of the family. Thank you for all that you've shown me. Her grit is measured in fortitude; her business mind is sharp as glass. She's the reason I strive for more and am not afraid to fail. In her past, she has laid it all on the line and seen her accomplishments devastatingly crushed, yet somehow relentlessly picked herself up and kept going, kept fighting, kept doing whatever necessary to keep her family afloat. She's the biggest risk-taker I know, and with my father, they cannot be broken. They are a team for the ages, my parents.

And finally, for all those who challenged me—good or bad—thank you.

Table of Contents

Prologue... 6

Chapter 1 — Summer of '74 10

Chapter 2 — Summer of '90 19

Chapter 3 — Summer of '97.. 24

Chapter 4 — Summer of '03...58

Chapter 5 — Summer of '05.. 106

Chapter 6 — Winter of '05 152

Chapter 7 — Summer of '06...178

Chapter 8 — Fall of '06 239

Epilogue.. 242

PROLOGUE

NONE OF US DALTON MEN saw eye to eye much. In fact, most of our lives we were in constant competition in one way or another. Didn't matter what. We were stubborn bastards. There was one thing we did agree on, though. One thing that always brought us together, even when times weren't so great. Baseball. It wasn't as simple as a game of catch between a father and his son to us. No. No, it meant much more than that. It was just a game, yes, but the unforgiving nature that makes you truly earn every reward, a team's battle, the choreography of it all; and there was always, *always* a winner and a loser. Yeah, that was living to us. There was nothing quite like it. To us, anybody that stepped foot on a field had to play the game right or they had no business being there to begin with.

Although we loved Major League Baseball, there was always great debate in our household of how the league was more business than play, which in turn generated a slower pace to itself. We always wondered what happened. The older we got we didn't care. Regardless of the league's evolution, it was still the game no matter what happened in that league. Besides, we had our own league to brag about. A league that broke all the rules and still succeeded. Reminiscent of old school baseball, it had more personality and flair than anything most had seen. Our league's success lasted for 91 years, in fact.

Publicity nor millions of dollars didn't keep it going. Instead, it took the heart of hard-working, blue-collar towns to keep it alive for as long as they did. The thought was that promoting the league would certainly lead to its demise. In that part of the country, the great game lived on without any disturbances from outside influence. Our league was the one thing untouched by Major League Baseball branding. And so it remained a precious little secret of the Midwest, first being called the Town Ball League, then just the Summer League.

Barrix, Kenmore, and Irons were three counties that formed it back in 1915 as a sort of company recreational program for iron ore miners. Those men of rocks worked rigorous eight-to-twelve hour days, five to six days a week. Much like the rest of America in the early 1900s, baseball grew wildly popular. So as the game evolved, so did the league.

The sort of game played was significantly different. It was played more passionately, faster and strikingly aggressive; and the crowds were livelier and rowdier than any other of its kind. There were rules in place to make sure that games moved along at a quicker pace: 12-second rule in-between pitches, batters had to stay in the box the entire time as soon as they entered, no intentional walks, limited pickoff attempts per inning, there was a two-and-a-half-minute inning break/pitcher change clock and there were time-out limits. These were the sort of rules that helped turn the Summer League into a rough and scrambling brand of baseball where hitters, pitchers and fielders were always moving, always going. Decisions were made on the fly.

There were no unions, and players received wages like any other job. As the league grew, so did its take. The better a player was, the more they would be paid. The highest paid player in league history only ever made $60,000 a year. More often than not, players had to take on second jobs in the offseason to survive.

There were no trades, free agent signings or drafts. Before every season each town would conduct tryouts for potential players that lived within township zones. For example, if a potential player wanted to play for a different town but lived in a different township, then that player would have to live in that team's town. In the event they did move, they would then have to attend a tryout. If they were already playing in the league, the player would have to be accepted by the town's team by a majority vote from coaches, players, and boosters.

Dress codes were simple. No accessories. Which meant no jewelry—that included earrings, chains, rings, etc. Each player would have to represent his town/team in a respectable manner. Going all the way back to the 1930s, the league incorporated the three-strike rule. If a player ended up being penalized three times for misrepresentation conduct, which included game conduct, he was blacklisted from the league forever. This happened only twice in the league's past.

The use of performance enhancing drugs carried a one strike policy. Players were randomly tested before and during the season. If a player tested positive for P.E.D's, he was banned from ever playing or being affiliated—in any fashion—from the Summer League again. Only one player has ever tested positive for P.E.D's.

Specifically, in my hometown of Rupland, which was a pioneer town of Barrix County, its history dated back to the nineteenth century, where the Rupland Iron Company founded it in 1883. Owned by brothers Arnold and Tyrus Rupland, the company was an iron and steel producer originally based out of Minnesota. The region was rich with iron-ore minerals, which took on many bids from producers before the Rupland Iron Company won and eventually hammered their stakes into the fruitful land. Towns were then established and branched throughout the three counties of Barrix, Irons and Kenmore. Dixon, Hillsdale, Gamme, Crockerty, Clarkston, Ransville, Ippling, Ellison, Holton, Iron Lake, Delta, and Rupland flourished for decades in a growing economy that brought families from different parts of the country and the world to the Middle American heartland. That part of the nation signified the American dream and what it meant to be proud of where you came from.

At its peak, the vast Rupland Iron range, which extended across the three counties, provided thousands of jobs. The quarry in Rupland was a one-by-two-and-a-half-mile footprint with depths up to 600 feet. China's growing demand for iron, along with the falling value of the U.S. dollar versus other world currencies had made the Rupland Mine the most profitable.

No one cared about that though. When entering downtown Rupland, it wouldn't take long to notice that mining wasn't even the locals' passion. And some would even argue its livelihood. It was baseball. Filled with the ghosts of the players and moments that had gone before, the elders there passed on ingrained stories of the league and the legends that acted as a Hall of Fame of sorts. Of course, there was the great Dom Brickey of Hillsdale and even the hitting machine Sammy Mercer of Crockerty. But if someone wanted to know about Rupland's greats, they would have to start with two legends that graced their field and made them relevant.

The first was Oren P. Rollins, a dominating pitcher of the 1930s. As word carried of his brilliance on the mound, the bigs came knocking one day. He ended up pitching two seasons for the Chicago Cubs before duty called and he enlisted in the Navy in 1941. Rupland's local ball field took on his name shortly after he was killed in action.

The second great was a charismatic shortstop by the name of Mikey Prevo. Mikey was the essential star for the town in the 1960s. Legend has it he once hit a ball so far during a regular season game that it was found in a dairy farmer's field the next town over. What was even more fascinating was that he was an idolized, respected black man in a working class community during that decade of the historic civil rights movements.

From May through August, baseball took precedence in the counties and would produce some of the greatest games people had ever seen. Each town's team had a twenty-eight game regular season schedule. There were four teams in each of the three county divisions:

BARRIX COUNTY	KENMORE COUNTY	IRONS COUNTY
Gamme Grays	Clarkston Black Sox	Hillsdale Wolves
Crockerty Crowns	Holton Bolts	Iron Lake Stars
Rupland Hawks	Ransville Reds	Delta Ottawas
Ellison Legends	Dixon Vikings	Ippling Miners

Playoffs consisted of three division winners and five wild card teams that had the next best seasonal records. After an eight-team, three-round, single elimination playoff one was crowned champion on August 31st. This was pure baseball royalty. Especially in Rupland, little boys dreamed of one day donning the orange and black colors of their beloved idols and becoming, what was always the team's mascot, a Hawk.

Watching a ball in flight or a pitcher battle against a hitter or the sheer timeless voice it maintains that makes you notice it is poetry. Nothing was more comforting to us Dalton men than that damn game. Every time we played, we were more boy than man. The child's game seduced us. Hell, maybe that was the problem.

Chapter 1 — Summer of '74

"It ain't over 'til it's over."
—Yogi Berra

Dear James,

With every passing day, the more excited I become. It means I'm that much closer to seeing you again. I always thought it was sort of corny when my girlfriends would dote about their boyfriends being the last thing they think of before they drift off to sleep or how they are the first thing they think of when they wake up in the morning. But I'm starting to come around to the idea now.

When I think of you, the feeling in my stomach can't go away, James. Especially when I pass by your family's house on the way to bible study. Last week my father caught me staring at the house. He has since chosen a different route to our church out of spite. He even said I'm far too young to be concerned with love or learn what it even is for that matter. These are the words from the great Pastor Moore himself. He knows how to lead his flock but doesn't have a clue about how women think—especially his two daughters. Don't think ill of him though hon, he's always done the best he could as a single parent. He's just overprotective. No matter how convincing he tries to be in steering me away from "that mischievous Catholic boy" as he likes to call you, the feeling I have in me says different.

It's so hard not seeing your face and touching you when I want. Who would've thought I'd miss your loud laughter or sitting in the stands watching your baseball games? I even miss watching them with you, if you'd believe it. The way you look at me, I miss most though. It's so hard, hon.

This will be the last letter I send you for a few weeks. My father screens the mail I receive now, so I have to find another address to correspond with you. No worries, I'll still be thinking of you, building the excitement of when you return from your tour. I'll still be here to accept your marriage proposal we've discussed before you left. I've been looking forward to it. My only worry, and I can see your eyes rolling now telling me not to worry, but my worry that you won't return plagues my mind frequently. Please, James, be safe and come home soon. I love you for all that you are, all that you have been and all you're yet to be.

XOXO, Sandy

A poorly bandaged, blood-covered hand places the crinkled letter in the front pocket of his jungle jacket, over his heart. The recipient of the letter is James Dalton, a dark- featured, brown-eyed, fresh-faced corporal with a short five-foot eight-inch frame.

The sun's blinding rays beam down on him and his platoon of twelve Marine soldiers, each banged up, burnt and bloody. Dressed in camouflage, with helmets strapped and guns at the ready, they march through Hell's heat in the overgrown jungles of Vietnam. Rags fill the hands of a few, with the lone use of wiping their blood, sweat and tears. A couple of soldiers limp. A few hold in grunts of pain from previous injuries sustained on the same day. Hours earlier, a Chinook helicopter crash left them stranded and three of their own dead. The blood from their wounds smear on the grass they trudge through. Every step is excruciating for these brooding twelve.

With a single-hand movement, a scar-faced, blonde-haired platoon leader brings his men to a halt alongside thick swampland. He is their lieutenant. The man is mildly eccentric but laid back as if he were a surfer or a California hippy of some kind. The swamp around them looks like something out of an acid trip, with twisted trees and exotic animal sounds. The lieutenant brings up his canteen from his side to pour water over his head and down his back. He rubs the week-old scruff along his war-weathered face, buying time before having to face his down and out platoon. When he does, he sees the exhaustion on their faces, like a marathon runner running their last mile. He doesn't break face and keeps his scan. Trailing behind the platoon, a very tall, sunburnt albino Marine with radio equipment clung to his back tries to tune in a frequency for a distress call.

"Any luck?" the lieutenant asks him. The albino simply shakes his head. The lieutenant then calls out to one of his other men, "Dalton!"

James approaches from his flank.

"We're swimming in shit," the lieutenant tells him. "Radio is down. We're about twenty miles out into the boonies. How are we on supplies?"

"Enough to get us through the day, sir," James replies. "That's it. Rest went down with the bird."

The lieutenant looks back at his men re-bandaging their wounds and watering up. Damn near defeated, he remarks, " Well, hell, we ain't got twenty miles in us today."

"What do you want to do, sir?" James asks.

The lieutenant extends his hand to him for the map James has in his possession. The soldier digs in his pack and unfolds a map splattered with coffee stains and they survey it.

"Terrain up the Red River might be our best bet," the lieutenant says. "Could keep us hidden well in the night too, if we stick to the banks." He points to another part of the map. "By morning, we start back up. Until then, we conserve water and rations."

James agrees to his superior's devised plan with a slight nod and rises with him.

"Two minutes," James says to the platoon while checking them over in his stride down the line. "Drink your water, wrap your shit. If you run out of bandages, spit on it, rub some mud in it and move on. We'll camp by dusk."

The next morning, the platoon wakes early to walk as many miles as they can. They clear the brush and mud off themselves that provided camouflage during the night and begin their twenty-mile trek to base camp. Staggering their formation in case of any surprise attacks, they look like some swamp monsters invading the thick in their suits of mud.

An hour into the walk along the riverbanks, a thick, heavy rain slants down in monsoon sheets. The platoon carries on. The ground they walk upon begins to become a soupy mud. They're pushed further away from the banks, so not to lose any men to the fierce rising tide of the river. Their surroundings become forbidding. Visibility is minimal from the blinding wall of rain. All that is heard is the heavy pelting of the drops. There is a moment where the lieutenant thinks of waiting the storm out, but with minimal rations and the current health status of his men, he knows they must trudge on.

Two hours into their journey, they come to a clearing. The rain thins, and the sun shows itself. They peer out into a terraced paddy field to spot three Vietnamese farmers tending to the area. So not to risk being visible to any potential threats, they work their way around the field, continuing on into the thick vegetation. They make cat-like strides as swift as humanely possible. When they reach the east corner, their exit point, they come across a small nine-year-old boy pissing on a tree. They freeze in their tracks, so not to make the slightest sound to surprise the child. The boy pisses abnormally long, making each soldier look at each other wondering when the hell he'll finish. When he does, he turns around to shockingly see the twelve large silhouettes' eyes hovering around him in the shadows. The boy falls back, and James scoops him up quickly, wrapping his hand around his mouth. The boy's muffled screams aren't loud enough to draw any attention to this part of the field.

"Fuck, man," one heavily-bandaged Marine whispers. "What are we gonna do?"

The rest of the platoon worries about their situation and potentially blown cover.

"Okay, okay," the lieutenant whispers to his men. "We'll take him with us and free him when we're far enough out."

James turns the boy about-face, calming him with a non-threatening smile. "English?" he asks him. "Do you understand English?"

The boy doesn't respond. His fearful eyes are big and never blink. But James' reactions at least have relaxed him for the moment.

"*Hien!*" The boy's mother, one of the farmers, calls out from afar in the field.

"Shit . . . " the lieutenant says under his breath.

The boy's mother starts to work her way towards them in search of her son. "*Hien?! Den voi tôi.*"

The lieutenant signals his men to duck and work their way back further into the thick jungle. When the boy's mother inches closer, she catches a glimpse of a few trailing Marines in the brush. This immediately rattles her, and she begins to hop up and down screaming for her son. The rest of the farmers in the field lift their heads, taking notice of the panic. James darts a glance across the field at the tree line to see two Vietnamese men with semi-automatic rifles emerge. They are opposition forces. The Vietcong.

"Let's go! Let's go!" the lieutenant yells at his men.

James releases the boy, and he dashes into the arms of his mother. The platoon wastes no time attempting to flee from the area. The riflemen fire their weapons into the air to signal the others.

"Sir!" one of the Marines hollers from behind.

The lieutenant looks back at what the man spots and witnesses a group of five Charlies rushing towards their position, guns at their sides.

"We're fixing to get into a hell of a dog fight," the lieutenant calmly tells his men. "Prepare."

He positions his squad in various spots along the brush, then crouches into a kneeling position and fires the first shots from his Colt M-16. The opposition hastily takes cover and returns fire. James and four other Marines shoot at the men across the field, who disappear into the jungle. Oddly enough, no shots return. The farmers have since vanished as well.

The volley of gunfire between the groups lasts for ten minutes, before two Marines that kneel next to James take shots from behind from a rain of fire that mows through them like a dropped anchor through water. They're killed instantly. James spots even more Charlies coming directly at them. He can't distinguish how many but relays to his superior, "We got ten . . . maybe twelve coming at us, sir. I don't know."

In between shots, they repeatedly hear the Cong yelling commands amongst each other, "*Di di mau! Di di mau!*" and "*Dong o tren chung!*"

The platoon separates into two groups of five, back to back, to handle oppositions closing in from both sides. Gunfire hails upon them repeatedly. A few become heavily injured but continue to fight. Marines don't quit.

Undetected, James works his way through the tall grass to set a sniper point. From the scope of his bolt-action Remington M40A3, he spots and takes aim on one Charlie who's lurking from the rear. He fires a single shot into his skull and then reloads. Another drops, then another.

The fire-fight ensues for a while, with a Marine lost every five minutes or so. The Cong restock their numbers, drawing more and more in to close in on the increasingly thinned platoon.

"I'm out!" a Marine yells, waving his empty shell cartridge.

"Me too!" another adds.

James and the lieutenant share what little ammunition they have to the ones lacking. The albino radio operator desperately tries to call for help, getting pings of broken communication, only to have his hopes crushed by signal drops and incomprehensible feedback. At one point, the lieutenant pushes the albino aside and grabs the radio to try himself, only to realize what his men already know—they're fucked.

Behind the lieutenant, James seems to have the best luck, picking off enemies left and right. So much luck, in fact, that he sees a possible retreat opportunity, and notifies his superior, "Sir, they're pretty thin on my side! We could fall back and cut across the edge of the field!"

The lieutenant has a Marine take his position in the line of defense, then joins James to see what he's talking about. The white in his eyes widen through his men's blood that's been caked on his face. "There it is," he says to himself, seeing some light to their hopeless situation. "How many we got?" he asks.

Again, James looks through his scope, finger pressed gently on the trigger. "Three. I-I'm seeing some . . ."

POW!

He shoots and racks his rifle. "Make that two, sir."

The lieutenant slaps James' helmet proudly and moves back towards his position, where he's shocked to find the Marine who took his place had his head blown clean off from his eyes up. His brains hang from his head like jelly.

"We're going to fall back!" the lieutenant barks to the men left.

They begin to fall back, each giving cover fire to both sides. James won't break eye contact from two meandering Charlies. Unfortunately, he can't get a clear enough shot.

Two more Marines drop before the platoon annihilates the remaining Charlies standing between them and glory. They run, run and run through the jungle until they can't feel their legs anymore. When they stop to catch their breath, the lieutenant notices he only has three men left standing out of the twelve he started with. Their breathing is deep and hard. They pass one canteen around. An odd sound draws their attention after a few seconds. It sounds like a tea kettle sifting.

"Hear that?" the albino radio operator asks.

Before they can even recognize the sound, a missile from a rocket-launcher whisks past their heads and explodes in a volcanic-like inferno against a few trees behind, torching their platoon's anchor. The engulfed Marine charges deeper into the jungle, burning alive.

When the platoon rises from the explosion that sent them to the ground, there are only three of them left. Their ears ring, drowning out the world around them. Muffled gunfire slowly begins to formulate in their dazed thought processes, and they flee once again. Fumbling to grip their weapons, their hands are slick with blood.

A covey of rockets streak past like comets in the sky, exploding and setting their formidable area ablaze. They're now moving targets running aimlessly through these mysterious inferno grounds. Each man leaps through the wall of fire in front of them, tumbling out of the jungle and into a large blast hole that's part of an empty, remote village.

Charred soldier remains are strung to large wooden posts throughout like decorations. It doesn't take long for the three to realize that this is still enemy territory. There is no escape in sight.

The Marines nurse the bullet and burn wounds that cover their bodies. They ache in pain. Each are serious, if not critical. Being the healthiest, with only a gunshot to his left shoulder and first-degree burns on his arms, James crawls on his stomach to check on the first Marine he can see—the albino radio operator. Wasting no time, he starts to treat the albino's wounds with what little he has left from his IFAK.

"Da . . . Dalton . . . " a shriveled voice calls out.

"Dalton . . . "

James spots the lieutenant's charred arm raise itself from the ground. His wounds bleed profusely, and he's clinging to whatever life he has left.

"Sir . . . " James responds.

"We're . . . not prisoners . . . " the lieutenant says. "We fear nothing . . . "

James nods, understanding. The burnt bodies that hang throughout the village are prizes to these savages. They don't take POW's here. Once more, fighting their way out seems as good an option as any at this point.

Static from the radio abruptly perks their ears. Someone is trying to talk to them from base. James crawls to the radio and speaks into the mic that still clings to the albino's back. A shot rings out from the jungle and hits the albino in the head. James rolls onto the lieutenant to shield him from any more unforeseen shots.

About ten Charlies emerge on the hole, surrounding it with various guns pointed at the last two Marines left. The enemies laugh and joke with each other, watching James and the lieutenant lie helplessly before them. James' heart is practically beating out of his chest. He doesn't want to die here. Hoping that this isn't the end, he raises his arms to surrender to the enemies, who continue to laugh and now spit and poke at them with their weapons.

"Fear nothing . . . " the lieutenant repeats to James.

In this moment that seems frozen in time, James glances over one of the enemy's shoulders. Light from the sun brightens past the enemy's shaggy hair and onto the Marine's face, rising ever so high from the dispersing gray clouds. The sun's warmth and light brings a calmness over him. A euphoric feeling takes control as if he were having an out-of-body experience. He watches the enemies pull the albino's body from the hole, then the lieutenant after a while. James wonders if his superior will be the first to die.

"Lord—" he says, looking to the sky, "there's been so much death today. Too much. Please, no more. I beg of you. I've got a girl back home that I love more than anything, Lord. I intend on marrying her. She makes me feel things I never knew I could. She knows what's best for me. And she's stronger than I ever could be . . . But I promise you one thing: if you let me live, I'll never take one thing for granted. If we have kids, we'll raise them right, and they'll do good things—great things. Please, I beg of you, let me live. Give me a chance to live the life I deserve. Please? . . . "

He begins to weep and says, "please" and "I promise," over and over again in his prayer. From the light over the shaggy-haired enemy's shoulder, a silhouette suddenly eclipses the sun, hovering. The silhouette is in the form of a USMC Bell H1-Huey Cobra helicopter. Bullets spray from the chopper, taking down many Charlies by the blast hole. Another fire-fight between it and the Cong intensely ensues.

Blood, bullets, and despair rip through the enemy village, killing anyone that stands. The shaggy-haired enemy watching his men die, steps into the hole to finish James.

"*Fuck bạn Mỹ lợn,*" the Cong says to him, as he brings the rifle to the Marine's head.

James takes a deep breath, dreading it's his last. A violent splatter of brain matter sprays his face from the enemy's head. The Cong crumbles dead into James' lap. Behind him, lying halfway in the hole on his belly, holding a smoking Glock, is the lieutenant. James breathes a sigh of relief.

"Fear nothing . . . " the lieutenant says one final time before he loses consciousness.

In the mess of bodies that litter the village below the chopper, James discovers he and his lieutenant are the only remaining soldiers still alive from the platoon. Pushing the dead enemy off him, James tries to stand but collapses to the ground. Exhaustion from running and his wounds keep him on his knees. He begins to crawl on his belly to help his superior. To his devastation, there is no pulse. The lieutenant has succumbed to his injuries.

A transport chopper behind the Huey Cobra lands in the middle of the village and a trio of medic soldiers rush to James' aid. As he's helped into it, he scans the carnage left in the village and tries to refrain from shedding any tears. He's the only survivor. Closing his eyes, he raises his head at the sun to take in the soothing warmth, and to thank who he believes saved him. God the Almighty.

CHAPTER 2 — SUMMER OF '90

"Ninety feet between bases is perhaps as close
as man has ever come to perfection."
—Red Smith

THE DAWN OF A NEW DAY breaks over the horizon, revealing a breathtaking countryside with rolling hills and a highway that seems to stretch forever. America's beauty at its best.

A gray 1989 Oldsmobile Silhouette with a family of five, travels down the lone road. The van is a rather small object compared to the vast country that surrounds it. "Up Around the Bend" by Creedence Clearwater Revival plays from inside its two opened front windows.

Now thirty-five, James Dalton is at the helm. It's been sixteen years since the war and ten years removed from being in the Marine Corps. Nowadays, he's a husband and a father as promised. His stocky frame is still solid but has added a small beer belly. His hands are absolutely huge, almost like Mickey Mouse gloves, from the harsh years of civilian life and welding work in the shipyards.

His wholesome beauty of a wife, Sandra, sits next to him. James calls her Sandy. She has long, dirty-blonde hair that rides down the middle of her back. Her features are soft, and she has freckles on her rosy cheeks that her husband claims resemble the Campbell Soup Kids.

Of the three children in the back of the van, two are asleep, each dressed the same, with colorful tank tops and matching shorts and sandals. Matching their outfits was something their mother did before they were old enough to complain about one brother copying the other. The one child awake is a five-year-old, dark-haired boy with brown eyes and a cluster of freckles that extend from one cheekbone across the bridge of his nose to the other side. He peers through the back passenger-side window, his excitable eyes fluttering at every scenic sight the van passes by. His name is Jack Dalton. Jack is full of energy and curiosity, and with curiosity comes questions only time will answer for the eldest son.

Seated next to Jack is his middle brother John. Much like Jack, he has dark features, but more so like their mother, he has rosy cheeks and Campbell Soup Kid features. The child holds a soft yellow baby blanket between his right thumb and index finger, rubbing it gently while he sleeps. It's during this age of two-years-old that the nickname Johnny would stick with him, after a favored-tune by the parents—"Johnnie B. Goode."

Tucked in the backseat by himself, baby Joe is sound asleep. He's much larger than most babies at three-months-old. Jack refers to him as a marshmallow due to the infant's chubby legs and arms.

The family rolls past a large, brightly-colored welcome sign that stands right at the county line. The sign is of a giant miner named Big Bo who stands 52 feet tall and weighs close to 16,000 pounds. Smack dab in the center above Big Bo's overalls and his pickaxe reads:

Welcome to Rupland
Land of Iron Ore and Baseball

Jack removes a small stack of Topps baseball cards he had tucked in his pants and flips through them. Boredom takes control after a time, and he projects towards the front, "Turn the station, Dad. I don't like your music."

James eyes him through his rearview, a smile hinted as he responds, "What's wrong with this? Everyone listened to this where I was from. Don't you know music, boy?"

Sandy scoffs with amusement.

James grins at her, "Oh, okay. I see how it is." He turns the station.

Sandy glances at her son, giving him a winning wink. She then runs her hand through her husband's thick, dark hair and comments that he needs to shave the month's stubble on his face. A boisterous, local Deejay is heard on his radio show, *This Week In Sports with Mel Grainger*:

"Hawks take another one last night, two-to-nil. Whatcha got on your mind, caller?"

"Mel, we've got something special going on this season," A high-pitch-voiced caller rambles with excitement. "Our boys are gonna ride the back of Hylman to the title. I can feel it!"

The family rides through downtown Rupland. In the distance, smoke stacks from the mine tower over their destination. A maple syrup smell that hangs in the air catches their attention almost immediately. The paper plant just west of town is the source of the smell. The smell awakens Johnny from his nap, just in time to see the sights. The downtown scene is quite busy, with a steady mix of locals and summer folk. The lakes that surround the area bring hundreds of families into town who have cottages on them. They even bring in many tourists looking to camp at the local campground for the weekend. Summer living is big business in this tight-knit community.

The van passes by these friendly locals that walk the sidewalks to window shop. Each stare at the newcomers a bit longer than most should, but it always ends with the same welcoming wave. They see children playing in the parks and running through the downtown streets on foot or riding on bikes. They spot quaint businesses, cute homes and traditional farming ways of life. Most buildings in and around downtown have fresh coats of paint, and their lawns are religiously mowed to a healthy trim. This seemingly perfect, tranquil community looks like something straight out of a Norman Rockwell painting. The Daltons fall in love. Its vintage, welcoming allure brings contagious smiles to all of them.

Jack's attention diverts towards a Little League field that's just outside the southern part of downtown. In the middle of the outfield, a county worker mows a stretch of grass. Beyond him, older children play in the infield. Jack's face lights up when seeing this, and he watches them until they aren't visible anymore.

The first stop in town for the family is to their newly-owned store. It's located at the end of a neighborhood street, across from a county workers garage filled with snow plows, backhoes, and mounds of sand and salt. The Little League field is just beyond the garage. Jack is already excited and figures he can easily walk there from the store in two minutes.

James climbs a ladder and hangs the American flag in front of the store so customers can notice the family's patriotic spirit the same time they notice the store's new lighted sign: Rupland Family Foods

Below the ladder and through the store's front windows, Sandy removes a *For Sale* sign. They give the space a once-over, realizing it is desperate for some tender love and care. They also find that coolers, shelves and freezers are some of the many things that are in need of an update. The 2,000 square foot store is quite the fixer-upper. The last time it was actually in use was nearly eight years ago when it was then a party store.

An elderly couple in their 70s ride up on vintage bicycles. James is the first to greet them. His once clean white T-shirt is now dirty with dust and gunk from cleaning the building. He wipes his hands on his shirt as the elderly woman asks, extending her hand, "Are you the new owners?"

"Word travels fast," James remarks, shaking hands with the two.

"Around here it does," the woman's husband says with a chuckle.

"We're so glad to see a grocery store finally open on this end of town," the woman comments. "I can just ride my bike here now instead of driving to the north side."

"We love to hear that, ma'am," James remarks.

"Do you have an opening date?" the man asks.

"A little over a month."

The couple "ooh" and "ah" as Jack and Johnny run from the store to join their father. Being the timidest one of the children, Johnny hides behind James' right leg. The outgoing Jack stands out front and doesn't have a problem speaking to the couple, "We just moved here!"

"We see that," the woman says with a smile, bending to his level. "I'm Barbara, and this is my husband, Cliff."

"Good to meet you," Jack says.

The woman digs in her pocket and reveals some candy, which she offers to Jack, who grabs it, and then to Johnny, who cautiously takes it from her.

"Jack, Johnny, what do you say?" James asks his sons.

"Thank you!" they reply.

"Your boys are very handsome," Barbara tells James, who in return gives her a polite smile.

"How old are you?" Cliff asks Jack.

"I'm five!" Jack replies, sucking on the fruity candy he ripped open as quickly as he took it.

"Five?" Cliff says. "You need to get a job, get married, settle down. You're almost my age!" The couple share a laugh with Jack and James. "Since you're new around here," Cliff says to James, "you oughta check out a Summer League game when you get settled."

"Summer League?" James asks.

"Baseball," Barbara adds.

James grins and replies, "Now you're speaking my language."

"You're a fan?" Barbara asks.

"I used to play some pro ball," James says.

"Oh, well, you'll fit in here just fine then," she remarks, sharing an excited look with her husband.

☞ ☞ ☞

Later in the evening, the Daltons arrive at their new home. They travel along a long private drive and park where the pavement ends. Beyond the pavement is a large hay field in need of a cut.

The family steps out to gaze at the majestic stretched-land their rickety ranch-style farmhouse sits on like a prop to the colorful country. Woods surround the field, and a few deer graze the edges. The house is in the open as are three other older structures that border it, one being an actual tin roof barn made of logs.

A once fully-operating farm with colonial history, the previous owners raised a few horses, pigs and chickens here. Much of the barn is intact with horse gates, feed and hardened mounds of manure, complete with chicken coops with feathers left behind. And as they would guess, the pig pens are still full of hard manure. Much like the store, there is plenty of work that awaits them. And regardless of its appearance now, or how it will appear when it's rehabilitated, they will always call this place the farm for as long as they live here.

A comforted expression sticks on James' face as he stares forward, taking in the beauty. The light breeze brings in a smell of nothing but nature. And that is something he remembers vividly from his childhood, bringing a happiness in him that he hasn't had in a long time.

"This is really it for us," he comments under his breath as almost an unconscious statement. "We're home."

He lifts baby Joe from Sandy's arms and points to various bits of scenery as far as the eye can see. The family stands side by side, staring ahead at the vast, serene property. This is their new chapter—something they've yearned for. This is their American dream.

CHAPTER 3 — SUMMER OF '97

*"You could be a kid as long as you want
when you play baseball."*
—Cal Ripken

THE CRACK OF A BAT echoes throughout all four corners of the farm's field. An older James, now forty-two, hits pop-ups to his sons in the deepest parts of a grassless, man-made, dirt-covered section. The family puppy Daggett chases bugs on the outskirts of the field. Daggett is a six-month-old black and white mutt of Sheltie and Springer Spaniel mix. He can barely be seen in the tall grass if not for his constant hopping of happiness.

A seven-year-old Joe hustles in to catch a shallow hit ball with his raggedy mitt on his left hand but misses. Jack, now twelve, and Johnny, now nine, each with gloves on their left hands, chuckle a bit at their youngest brother's expense. Joe retrieves the ball and throws it back towards his father. The ball ends with a trickle at James' blocking foot.

"Joe, you gotta get under those!" James says. "Two hands now—c'mon."

Joe nods. His eyes are wide with anticipation for the next hit. The youngest of the clan has developed broad features, much like his father. He's a large boy, not fat, but thick and solid with chubby hands, long legs and big feet. Unlike his brothers, he doesn't have a temper or hardened passion for the game. Instead, he tends to be more jolly and lighthearted; the comedian of the trio.

Admiring her family from the porch steps of the house for a few minutes, Sandy yells to her boys to come inside for dinner.

"Bring it in, boys!" James tells them.

His three dark-haired sons hustle to take a knee before him. James scans them, a long day of practice showing on their prideful faces. Sweat and dirt drip as a sort of badge of honor for the work they put in on the field today.

Earlier they went through a drill called Pepper where each took a turn hitting and fielding brisk ground balls to each other. This is a drill James puts them through frequently to improve hand/eye coordination. It's also a drill that tires them the most as it's run repetitively for an hour without breaks.

"Feel good?" James asks, a smile hidden, ready to break. The boys nod. "Having fun?" The boys nod again, this time anticipating the real question. "Got a man on third. Two outs," James explains a scenario. "Where's the play going?"

Johnny pipes up first, "Home!"

James shakes his head.

"First," Jack says confidently.

James nods. Johnny shows his disappointment with a sigh. Jack antagonizes him for getting it wrong, which results in the two having a shoving match that James has to break apart.

"The three of you are lucky," James states when they are calm again. "Do you know that?"

His sons don't know how to answer this question.

"Your biggest strength is each other. Remember that. When your mom and I are gone, the three of you are all you have left. My brothers and I can be assholes to each other, but we love each other. There is no bigger bond than brotherhood . . . So enough of this fighting shit."

Frantic neighing from across the field suddenly grabs their focus. Though far away, they can detect a deer trapped in the rusty barbed wire fencing that surrounds the western part of the property. The competitive Jack and Johnny decide to race each other towards the struggling doe to find her in rough shape. James and Joe join them not long after.

"I'll go get the cutters!" Jack says, making a move towards the house.

"Wait, Jack," James tells him and steps cautiously to the doe.

She struggles frantically when he touches one of the many gaping wounds on her body. The barbed wire digs into her skin even more, becoming embedded.

"See these?" James says, removing his hand from her. "Must've ran into a bear or cougar or something."

"She's in a lot pain," Johnny comments. "What should we do to help her, Dad?"

James looks down at the bat he holds in his hand and brings it above his head to hammer down, "Boys, stand back."

"You're gonna kill it?" Jack asks his father, his voice straining.

James breaks his stance and faces the three, "She won't survive. Best to put her out of her misery."

Joe begins to tear up and his lips quiver. Jack also can't stand the sight of this. He turns away. But Johnny doesn't say anything. He's curiously focused on the situation.

"There's going to be times in your lives when you're going have to do things you don't necessarily want to do," James explains to them. "Don't dare back down from it. Understand me? Fear nothing."

The boys nod to him that they understand. James turns to the doe that snorts and squeals violently. He rests his hand on her head to calm it some, "Shh . . . " He then raises the bat again. Jack and Joe can't stand the sight of what's about to happen, and they turn away once more. Johnny doesn't. He stands still and watches without a flinch.

"Jack. Joe," James says in a deep, commanding tone to look at what he's about to do. "Turn around. Face this."

The two obey, and James follows through with three mighty swings to end the doe's suffering. Jack begins to feel sick to his stomach, while youngest Joe can't help but cry uncontrollably.

"We'll leave the carcass for the coyotes," James says, winded as he wipes the blood from the bat in the grass. He then picks up Daggett who has followed them to this part of the field and hands the puppy to Joe to end his bawling as best as he can.

"Johnny, let's go inside," James says, realizing his son hasn't moved.

Johnny stands in the same spot and just stares at the slain deer. He comes to and joins his father and brothers. On their way back to the house, he notices two fawns standing timidly on a hill, several yards from the fence—witnesses to their mother's demise.

Sandy leads a Catholic grace at the dinner table. Chicken, mashed potatoes, corn and other fixings populate the hearty spread. The family joins in while

Jack and Johnny fool around, kicking each other under the table. James shoots a heated glare at them, interrupting grace. Both immediately stop their nonsense and join in on the rest of grace.

Daggett takes his normal seat under the table to eat any scraps that fall his way. Joe is the pickiest eater, and Sandy often catches him trying to feed the dog. For the most part, the family indulges in their meals for several minutes. The Dalton men eat similarly, with their arm wrapped around their plates and hovering over their food like they're in a prison cafeteria. They primarily focus on their own meals. Every once in a while, they raise their eyes to engage each other. Maybe it's Sandy's excellent home cooking or maybe because James comes from a large family himself, who all ate the same way. Growing up in his household, if you didn't finish in time, there wouldn't be any second helpings. The mood tonight is somewhat grim. Regardless of how good and filling the meal is, the three sons can't seem to shake the thoughts of what their father did to that deer earlier.

July's muggy air is so thick one can eat it with a spoon. Nine kids gather in the field-level Little League dugout. More ride in from the parking lot on their bikes. Strapped on their backs are book bags and others batting bags with their mitts latched to them. Each one of these boys carries their mitts with them everywhere they go in case a pick-up game breaks out or to play catch when the mood calls. Wrapped around a few bikes' handlebars are plastic grocery bags filled with practice essentials: Surge pop, assorted flavor sunflower seeds, Airheads, Sour Warheads and the most important of them all, Big League Chew. On the way to practice, it's tradition to collect empty pop and beer cans and bottles along the roads to turn them into Rupland Family Foods for the ten-cent deposit they'd receive in return. Getting two-to-three dollars' worth of returnables is all a boy needs in his youth. They can stretch those dollars further than anyone if it means scoring baseball cards, pop, candy or the occasional toy. Besides, no parent in their right mind would give the money to get their children hopped up on sugar, especially if it wasn't a game day.

The boys range in ages from eight to twelve years old, and they carry themselves with a tough country boy attitude, much like New Yorkers or Texans. On the dugout floor, pairs of batting gloves, clusters of bats and a couple baseballs lay scattered, reminiscent of their messy bedrooms. Ahead of them lies the freshly cut, chalked Little League field. A rusted 275 sign is hung in dead center field. Baseball season is in full bloom.

A couple of teammates carve their names with Swiss Army knives into the wood dugout wall that's painted dark green. The wall has many names carved into it from Rupland Little League players past and present. It stands as their own memorial so that the newbies who follow them will know their names for years to come.

The majority of the team watch two boys in the middle of an intense card trade. One of these boys is Lou Webb. He's a physically gifted black shortstop who is twelve years old and in his last season of Little League ball. He fans his newly store-bought cards before his trading partner, who also reveals his impressive collection.

"All right, Brian," Lou speaks up. "I'll trade you two of my '84 Kirk Gibson's for that Kirby Puckett."

Brian thinks for a moment, scanning his cards and then Lou's, before accepting the proposal. The rest of the team gasps with disgust.

"Lou, what the hell?!" A teammate remarks.

"Dude, I'm a Twins fan," Lou responds, grabbing his new card. "Get over it."

Meanwhile, a gray, '95 Jeep Comanche and white late 70s Trans Am pull into the parking lot of the field at the same time. James shares a nod with the driver of the Trans Am. Both are dressed the same in filthy work overalls covered in rock dust and grease. They've just finished a long shift at the Rupland Mine. A cloud of cigarette smoke fogs the man in the Trans Am. His name is George Kosko. His face is leathery from his earlier days working on the county road crews, and he has a grizzled beard in much need of a trim.

When George flicks his butt and rolls his window fully down, James can see a twelve-year-old boy sitting next to him through the cigarette smoke that lingers. The boy is George's son Nick. He ties his cleats, readying himself for practice. Nick is tall and thick. He's strong but gentle and is everyone's friend; a very popular kid. Throughout the past four seasons, his mother has had to carry a birth certificate with her to every game to verify his age to other teams, who challenge that he resembles a high-schooler.

James and his sons exit the truck and grab a few bags of equipment from the truck's bed. Johnny hurries off towards the dugout, neglecting to help his father and brothers.

"Johnny, get over here and help!" James says.

Johnny turns around, sighs and heads back. James stops by his coworker's window on his way to the dugout.

"Hi-ya doing, George?" James asks, then nods to the boy. "Nick."

"Big game coming," George remarks.

"Yup," James replies. "We sure could use all the support we can get. You coming?"

George lights another Marb Gold cigarette. His coldness towards any social interaction is apparent. He responds without even looking at him, "Maybe, yeah."

James notices the excessive mess of empty beer cans and alcohol bottles that litter the backseat of this once classic Trans Am. The car is undoubtedly devalued with scratches, dents and engine problems from George's devil-may-care attitude.

"Good to hear," James says. "Take it easy, George."

James adjusts the bag of gear over his shoulder like an ancient peddler and continues towards the dugout. His sons have since entered, taking part in the team's chatter. The Little Leaguers chant "Zoom-Zoom" again and again to Jack to grab his attention. The nickname has stuck with the boy since he was six. Light-footed and quick, he can round the bases faster than any kid and is known to always make baseball card bets for foot races during recess or practice. By the confident way he carries himself and how his teammates respond to his presence, it's apparent he's the level-headed leader of this rowdy bunch.

Back in the lot, Nick has finished getting ready and exits the car to join his teammates. George's eyes harden on him, and he says, "Come over here, Nicky-boy."

Nick walks back towards the car window where a few grimy, crinkled dollars are handed to him.

"After practice, I need you to go to the store and buy some bread for your mother."

"You're not picking me up?" Nick asks.

"I'm back on thirds tonight."

"Yeah . . . " The boy replies with some cynicism.

Nick turns around to leave, but George reaches out his window and jerks him back towards the car. "Hey! Do not turn your back to me."

Nick's jaw tightens, looking away from George. He is very upset but calm, not wanting to anger his father any further to avoid an embarrassing scene. "Quit pouting," George says. "You can ask Coach for a ride home." Nick accepts his answer. George slams his car in gear and says, "Go on," before he tears out of the parking lot.

From the dugout entrance, James has witnessed the altercation between the two. He redirects his attention back towards his team and begins to pick the mitts and bats off the ground that aren't his. As Nick reaches the dugout, his demeanor lightens when his teammates greet him.

"Who's got the seeds?" he asks.

Lou tosses him a bag. Nick pours a handful of jalapeño-flavored seeds into his palm and tosses them back, giving him a watery-eyed, packed-cheekful. He then moseys to the wall where the carved names are and grabs his pocket knife to carve his own name just below Jack's.

Suddenly, a Jeep without a muffler can be heard roaring into the lot. The team recognizes that sound, which triggers them all to stand on the bench to peer through the partially obstructed view the roof maintains from the back of the dugout.

Alicia Masterson steps from the Jeep to grab a blue bat bag from the backseat. She is a young, attractive woman in her early 20s. She wears a cropped Bon Jovi tank top and ripped Daisy Duke jean shorts and cowboy boots. From the other side of the Jeep, her son Eli Masterson exits. He is a blonde twelve-year-old boy with colorless eyes and a thick jawline. A shaved, trend-setting lightning bolt highlights the right side of his head. He's considered the cool and rebellious one out of his teammates, who's quick with his words; often considered to have a sharp tongue.

He hastily swipes his bag from his mother, giving her an obvious look to leave. Ignoring him, she removes her aviator sunglasses and plants a giant kiss on his cheek, leaving behind her blood-red lipstick outline. Eli breaks free of her for the dugout, where his teammates give him shit. Alicia then glistens a pearly white smile at the infatuated, prepubescent boys. They can only ogle and drool over her as they watch her leave.

Eli pulls a couple of teammates down from the bench; each laughing at his expense. "All right, horn-balls!" he says.

At the other end of the dugout, James dumps baseballs from the equipment bag to the ground. They scatter everywhere like spilled milk.

Diverting their attention from Eli's bombshell mother, he says to the team, "Dig in."

Each grabs a ball to head into the field to warm up. Eli places his bag next to his best friends, Jack, Nick, and Lou.

"Man, when I'm old enough to drive, I'm definitely asking your ma out." Nick jokes, his loud laugh echoing as he goes to play catch with Lou.

Eli playfully pushes his friend further into the field, almost tripping himself.

"Louis." A man speaks softly from the fence in front of the eight-row home side bleachers.

Lou stops to see his father Hakim dangling a batting glove over the fence for him. He is the only parent of the team that usually attends these practices to watch his son play.

Lou takes the batting glove from his dad and puts it on his glove hand, then squeezes his loose-fitting mitt on over it to provide him with more of a snug fit.

In the dugout, Eli reaches between his legs and snags one of many loose baseballs. As he and Jack make a move for the field, James swipes something from his back pocket. A pack of cigarettes lies in his coach's palm. James' cold stare affects the unwary child, and he clams up. His mouth turns dry fishing for an excuse as if there's one hanging in the air. Stumbling over his words, the boy finally blurts, "Uh. Think I should of hid them better, Coach."

His answer throws James off, but this coach wouldn't expect anything less from his cockiest of players. James knows Eli has always carried a chip on his shoulder. And while he gets away with an excessive amount of mischief, the only two people who he's never been able to fool are him and his mother.

"Should have what? You like pitching, son?" James asks.

"Love it," Eli replies.

"No smoking while you're part of my team. If I see or hear anything like this again, you're sitting Saturday's game. Understand me?"

Eli nods, trying to fish for an answer to James' rhetorical question. He would never go toe-to-toe with his coach, a man he's always admired and respected. James is the only real and constant male figure Eli has had in his life to this point.

"Wait," James says to Eli, noticing a group of bruises on the boy's shoulder that creep near his neck. They seem purposely hidden by his long-sleeve shirt, while the rest of the team wear cutoffs and baggy tees on this hot day. James paws at the shirt a bit more to reveal Eli's entire shoulder is black and blue.

The boy jerks back, quickly pulling his shirt back over the marks. He shows some embarrassment towards this and tries to spring another story, stumbling, "Took a tumble off my dirt bike yesterday near the gravel pits."

Skeptical, James ponders this before he nods the boy away to save the interrogation for another time. He steals a cigarette from Eli's pack and lights one for himself. His concern for the troubled child ruminates a little before refocusing on the rest of his team warming in the outfield.

"'Should have hid them better,'" he scoffs to himself, slightly amused by Eli's excuse.

Johnny follows his brother and Eli into the outfield undetected. His words trail quiet and unsure, looking for acceptance from the big kids. "Can I throw a few with you guys? "

Jack and Eli glance back at him as they step into the outfield's grass.

"No rookies," Eli responds to Johnny.

"Shut up, Masterson," Jack remarks, then waves his little brother to him. "Come on."

Before Johnny can even throw his first ball, James yells to him from the infield, "Johnny! Let the pitchers and catchers throw with each other. Go join the others."

Johnny's face drops with disinterest. He casually begins to depart, dragging his feet as slow as he can. To add to his misery, Eli snickers at the boy's expense.

"Let's move!" James keeps on him.

"Go, Johnny," Jack tells him.

Johnny's drag turns into a hustle, and he makes his way to the deepest part of right field with the other players.

James stops his truck near a curb. He waves at a few coworkers passing by that head in for third-shift at the mine. In the front cab, Joe holds a bag of groceries on his lap. Out of the bed hop Eli and Nick, leaving Johnny and Jack behind.

Rupland's second biggest river runs around this section of town the locals call Black River Alley. The rundown houses in this slum still exhibit a few signs of a once-prospering neighborhood. Porch lights provide the only source of light on these uneven streets as a colored sun without feature inches below the horizon.

"Black River boys out!" Eli says with a wink.

"See ya, Zoom," Nick says to Jack.

James glances at Eli's house, an unkempt domain that blends in with the rest of the area. "No one home?" he asks, concerned that the driveway is empty.

Eli keeps his stride towards his house, not looking back. "Mom works late on weekdays."

"You gonna be all right here?"

"Yup. Always am, Coach."

James accepts the quick answer and follows with, "Make sure to take care of that arm!"

Eli nods, continuing on with Nick, who's struggling to put his glove in his book bag.

"Kosko!" James calls to Nick and tosses a loaf of bread from his own grocery bag.

The light goes on upstairs and brightens the kid's face. "Oh, man, I forgot about that! Thanks, Coach!"

The Black River boys slap hands before parting ways to their houses, across the street from one another. Sitting back watching them, James can only speculate the lives they live outside the field. Everything outside the game is a jumbled mix of consequences and responsibilities that he cannot control. On the diamond is his own sanctuary. It is there his team—his players—are hungry for knowledge of a game that is reminiscent of life.

Qualities of teamwork and sportsmanship are the foundation for them to learn what it's like to earn something and be proud of it. On the field, these are put to the test by situational thinking, leadership, trust and accepting success as well as defeat. For a coach at this level, James' job couldn't be more important. He's shaping these young men with qualities he hopes will remain with them throughout their own lives.

Eli walks into his house. His face turns a ghostly white when he hears the television on in the living room. He closes the front door ever so quietly. Creeping past the dark room's doorway, he tries to make it to the staircase.

A man's grizzled voice clears itself and projects, "How was your game or whatever?"

Eli stops dead in his tracks, swallowing a hard lump in his throat. He can see the blurred television screen on through the smoke-filled room. The sound of a local newscast can barely be heard.

"Come in here a sec," the man says.

Eli's eyes drop, and his face drains further with fear as he reluctantly drags his feet towards the man. His usual confident, cocky demeanor is knocked down, revealing a scared boy, ill at ease. He positions himself in front of the man in his mid 40s. With a crew cut and belly that can't quite fit under his Dallas Cowboys t-shirt, it's the bright red, bloodshot eyes that stand out the most on him as if he were a monster ready to pounce on his next victim. The chair he sits in is sunken around his ass, indicating he's been in that spot for most of the day.

"I thought my mom kicked you out, Greg," Eli says quietly, almost under his breath.

"Couples fight, kid," Greg responds. "It's just grown-up stuff, that's all." He takes a long drag from his hand-rolled cigarette, staring at the boy. Eli can't bring himself to raise his eyes to him.

"I'm sure your mom wouldn't want you dragging dirt through the entire house," Greg adds. "Do her a favor and put your clothes in the laundry."

Eli takes these words as sort of an exit strategy, jerking his body back towards the stairs behind him.

"Here," Greg demands.

Eli freezes his movements, unsettled, knowing very well what Greg is insinuating.

"Drop them here. Last thing I want is your ma getting on my ass about the dirt. Bad enough she gets on me about cleaning this sty."

Eli hesitates on Greg's incessant looks, which become more pressing as every second goes by. Almost like an eternity. Looking away, he slowly strips his clothing: baseball pants, long-sleeved shirt and shoes. With every piece that's peeled off, the bruises James noticed earlier are greater and more disturbing. They run from his shoulder to his armpit. Down to his underwear now, Greg gestures him to remove those as well. The boy reluctantly does so, and now stands naked and ashamed. Much like his clothes, he is stripped of decency. Greg observes his body, making him even more uncomfortable than he already is.

"Get on upstairs and wash your ass," Greg says.

Eli wipes away a lone tear that rolls down his cheek. He then grabs his clothes to hold them over his privates and shuffles away. Greg takes a moment before he turns off the television and rises from his chair. He then gradually moves in the boy's direction to follow him upstairs.

A scuffle is heard outside Nick's own bedroom in the wee hours of the morning. Already half awake, he hops out of his sheets to peek out his door. The house is pitch black. He can only see that the house's front door is wide open, so he decides to leave his room to go and close it. The scuffling noises continue, which drives him to investigate further on his own. When he walks past the dining room, he notices an untouched plate of cold food left for his father. The loaf of bread Coach gave him earlier lies untouched next to it.

A yellow light glows from the living room. Some Merle Haggard music lightly plays. Nick tries to creep past so he doesn't wake up his mother, Judy, who is lying on the couch where she fell asleep listening to Merle Haggard while waiting for her husband to come home from boozing.

Nick finally reaches the bathroom where the noise was coming from and stops. He opens the door to find George unconscious on the floor. The boy's expression doesn't crack. He isn't surprised, nor is he upset. Out of routine, he just bends down to help his father. In doing so, his hand grazes some puke on the toilet seat. He ignores this and fights to lift his six-foot, 250-pound father off the cold floor. When he does, he leads him to his parents' bedroom. For a moment when the two pass by the living room a second time, Nick makes eye contact with his mother, whose eyes are now open. She immediately closes them to ignore the re-occurring situation at hand.

Nick drags his father to the bedroom and then struggles to situate and tuck him into the bed. He takes a much-needed breather after he does.

"G'night, Dad," he whispers.

He then reaches under the bed and slides a previously placed puke bucket to George's side.

The dusk skies over Rupland are a giant pastel painting on this festive 4th of July day. Through the chain-link gates of the Rupland Mine facility entrance and into the giant parking lot where cracks in the cement have since spread like glass spiderwebs, miners retreat from the changing sheds to their vehicles following a shift change. Most of them are men, some women, each with a workday's worth of crud on their faces and hands. One can only imagine the scrubbing it takes to remove the filth. The grime underneath their fingernails will always remain though. Cigarettes dangle from various lips; each are chattering amongst each other. The only conversations worth listening to throughout the lot are about tonight's Summer League game. Eventually, the group of miners breaks away in, what can only be a trend of large work trucks with metallic tool boxes bolted on the backs of the cabs. And if not trucks, muscle cars that are about as maintained as well as their lawns.

James opens the driver side door of his truck, tossing in his thermos. He looks up when hearing a vehicle roar out of the lot. George's Trans Am hits the corner and is gone in a blink of the eye. The sound of the distancing revs of his 301 Turbo V8 engine fade with it. Within minutes the rest of the vehicles file out of the gates too, leaving the lot a mess of exhaust, cigarette butts and tobacco spit.

George rolls in behind a few abandoned warehouses that were once furniture facilities. The lot's grass is almost jungle-like. Symphonies of crickets and a few birds that fly above are the only sounds in the area.

The rough-hewn man steps out of his car to lean against it, cracking open a Pabst beer can. By the way he eyeballs every edge of the lot, it appears he's waiting for something or someone. Ten minutes go by, and a second vehicle approaches. Spitting and sputtering up the hill, a multi-colored heap of an '88 Ford Escort barrels towards George's spot.

George downs the rest of his can in one swallow, tosses it in the brush, and walks in the open just as the car parks adjacent to his. The rusted yellow door creaks ajar and out walks a sickly thin, timid man in his mid 30s with wind-chafed skin, dead eyes and long, greasy brown hair that doesn't move when he walks. A paper bag is firmly tucked under his bony, skeleton-like arm. He obsessively checks his surroundings with each stride towards George. Any awkward sound would surely spit him out of his boots.

"Took you long enough," George remarks.

"I- I- I- appollogggize," the man stutters.

He unfolds the paper bag, revealing a couple crumpled dime bags of crystal meth.

"Calm your ass down, Little Zeke," George tells him. "Everybody's headed to the game as we speak."

"Yyyou nnever knnoow."

George rudely rips the drugs from Zeke's hand, "Well, I do know," he states, replacing the bag with eighty dollars worth of twenties. He begins to walk back to his car but not before commenting, "You could increase your clientele if you'd attend some of those ball games, you know. Could be a gold mine just waiting for your old man."

Zeke sheepishly replies, "I h-hate baseball."

"Well, that's just un-American, Little Zeke," George replies, plopping in his car. "Tell your pops I said hi."

Zeke stammers a reply, "Quiiit calling . . ."

The intentional rev of George's engine drowns his words, and the vehicle kicks up a mess of grass and dirt exiting the lot.

"Little Zeke," Zeke says, finishing his sentence that no one but himself heard. Agitated, he tosses the paper bag aside and returns to his own car.

☞　　☞　　☞

On the other side of town, Sandy locks the front doors of Rupland Family Foods, then wipes away the daily fingerprints smudged on them. Afterwards, she pulls the string to the illuminated open sign that hangs above the inside of the door to turn the lights off.

Before she returns to her closing tasks, she peers through the window and notices the downtown street has emptied. Scattered *Closed* signs litter business fronts. In the distance beyond town hall, she looks at a neighborhood street that's also empty. Silence is everywhere. Not a vehicle nor person is in sight. Rupland resembles a ghost town on game days.

☞　　☞　　☞

Six field tower lights explode on to reveal a cathedral of a ball park carved into the old mining town. It's here at this sacred fortress built of brick and steel that memories of the town are lucid. Here is where the game has more meaning than anywhere else.

Extravagant fireworks explode in the sky, reflecting a colorful display on the field and on the fan-filled bleachers. This is as American as America can get. Several thousand anxious fans pile in like a cattle drive. They direct themselves around a large bronze statue of the late, great Oren P. Rollins. The sixteen-foot monument stands in the center of the entrance, forcing every single patron to acknowledge it before they enter the confines of the park. Most fans touch it for good luck, a superstition that hasn't faded over the years.

This sanctuary embodies the rich baseball history that Rupland is known for. Scattered memorabilia include framed pictures of Ty Cobb, Babe Ruth, and Satchel Paige that once barnstormed here in the 1920s and '30s. Giant posters of every Rupland team since the start of the league are nearly everywhere. Decorated with memorabilia are local sponsorship signs posted around concessions and outfield walls: Middleton Realty, Karen's Diner, Rupland Family Foods, MC Sports, Jaeger Optics, Ronson Leather and Heritage Bank are just some.

A row of championship banners hangs high in center field on a second wall that stretches from end to end, below the outfield bleachers:

1915, 1924, 1934, 1939, 1955, 1967, 1968, 1977, 1983, 1988, 1995

The diamond's structure is reminiscent of the former Polo Grounds of New York. The deepest part of center field is 442 feet and has a 90-foot wide incline that everyone calls Prevo's Peak after the legend Mikey Prevo, who hit the majority of his home runs to center. Only the best center fielders in the league know how to play this spot. The right field section extends to 326 feet, while left field is the shallowest part of the park at 315 feet. Deep dugouts are sunken well below the stands, leaving only a small railing noticeable out front of it. The tops of Rupland's dugout displays their team name, while the other reads "Visitors." The Hawks dugout has a distinct vertical crack on the closest wall near the on-deck circle. It's been there since 1972 when Rupland catcher Roy Thurman knocked himself out trying to catch a pop-fly in the playoffs. Needless to say, he did not catch it. This flaw in the brick has since been dubiously named Roy's Fault and stands proud to this day. Welcome to the kingdom.

Off the center of the backstop, covered in Plexiglas, is the pitch clock. Its lone purpose is so pitchers can time themselves in-between throws, so they won't be penalized. Behind the backstop, sitting high above the stands is where the announcer's booth resides. Inside it's filled with broadcasting equipment, historical moments in the League's history and cartoonish bobble-heads. Built against the wall, below a string of windows is a table that has about every baseball stat book known to man. Notepads are also scattered about. Sitting at this table are a few press members and Summer League officials, each whispering to each other about player stats, league predictions and good old-fashioned baseball debates.

At the far end of the table, seated behind the largest windows are two famous radio broadcasters. Each are well into their 50s. Play-by-play announcer Frank Reese and his colleague Reverend Mel Grainger, who provides color-commentary, have been calling games since the late 1970s. Frank is the clean-cut, mild-mannered one. He's a fair and plain facts man. Before him is a scorebook with pages of scoresheets from previous games, each marked with chicken scratch writing that has no organization or end. The lost art of scoring a game this way lives on through him alone.

Mel is a former Summer League player turned announcer. He's an opinionated, jolly soul with a silk voice. And when he's not hosting his daily morning show that broadcasts over the three league counties, he's preaching epic sermons at the New Hope Baptist Church. Unlike MLB announcers, both dress casual with polos and khakis as if they're preparing to play 18 holes of golf. He and his partner are throwbacks to the days of the great New York Yankees announcers Mel Allen, Red Barber and Phil Rizzuto.

"Mel Grainger and I, Frank Reese, are here on behalf of 107.3 W.L.A.K." Reese rolls from his tongue into his Lip-ribbon microphone with finesse. "It is a beautiful night in Rupland, Mel!"

"Indeed," Grainger follows. "The Rupland Hawks come in tonight looking to sweep their county rival, the Ellison Legends."

"Manager and former player Fred MacIntyre is trying to add another win onto his impressive eighteen-year career," Reese comments.

"Let's see how his team fares tonight."

The Dalton clan are among the fans entering the park. They make their way to their normal spots in the stands behind the Hawks dugout. Joe holds his mother's hand, while Jack and Johnny stand in front, mesmerized by the sights they've seen so many times before. Although, by their joyous expressions, it appears as if they're seeing this place for the very first time. The atmosphere is a classic spectacle of competition at its finest. A sea of orange and black in the bleachers that roars at the sight of their hometown team is something the Dalton boys idolize more than anything else. To them, the Hawks are giants among men. Everything they do is perfect.

When the fireworks die down, and almost everyone sits, the pre-game ceremony begins. Everyone's attention focuses on the field. Both teams stand on the foul lines and remove their caps. The boys look at the players in awe.

The Hawks' home uniforms are mainly white button-ups with "Hawks" spread on their chests in orange with black trim. The pants they wear are white with a thick black and orange stripe down the sides, complemented with an orange belt. Some players elect to tuck their batting gloves in one or both back pockets, leaving them half-hanging out. Their socks are black, and some players style them with orange stirrups. To complete their attire, they wear black hats with an orange brim that has the letter 'R' on the front in an orange Old English font.

The Ellison Legends uniforms are also traditional button-ups, but theirs are purple with gold lettering and white trim. "Legends" stands out on their chest. Unlike the Hawks, they do have names on the back of their jerseys. Their pants are white with a single gold stripe down the side along with purple belts. And their hats match their tops with a gold, Brush Script-fonted 'E' stitched on the front of them.

The Rupland High School marching band marches into the outfield. They position themselves and begin to play "The Star Spangled Banner." Proud American families of miners and veterans place their hands over their hearts. They acknowledge the incredibly vast American flag in center field that waves above all, atop the 36 x 16 black and white digital scoreboard.

Sandy sings along with the anthem as she does every time. Her husband instinctively stands firm, his eyes pierced forward with his right hand saluting perfectly and his other hand properly straightened at his side. Other veterans do the same. Johnny fidgets next to James. Before the anthem ends, James places his hand on his son's shoulder to keep his attention for the rest of the song. When it concludes, Jack joins Eli and Lou, who stand on the side of the bleachers near the bottom, eagerly waiting for their friend. His younger brothers get the okay from their parents, and they follow Jack down.

"Where's Kosko?" Jack asks when he meets his buddies.

His friends shrug their shoulders, and the pack of five almost trample beer vendors that roam the crowd to try to find a seat closer to the field. They maneuver by the Rupland Rowdies, a club of fans that fill three rows of bleachers. They are known to have the most creative signs and begin most of the chants that start at one end of the park and ripple to the other in waves. Closer to the field, next to the home team dugout, they pass by Mr. and Mrs. Greenberg. The elderly couple have sat in these same seats for over sixty years. Their names are engraved on plates on the back of the seats. The friends eventually sit behind the backstop, in front of the section reserved for coaches' and players' wives and girlfriends. In this group of various ages and maturity levels, team and town gossip, game strategy, bragging about their significant others and recipe sharing define these timeless beauties.

Top of the 5th inning. A screaming fastball sails by an Ellison hitter at the plate to ring him up for the third strike. The hitter hangs his head while making that long, lonely walk back to the dugout. Passing by him is the rest of the Rupland fielders making their way off the field to bat. Last in, the fierce throwing, right-handed ace, Charlie Hylman, walks from the hill. He takes a few slaps on the back from teammates. The thirty-three-year-old keeps his eyes down to stay focused. He's in the zone. Charlie is a kind-eyed Southern gentleman with bushy brows, short brown hair and a goatee. He wears thick, black-framed glasses that fog when he goes into the deep innings. His nose is also crooked, having been broken more than once. No one really knows if it's a baseball injury or from a brawl from his heavy drinking days back in Texas. All eyes in the dugout and in the stands stay on the star pitcher throughout.

In this dugout, it is a world like no other. There's loud chatter and the occasional swearing, spitting and testicle scratching. Manners don't apply. This is no place for one's mother. Almost always there's an injury being treated by the local trainer at one end of the bench. And of course, there are those sweet sounds. Sounds of cleats scraping across the ground's rubber mat and on the cement stairs and the endless clunking and rattles of equipment and bats are theme music to the sport. This particular dugout is a place where teammates are like brothers, and the art of winning is a finely-tuned machine. It's not just a holding place for nine innings or more to them. It's familiar, and it's safe. Some consider it home.

A short, black, clean-shaven man in his mid 50s with droopy green eyes leans against Roy's Fault, keeping one foot on the step and the other in the dugout. As he observes his bench, the gears turn in the genius' head. Thoughts of devised strategy are building—weighing this and weighing that. He understands baseball more than anyone in this park, and he knows it too. His philosophy has always been to keep the pace moving at all times, which led to a hit-and-run mentality for offense and a nonstop attack approach for defense. Before every pitch, the defense is shifting, and after every hit, they're moving somewhere. Each player has an assignment. A firm believer in playing with maximum effort, one must run out fly balls and grounders as well as touching first base no matter the circumstance—even if they are an imminent out. His players have learned to keep fighting regardless of the score, and at the end of the game to look their opponents in the eye and shake hands. He's a hard-nosed relic of the great game. Fred MacIntyre is the manager of this ball club.

Watching Charlie closely, MacIntyre sees his golden boy cover his pitching arm with a warm-up jacket to keep it nice and toasty. Obsessive thoughts race through his mind—*How many more innings can he keep Hylman in for and will his once-superior, now fading curveball be able to withstand the middle of Ellison's lineup consistently?* These are the sorts of thoughts that lead to many sleepless summer nights for the skipper. There are a few who think this is a curse, but to him, it's a way of life.

When seated, Charlie notices his manager's deep stare on him.

"Good?" MacIntyre asks, breaking the silence.

The veteran gives a slight nod. MacIntyre then paces in front of his players on the bench, his lip snarled with disgust suddenly, and he yells, "I don't wanna see any goddamn smiles after that shit inning! Wipe 'em!"

"Let's wake up our sticks now!" the third base/pitching coach Lloyd Roberts injects, clapping. "What'd you say?"

Roberts is a lanky and goofy-looking white man in his mid 40s. He has a grayish beard and a ridiculously giant chaw of tobacco wrapped in chewing gum that's packed tight in his cheek. When he spits, it makes an almost comical sound leaving his mouth and splattering onto the ground. The mess left is a dark-colored puddle that will leave a stain before game's end. Some refer to him as the next coming of Yogi Berra. Not for his former play, but for his eccentric and odd-thinking manner, for which he blurts senseless, sometimes, meaningless facts to anyone that'll listen.

A Hawks shortstop named Gomez grabs a bat and helmet on the way out of the dugout. A second player nicknamed Fozzy follows, twisting his hips to loosen his muscles while he adjusts the fit of his batting gloves. Following them are Roberts and the first base coach, thirty-year-old Sarah MacIntyre.

Sarah is Fred's only child and is of mixed-race: African-American and Caucasian. She is the current manager of the high school girls' varsity softball team and is a replica of her father in every way. Fred brought her up learning every aspect of baseball and prepared her for the struggles of being a woman in a man's sport. Nevertheless, her knowledge and ability to play, and play well, earned her respect among her peers, the team, and the town. Sarah is a tomboy at heart. Her hair is short and brown and plain without any styling. To her, makeup is gross, and she'll never touch the stuff. She isn't very tall, freckles cover her whole face, and she is in impeccable shape. Back in her softball playing days, she led Rupland High School to four regional finals as a terrific hitting outfielder. She brought that same success to UCLA where she won back-to-back-to-back college softball World Series championships in 1988, 1989, and 1990.

Fans suddenly rise to their feet with praise. Jack, Johnny, Joe, Eli, and Lou have made themselves comfortable behind the backstop, spitting sunflower seeds on the concrete around them. They watch the game with enthusiasm before they, too, stand from their seats when the wave of standing fans reaches their section.

The contagious excitement in the air is towards beloved player Cain McCloud. Cain struts to the box, windmilling his bat around like a helicopter; his walk-up ritual. This excites fans, whether it's meant to or not. He's a white, spiky, blonde-haired, blue-eyed twenty-five-year-old with movie star looks that break the hearts of just about every girl in the house. But he isn't just looks. Cain is a gifted athlete, whose talent level still hasn't peaked. The letter 'C' is stitched on the left breast of his #5 jersey, revealing him as the captain of this talented squad. He adjusts his orange wristbands and positions himself on the right side of the plate, digging in deep. His intimidating, Clint Eastwood-type squint at the opposing pitcher sends chills.

The first couple of throws are fastballs that barely miss the zone. Cain displays great plate discipline not to swing at these. Ellison's pitcher refuses to get in a 0-3 hole, so he changes his selection and slings in a curveball that hangs over the heart of the plate. Cain takes advantage and crushes it, exploding out of his post-swing stance, hopping. He watches the ball travel deep for a solo home run. Several kids go nuts trying to claim the prized ball up for grabs now. Foul balls are one thing, but home run balls are the most valued of treasures.

Rounding the diamond with his usual unfazed expression, Rupland fans go wild for their rising phenom. As if someone cued a massive choir, they begin to sing the Hawks' theme song "Thunderstruck" by AC/DC over and over. The chants are so loud they can be heard clear across town.

"Touch 'em all, Mr. McCloud!" Reese announces from the press box. "That's home run number 10 on the year for the young catcher."

"He's gonna make Rupland a threat for seasons to come," Mel Grainger chimes in.

Remaining fans are still filing out after the last fireworks of the night conclude the postgame. The final score on the scoreboard reads:

Hawks 7

Visitors 1

An endless convoy of headlights in the distance leaves the lot towards the highway that wraps around it. Remaining on the field, the Hawks kneel around the mound to listen to their manager, like knights before their king.

The dozen fans left in the park are kids that gather on top of the Hawks' dugout, each hoping for an autograph from their favorite players. A few local reporters—a beat reporter for the Rupland Journal newspaper and a television reporter that covers the three counties for a small market station—wait near the dugout. Next to the dugout, the three Dalton brothers press their faces against the fence to try to get a listen to MacIntyre's postgame speech.

Stone-faced, MacIntyre grips a game ball while scanning his team, "There isn't much to say," he tells them. "That was a hell of a win tonight."

His players' eyes stay glued on him, engaged in every word he speaks.

"Baseball is the cruelest game," he continues to explain. "Even the best execution can result in failure. But when we do the small things right and our execution is sound we'll keep having nights like tonight. It was a team effort here. We are one unit, gentlemen. Pure. Odds will be in our favor if we stick together. We do that, I guarantee we bring the title back here." Making a move away from the mound, he turns back before leaving, hinting a grin. "You can smile now."

The players shed a few grins of their own and they rise to leave to sign autographs and talk to the media. Every little boy and girl, including Johnny and Joe, lean over the dugout when seeing the players approach. Most stretch on their stomachs and reach out with whatever memorabilia they have for Cain to sign.

MacIntyre avoids the media altogether as he so often does, and heads straight for the dugout to the locker room. Before he enters, he makes eye contact with a fascinated Jack, who stands alone in his same spot. He isn't interested in autographs like the other kids, he's interested in the atmosphere. He's still lost in MacIntyre's words to his team as if he were there kneeling with the players and listening himself. MacIntyre tosses the ball he was holding over the fence to the kid. Jack looks down at his gift, admiring the dings and dirt it collected during the game.

Buckled in and asleep in the back of the van are the children. Jack holds his prized game ball tightly in his hands. Sandy massages her husband's neck, while the calmness of the warm summer night ends with the rumblings of thunder from an impending storm sweeping the county. Memories of tonight's game play fresh in their minds.

James' eyes drift for a moment before he notices multiple lights flashing several yards ahead. He stops at a road block to see the Sheriff's Department and State Police cruisers have contained the aftermath of an accident. Past them, an ambulance and a fire truck sit. James and Sandra's faces turn white when they spot a Trans Am lying on its roof in the ditch. They know the owner of that very car.

James wastes no time in exiting the van.

Rupland's elderly Sheriff Bill Orson blocks his way. "Hold on, Mr. Dalton," Sheriff Orson tells him.

"What's going on over there, Bill?" James says with worry in his voice. He pokes his head past the sheriff's shoulder to witness a bloody George in handcuffs, being escorted into the back of a squad car. He sees a noticeable limp to his stride, partly because he has only one shoe on.

"George!" James screams to get his attention. "George!"

Sheriff Orson struggles to hold him back, "Mr. Dalton, please!"

"Where's his son?!" James cries, scoping the scene for the child. "Where's Nick?!"

The sheriff points at his own squad car, where Nick sits in the backseat, bawling into the blanket wrapped around him while he's checked over by paramedics. A small amount of blood streaks down his face.

"He'll be fine," Sheriff Orson claims. "Just has a few scrapes. In shock too. Watch yourself—"

He moves James out of the way to let a black cargo van through the road block barricade. James reads the side of the vehicle: "Coroner."

Taken aback, he stumbles backwards some.

"Judy . . . " Sheriff Orson reveals with his eyes dipped.

Shocked, James locks his hands together and places them over his head to get air back in his lungs, " My God . . . "

He backpedals towards the van. Sandy hasn't taken her eyes off her husband this entire time. The children in back begin to awaken one by one, each unbuckling their seatbelts to get a better view of the accident. When James enters his vehicle, he sinks into his seat and drops his head on the steering wheel.

Sandy stares at him with a lost expression, not knowing what to say. Her eyes fill with tears, figuring something tragic has happened. James takes a moment to gather his composure and puts the van into gear.

"Sit back and buckle yourselves in," he tells his kids.

They do so, and James turns the van around to head back in the direction they came. He glances at his wife; her eyes still haven't left him.

" Judy," James says with grief.

Sandy expels a small gasp, soft enough to not alarm the children.

Heavy breaths. Feet running. James' heart is racing. He sees the bamboo rooftops of the familiar savage village. Vietcong soldiers pace around the blast hole he lies in. He stays still as if he were paralyzed. His eyes are the only part of him that moves. The shaggy-haired enemy examines his area as he steps past his body. James panics, thinking he'll be executed next, but the soldier just walks on as if he were invisible.

James lifts his head from the mud and rises cautiously. He witnesses past platoon members that died previously, helplessly massacred by the enemy again. Some are instantly killed. Others die much slower deaths by knives and machetes. Unscathed, James is a witness to it all.

He touches some blood on his face and discovers his entire body is covered in blood. He looks back to where he was lying to grab his rifle, but it's gone. Replacing his rifle are two live Marines on each side of him. They lay on their stomachs, squirming from apparent and unseen injuries. James reaches to one side to help his comrade, but the body is abruptly drug out of the hole by the shaggy-haired enemy. James fails to grab the Marine's hand. He then focuses on saving the second Marine, but he, too, is swiftly taken away in the same manner. Watching the horror of these two damned soldiers being dragged away to their inevitable murder, something in James urges him to keep trying to help them. He knows the rest of the platoon are goners. But there's a chance he can at least save somebody.

He claws himself from the hole just as a piercing voice heard through the gunfire screams at him, "You can't help them, Jimmy!"

James stops and turns around to see a man not much younger than himself, standing casually with his hands in his pockets. The man looks similar to James and wears an earth-toned shirt with camo pants tucked into spit-shined black boots and nothing else. He's clean. There isn't a mark on him nor any gear or guns. Around them, the Vietcong continue their massacre of the platoon. James and the man stand removed from it all as if they're an exception to war.

"J-Jacob?" James asks, recognizing the man. His eyes are wide with surprise. "What are you doing here? It's too dangerous for you here!"

The younger brother stares at James without saying another word. James makes a move back towards the Marines that are still being dragged away, "Don't just stand there! Help me, damn it!"

"We can't help them," Jacob says. "Let them be."

James becomes infuriated, turns back, and grabs Jacob to shake him. "What's wrong with you?! Grab a fucking gun and help me, little brother!"

"They can't be saved, Jimmy . . . "

Confused, James lets go of him. "Why? Why can't we try?"

After hacking down a Marine, another enemy's eyes have turned toward the brothers. He charges at them with his machete raised high over his head. James notices this happening from behind his brother's shoulder. Just as the enemy is about to make contact with Jacob, James lunges to push him out of the way.

"Jacob!" James screams.

He gasps out of his dream swinging his fists frantically. Sandy leans on her husband to calm him and takes a punch to the side of her face, sending her back against the children that lie next to them in a heap of blankets on the living room floor. Outside, the storm is at full strength. Wind, rain, lightning, and thunder won't let up.

"Jacob!" James continues to painfully scream. "Jacob! Jacob!"

Sandy recovers from being struck and repeatedly slaps James in the face to snap him awake. It doesn't work. The children are wide awake, watching the situation between their parents. They aren't scared, nor are they surprised. All they can do is watch their mother try to manage their father's episode.

Sandy cocks back her fist and brings a thunderous jab to his face that knocks him into consciousness. His hyperventilating subsides with each passing second. Sandy then wipes the beads of cold sweat on his forehead with her nightgown.

"Same dream, Dad?" Jack asks.

James' quietness gives everyone their answer. Sandy puts her arm around him, and he rests his head against hers. She strokes his hair continuing to calm him down.

The storm has knocked out the electricity in Rupland on this night. While the family has done this during previous power outages, staying close together just seems right after witnessing the Koskos' tragedy earlier in the night. They make themselves a den of blankets in the middle of the living room.

"It's been a while since you had that dream," Sandy says.

"I know," James replies. "Maybe tonight just . . ."

He stops himself from going into deeper emotions. He considers showing these kind of emotions in front of his children a weakness. That's the way his father was with him and his own brothers.

It doesn't take him long to discover the shiner he left on his wife. He sits straight up and kisses the mark, concerned. "Are you okay?"

"Always am," she replies with a smirk.

Jack has brought his parents each dish towels full of ice from the freezer to nurse their swollen marks.

"Sorry, sweetie," James apologizes to his wife.

"Don't be. Yours is going to hurt far worse than mine in the morning."

James grins and kisses her mark again, which makes her giggle a bit.

"Oh yeah," James says holding the side of his face. "I'm starting to feel it already."

They tuck their children in for bed again.

☞   ☞   ☞

Saturday—July 12th, 1997

There's hardly a breath of air on this hot Saturday afternoon. The American and Little League flags mounted on top of the foul pole in right field are dead with seldom movement. Below them a row of seven-foot wide championship banners cover the entire outfield fence:

1997 LITTLE LEAGUE CHAMPIONSHIP

LITTLE HAWKS V.S. LITTLE WOLVES

Bottom of the 6th inning. The Little Hawks hustle in after a fly-out to center. Families populate the small group of bleachers on each side of the field behind the chain-link fences. A few claps of excitement are heard here and there, but the obvious sorrowful cloud of death hangs over their heads. The community is still in a state of shock by the accident that occurred last week.

Several players' moms work the concession stands, baking and registering sales. Gossip and smoke fill the building; a mother's game ritual of sorts. Among the group are Sandy, Alicia Masterson and Lou's mother, Denise. Denise's account of what she witnessed at the emergency room the night of the accident is a hot topic of discussion this afternoon.

"Heartbreaking," one mother with big hair says, puffing on her smoke.

"Absolutely crazy," Sandy remarks. "I just feel for Nick, you know? Who is he going to live with?" Sandy's shiner has faded and any darkness left has been covered with makeup.

"I heard he's going to stay with his grandmother," Denise says while pulling a new batch of brownies from the fridge.

"What happened to George when you saw him, Denise?" another dolled-up mother asks.

"He only needed a few stitches," Denise explains. "We ran tests on him. I shouldn't say anything, but the man was about as drunk and high as I've ever seen anyone . . . When they got the results, they sort of just hauled him away."

Shocked and worrisome gasps erupt from the moms.

"He's probably going away for a long time, you would think. Right?" Sandy says.

"That is so sad," Alicia says as she greets another male customer through the concession's sliding window.

Throughout the game, some of the husbands flock to the concessions. Each chat with Eli's flirtatious mother. It's hard for them not to notice this stunning woman wearing shorts so small that her ass cheeks hang out of them; not to mention her hard nipples easily seen through her tank top she sports without a bra. Many of the other moms aren't amused by her antics. Most of them just shed dirty looks at her with their judging eyes.

"She gonna blow him too?" the big-haired mother whispers to a few others, each chuckling at Alicia's expense who is oblivious to it all.

Joe lingers with a couple of friends near the entrance. Sandy hands him and his friend each a plastic cup of Kool-Aid before sending them on their way. The youngest Dalton breaks away from his friend and enters the dugout.

"Where's my bat, Joe?!" Johnny snaps at him, searching for it with a helmet on his head. "I'm leading off!"

"Don't know," Joe replies. "I think it was at the other end of the bench."

"You suck at being a bat boy!" Johnny tells him before he finds it.

Dark blood stains forever smear the barrel of his favorite bat. This is the very bat James killed the deer with. Since then, Johnny has taken to it, even naming it the deer slayer.

The last player off the field is Jack. He appears winded, and his strides are slow as he passes by his father and plops on the bench in his pool of sweat. James observes the exhaustion in Jack's body language while watching him shed his catcher's gear.

James sits next to him and asks, "How is it out there?"

"Masterson's hanging in," Jack responds. He tosses his shin guards aside, giving his usual report of his pitchers to his coach. "His throws are starting to rise a little, and—"

"It's pretty hot out today," James interrupts. "Think I'm gonna pull you."

"What? Dad, no!" Jack pleads, not expecting these words from his father.

At the plate, Johnny watches the ball go by for a strike. He glances back at his father who is not paying attention to him.

Jack continues to beg James to stay in, "Come on, we got this game. Please?"

James contemplates. It's hard for him to reject the want he sees in his son. The thought of taking his last Little League game away from him, not to mention benching one of his best players when needing his bat this inning is far too cruel.

" . . . Get on deck," James reluctantly tells him, giving in.

Jack throws his chest protector aside without hesitation, grabs a batting helmet and bat, and heads to the on-deck circle. James redirects his attention towards Johnny's atbat in time to see him hesitate, bringing the bat around for a second strike.

"Let's go, Johnny!" James says.

Pressure sets in to the youth. He knows his father's attention is finally on him now. Glimpsing at the scoreboard that reads 1-1, he reminds himself that the moment could be his, victory or defeat. Unfortunately, with an 0-2 count, the odds are in the pitcher's favor. There is no turning back now. Johnny understands what he needs to do. He's determined to get a piece of aluminum on that ball. Setting himself in the batter's box, he tries to be confident with a long, steely-eyed stare he beams back at the opposing pitcher. To him, there is nothing else in the world more important right now than hitting that damn ball good and hard.

The pitcher winds up and unleashes some serious heat that blanks him as he swings way late for a third strike. Johnny glimpses back at the pitcher who stands tall in victory. It's over. Johnny's chance to shine is diminished. With his head dropped, he sadly drags his bat back to the dugout. Leadoff hitter Jack passes by on his way to the plate, but Johnny doesn't pay any attention to him. The last thing he wants is to acknowledge his brother and vice versa.

Before Johnny can get both feet into the dugout, James snatches the bat from his trembling hand. In one motion he forces his middle child to the bench, "I didn't teach you to walk. You'll never get a hit if you're not aggressive!"

The embarrassment is far too much for Johnny to bear. He can't even look over at his teammates staring at him, let alone his own father. Keeping quiet and wallowing in his self-disgust is all he's interested in.

James flings Johnny's bat against the dugout's fence, and the team moves on from this altercation to cheer on Jack. James does too, squatting down at the dugout entrance, closely watching his atbat.

Jack rocks a liner off his heels on the second pitch for a stand-up double. James and the parents rise clapping. New life is breathed into the team.

Lou steps to the plate next. The opposing pitcher takes a few more breaths in between throws, showing his exhaustion. He musters enough stamina to toss the ball near the zone. Lou smacks the ball deep for another double, bringing Jack home to give the Little Hawks the lead. Jack runs so fast he brakes his momentum and ends on the balls of his feet before colliding with the fence.

Top of the 7th inning. James gathers the team on the bench before they head back out in the field. He scans their faces. They sit anxiously with their legs shaking, knuckles cracking, eyes fluttering about.

"Game is yours if you want it," he tells them, loosening his jaw for a smile. "How bad do you wanna win?!"

"BAD!" the team yells.

"Doesn't sound like it. How bad?"

"BAAAAD!" the team yells even louder, their smiles ever so bright.

They're having fun, which was James' first lesson when he took on this team.

"All of your hard work this season needs to pay off in these last three outs. For you twelve-year-olds, I've taught you everything I could these past four years. Let's finish this right."

James steps away from the entrance to let the fielders hustle past him. He blocks Johnny before he too can join them and coldly says, "Take a seat, Johnny." He then calls another player, "Sanders!"

A smaller kid rises from his normal spot on the bench. He's around the same age as Johnny but isn't very coordinated, nor has a lick of athletic ability. But he plays hard for his coach, which gives him ample playing time every game.

Pissed off and hurt, Johnny stands firm behind his father.

"Sit," James says a bit more sternly. "Now."

Johnny sighs, then steps back to let Sanders go by to take his position in left field. He stomps to the bench and chucks his glove at it.

James quiets his angry son with one loud and startling word, "Enough!"

Jack jogs next to Eli on their way to the mound together. He notices Eli isn't running his mouth per usual. The nerves of the close game have taken its toll on the young pitcher. Eli positions himself behind the rubber, which has a light dusting of dirt. He sweeps it with his cleat, revealing the pearl white color it had been before the game.

"Relax," Jack tells his friend as he puts his arm around him. "It's like playing catch, bro. Just you and me out here."

He then places the ball in Eli's glove. Eli exhales, giving his friend a reassuring nod. Jack taps his buddy's chest with his mitt and returns to the plate.

A Little Wolves batter steps in. Eli goes right to it by getting ahead on the count 0-2, with just two pitches—each painting the corners of the plate. He sets again and then delivers a kill shot curve that seems to drop off the table, which the hitter bites on and misses. Jack drops to his knees to block the ball when it hits the dirt, scooping it up with ease. Behind him, an elderly umpire punches a third strike.

Eli walks around the mound a tad more relaxed now that the first out is behind him. He's one step closer to ending the game. Retrieving the ball, he watches the Wolves' cleanup hitter walk to the plate. Like most cleanup hitters, this kid's got a lightning quick bat and explosive power. Eli knows the hitter well. Back in the third, he rocked him with an opposite field hit to right that brought in an RBI. Eli refuses to be outmatched again. He sets and delivers another curve in hopes of getting this hitter to fall for it too. To no avail—the cleanup hitter tees off and sends the ball past Sanders' head. Sanders has a difficult time retrieving the ball, bobbling it when he picks it up. He eventually gets control and tosses it to his cutoff Lou, who holds the hitter at bay for a gut-wrenching triple. Sanders shakes his head in self-disgust, knowing he gave up the extra base and put his team in jeopardy of the Wolves tying the score.

On the mound, Eli punches the palm of his glove hard in frustration, holding strong on the middle of the rubber, isolating his anger to himself. He won't look at Jack as he knows his friend will try to calm him down. With the game being as close as it is, Eli doesn't want to show any sign of weakness. He wants to show he can finish this himself. He's used to handling his own situations. This time is no different. He sucks it up, retrieves the ball from Lou, and gets ready for the left-handed five-spot hitter.

Wiping the sweat from his brow, Eli winds with a short kick of his left leg and tosses one in to the hitter that's called for a ball. Jack throws two fingers down between his legs. Eli shakes the sign off. Jack then throws down a one, which Eli agrees to and then fires in a fastball that the hitter knocks hard and high to left field.

Here we go again, Eli thinks to himself, watching Sanders waddle to it, unsure of his positioning to get under the ball. Parents, coaches and benches are in suspense as the game has just turned ugly. Jack waves in Eli to back him up and stands partially blocking the plate with his left side in the line of fire. Sanders, surprisingly, catches the fly. The cleanup hitter on third tags up for the sacrifice and heads home, pumping his arms fast and hard, in hopes to tie the score. Lou has since run deep into the outfield for the cutoff. Sanders relays the ball to him.

"Get it in!" James and a few parents shout.

In one motion, Lou wings it to Jack at home. The runner goes into his feet-first slide as Jack sweep tags him. A thick dirt cloud shrouds Jack, the runner and the umpire. The cloud settles, and the umpire signals the last out.

Rupland fans and dugout players roar in triumph. The rest of the Little Hawks crowd the plate as Jack stands with the ball almost embedded in the webbing of his mitt. James runs in the middle of his team to pick Jack up and holds him high for everyone to cheer him on in his moment of glory. Jack looks as if he's floating high above them all. He embraces his moment to shine.

Alone, Johnny lingers around the outside of the team's celebratory pile. He observes his brother. He observes his father. He observes his teammates. The moment is bittersweet for the nine-year-old. While there is an urge to join in on the celebration, there is also a feeling that it's not his place. Or simply, it's not deserved.

☞   ☞   ☞

CHING . . . CHING . . .

Clinks of the fence rattling are the only sound in the empty Little League field that was at capacity not more than two hours ago. One by one, baseballs hit the backstop fence, either straight on or rolling. Feet behind the rubber of the mound, an exhausted James grabs a ball out of a bucket sitting on the ground next to him and throws it unusually hard over the plate. Still in his grass and dirt-stained uniform, Johnny watches the ball wing past him, without ever lifting the bat off his shoulder. He can barely move, and tears roll down his cheeks at a rapid pace.

"Swing at the goddamn thing!" James shouts.

Jack sits on the home dugout bench, still in his game attire too. The sweat has hardened the dirt on his face, arms and hands. His head hangs, and he kicks around whatever trash has been left on the ground. Next to him, Joe carves his name into the wood of the dugout with Jack's Swiss Army knife to add his name with the other players. He'll be playing for the Little Hawks next year when he turns eight, so now is as good as a time as any to join the wall. While both feel for their brother, they each try to ignore what's happening on the field in their own way. They've been through this situation plenty of times.

James tosses another that Johnny decides to take a cut at and misses, spinning in the box.

"We can be here all night!" James says, throwing up his hands. "Don't just take a hack at it for no reason. Don't just work the bat, control the bat!"

Johnny tries to compose himself back into his stance, while James reaches into the bucket for another ball. It's empty.

"Go shag 'em," he says to his son.

This instantaneously cues Jack and Joe to rise from the bench to help Johnny retrieve the balls that litter the backstop.

"No!" James shouts. "Johnny will."

The two brothers freeze in their tracks. They're forced to watch their brother tirelessly fetch the balls alone. At this time, the family's van pulls into the parking lot. A concerned Sandy exits and approaches the fence. She's been waiting for the Dalton men to return home for dinner for a while.

"Hon?" she calls to her husband.

James ignores her and places the balls Johnny throws back to him into the empty bucket.

"Thought you and the boys were on your way home," she says, entering the dugout from the entrance.

Joe looks back at her, a distressed expression on his face. Jack locks his hands on his head while watching the still tearful Johnny grab his bat again to return to the batter's box for another round of pitches. Sandy now realizes what's going on. She rips open the gate's door, pushing it hard to get through and marches on the field behind Jack and Joe. James ignores her and continues on with his strenuous lesson.

"James, enough!" she angrily lashes out at him.

Once again James neglects her. He points at a ball against the backstop Johnny forgot. "You missed one . . . "

Johnny releases from his stance and takes a glimpse back at the lone ball he must have overlooked. Annoyance sets in on him as his last tear falls from his face. He throws his bat hard to the ground, bouncing it on the plate. A heated-glare beams at his father.

"Well?" James says to him, growing tired of waiting for the last ball.

"Do we have to do this again?" Sandy asks James. "Our boys played hard tonight. They won for Pete's sake!"

James focuses on Johnny instead, leaving his hand extended to him for the ball. Johnny slowly walks to it and is even more sloth-like when picking it up, taunting his father.

"Got cement in those cleats, boy?" James zings. "You're moving as slow as your swing!"

Annoyance turns into anger, which fills Johnny's demeanor like a cartoon thermometer exploding when it's too hot. Oddly enough, he grabs the ball with his left hand and unleashes an ungodly throw *at*, not *to* his father. James tries to catch it bare-handed, but it smacks his palm hard and ricochets somewhere into the infield.

Sandy, Jack and Joe stand back, stunned by this act of rebellion. Silence hangs in the air for a time, while James shakes the sting from his hand. He darts a surprised look at Johnny, who just finds his bat to step back into the box. Anger still has a hold on him.

"Come here . . . " James says with a serious and expressionless tone.

Johnny does so and plants himself right in front of his father. He doesn't hang his head or look away; rather, he stares him dead in the eyes. No words are exchanged at first, and this moment makes James realize something more than the dried tears on his son's face. He realizes he rattled him. He got under his skin. And from that something beautiful happened.

"What was that?" James scoffs.

Johnny sniffles and shrugs.

"You all right now?"

Johnny shrugs again. James waves his other two sons over to join them on the mound. His expression softens when he sees all three of them looking up at him with their innocent eyes, anticipating what he'll say next, as they've always done.

With a lighter tone, James explains, "If each of you are going to step on any field, you must play this game right. When played the right way, believe me, there is nothing more perfect. It can teach you a lot about life . . . About yourself even. Sometimes it can be your best friend, and other times your enemy. Being unpredictable is what makes it that much more beautiful . . . That's why you will respect it. Respect every opportunity it gives you . . . All of you will have to work hard. Just . . . I'm telling you now, you gotta work harder than anyone else at this to make your own opportunities. Do that, and good things will happen. I promise. My dad played this game. His dad played and so on. It's meant a lot to our family. And boys, your mother and I can't give you things that people with money have. In all honesty, we don't want you to follow in our footsteps. We want better things for you."

He bends down and picks a baseball from the bucket. Looking at the ball while he rotates it with his fingers he adds, "Baseball is the only thing I can give you that might be worth something in your lives." He glances back at Sandy, then back at his sons, "Let's go home."

The boys walk side-by-side with their father leaving the field, the sun setting behind them. James gives an apologetic look to his wife, knowing he's in trouble. She says nothing though and heads back to the van to go on ahead of them.

Johnny falls back to grab the deer slayer.

"Leave that ugly thing for the neighborhood kids," James tells him, and he returns, giving one last glimpse at his favored bat.

James breaks his attention from it when he asks, "Southpaw, huh? Where did that come from?"

Johnny remains silent, not knowing how to respond.

"I think you have something there. "

Jack interrupts him, "Do you think I'll play for the Hawks one day, Dad?"

"Me too?" Johnny and Joe add, trying to emulate their older brother.

"Yes," James answers. "I think all of you will."

"Man, I hope so," Jack replies.

They continue off the field together. James understands his sons are young and untouched by the hardships of life. He doesn't know it now, but Rupland is changing. It's only a matter of time before it changes them too.

CHAPTER 4 — SUMMER OF '03

"You wait for a strike, then you knock the shit out of it."
—Stan Musial

THE PARKING LOT of Rupland High School is a large two-squared space that is dimly lit. Rows of student vehicles fill the lot on this starry night that happens to be prom night. Near the back of the lot, a giant, rusty black Dodge Ram diesel sits under the dimmest of lights. It's an excessive beast of rubber caked in mud. "Mama Tried" by Merle Haggard plays from the radio inside. Banter among six teens sitting in the bed of the truck in tuxes and dresses drown out the music. Among these high school seniors are a few familiar faces. In their rugged handsomeness, there's an obvious change from the Little Hawks of six years ago.

Jack Dalton sits on the bed's edge, fisting a Labatt Blue can. He now has shoulder-length, beach wavy-styled hair, which has been gelled back for the dance. His body is athletic with tree trunk thighs. His features are dark, and he has long eye-lashes. That same cluster of freckles across his cheekbones remain, and even though he's eighteen-years-old now, the child he was remains on him. A highlighted brunette with a short, black formal dress that fits exquisitely on her tight body rests her drink on his knee. Her name is Savannah Ricci. Every once in a while, she and Jack's eyes meet. These looks are more than just casual.

Sitting against the cab's window, strumming an acoustic six-string along with the radio in between taking pulls off his beer, is the owner of this rig— Nick. He's grown to a massive six-foot three, 250-pound teen. His façade is stoic and uncaring when the attention isn't on him; thoughts of the past still haunt his mind. Merle Haggard is about the only artist he listens to anymore. Memories of his mother playing his music in the house almost every day have stayed with him. When the attention is on him, he goes right into that fun-loving, boisterous friend he's known for. A few stains on his tie from dinner add to the mess of his disheveled black tux. His short-hair is a stylistic mess, and his belt is undone to let his beer belly breathe. A noticeable scar is on his chin; a torturous reminder of the accident that took his mother's life.

Rising from the opposite side of the truck's bed is Lou. He speaks softly and is more of a gentleman than his friends, saying, "excuse me" when he needs to get by the girls and asking them if they'd want another brew. Ladies flock to his easy-going charm and love the fact that he's an accomplished student with a bright future ahead of him. His physique is trim and his hair cut to a trendy Mohawk but closer to a Faux-Hawk.

He kicks around the cemetery of empties that lie in Nick's truck bed. "Taking a collection back here?" he jokes to Nick.

Nick chugs what's left in his can and reaches to Lou for another cold one.

"Bro, you using your cover bun as a koozie?" Lou asks Nick with a bit of a chuckle.

Nick observes his jerry-rigged koozie that's wrapped around his empty can and explains, "Lost my Hooters one. Had to MacGyver this bad lad for the occasion."

Lou tosses Nick another can. He empties his koozie and replaces it with a new brew. Cracking it open, it explodes, spraying foam and inadvertently splattering his petite junior date and Lou's senior date. Each throw their hands forward in front of them to block it. Nick stops the flow with his mouth, before placing it down to strum a few more notes.

In between songs, news radio broadcasts, "And over in Rupland County, further budget cuts at the mine make their impact. 80 more jobs were cut from this year's budget . . . "

The banter dies some, each person focusing more on the radio.

"This marks only the second time in fifteen years the mine has suffered these sorts of cutbacks. This is in preparation for the Toledo Cliffs merger that recently took stake in support of minimizing production . . . "

"My uncle was a part of that," Savannah chimes in.

The somber mood turns to a dead quiet. Nick breaks the silence, "Wait Savannah, isn't this the same uncle who made it with a goat on New Year's Eve last year?"

Everyone erupts in laughter.

"You're an asshole!" Savannah says.

Jack tries not to break face on his way to the cooler.

"Babe!" Savannah yells, seeing he's trying to suppress his laughter at Nick's comment.

"What?" Jack asks with a chuckle. "That shit is funny. Wouldn't be surprised if it's true, too, babe."

Savannah throws her empty at Jack. He grabs a full can and opens it for her. Then he puts his arm around his honey and plants a kiss on the side of her head.

"Seriously, Zoom," Nick starts again. "Sheriff caught the dude ass-naked in Potski's barn. Spent two days in the cell or something."

The contagious laughter forces Savannah to even hint a smile after so long.

"No worries, honey," Nick tells her. "Tell your uncle to stick to goats. Heard they're better screwing than most of the girls around here anyway."

Beer spits out of Lou's mouth, causing him to choke on some during his breathy laugh.

Nick then jumps out of the bed to piss in the corner grass. "Zoom!" he calls to his friend. "Come here!"

"Dress pants ain't that hard to figure out, pal," Jack quips with a sneer.

"Just get your ass over here, pard."

Jack decides to relieve himself as well, a few feet away from Nick in the opposite direction.

"Hey, so, uh . . ." Nick sputters into a serious tone, trying to spit out the words as he finishes his piss. "Your folks hiring at the store? My pops could use the work."

"Not sure," Jack responds. "I can ask if you want."

"If you could, that'd be dope. Thanks, man."

Jack gives him a reassuring nod and zips his pants. The two head back to the truck where the clicking of heels approach from the dark shadows of the lot.

"My bitches!" a girl's shrill voice rings aloud.

A tall, blonde senior who could be a model emerges, arm-in-arm with her younger date, a fifteen-year-old Johnny Dalton. Johnny sticks out like an eyesore in his white tux that isn't fitted quite right. It hangs loose on his scrawny body, appearing as if he's swimming in it. He's grown a lot over the years. He's taller than Jack by three inches. Though Johnny's a sophomore, he's still developing into an adult's body; that awkward end stage of puberty. His nose is broad, and his lips are wide and meaty, and he has a buzzed haircut to go along with his million-dollar smile that lights up any room. Even though his outfit will draw attention, Johnny is more reserved, observing his environment, never speaking in it.

"Katie!" Lou's date shrieks, leaping from the tailgate into her friend's arms.

"You fuckers ready to get shitty tonight?!" Katie asks to the others over her friend's shoulder.

She then blows kisses to the others and pulls a game changer from her sparkled clutch purse—a fifth of Jameson Irish.

"Time to raise the stakes up in here," she says before taking a swig and passing it around.

Jack gives his brother an obvious but casual *are you serious* look about his pistol of a prom date, knowing very well the kind of party girl Katie is rumored to be. Katie Purnell is a free-spirited, outgoing, wild child. Johnny mischievously smiles back at Jack, loving every minute of it. Even better is that she's an older woman, which in high school will give him legendary status among his fellow classmates.

"Y'all coming to my camp after?" Nick asks the group.

Yeses spread. Jack helps Savannah off the tailgate, locking hands with her, and suggests to everyone that they head inside the school.

"Yeah, I've gotta good buzz going now anyway," Nick adds, staggering to a stand to grab at his loose belt and unbuttoned dress pants. "If I pass out, just rip me outta these." He takes a deep breath and sucks in his gut to complete the rigorous task of buttoning and buckling himself into his tight pants.

Walking next to Johnny and Katie, Jack observes his brother's duds, less than impressed with his loud appearance. He remarks to him, "You look like an asshole."

"Better than looking like someone's butler," Johnny zings back without skipping a beat.

An edited version of "In da Club" by 50 Cent blasts on the speakers of the gymnasium when the group arrives. They stand under the stretched font prom banners that hang above. Crowds of well-dressed teens dancing and carrying on fill the place. Cheap, disposable cameras sporadically flash about. Orange and black streamers, inflatable arches and columns complete with decorative lanterns and backdrops highlight this dream-themed prom. Looking beyond the dance floor, under the lifted basketball hoops, a professional DJ booth is front and center on a stage. He spins mostly Top 40 and takes requests the entire night.

Nick watches a chaperone pass them, and when it's clear, he snags the fifth from Katie's hiding grasp to sneak a sip, before passing it around to his friends. A pair of arms with fire tattoos peeking onto the hands suddenly wrap around Johnny's neck, putting him in a headlock.

"What are you doing here, little Dalton?!" Eli Masterson jokingly hollers. "Huh, boy?! Huh?!"

Johnny pushes Eli. The eighteen-year-old belts a warm guffaw that is all too familiar. The innocence he once had as a boy vanished, now replaced by a wild, independent teen on the verge of freedom from high school.

When Eli sees Katie locking arms with Johnny's, his smile melts off his face. He now understands why the youngster is attending the upperclassmen's prom. There's some jealousy hidden in Eli because he used to have a huge crush on Katie. Last year she rejected him when he tried asking her out for the millionth time. This is something that doesn't happen often to Eli, so the sting of rejection is still fresh.

"Yo, look at the sophomore getting the older ones," Eli says, his smile reappearing. "Man after my own heart."

He then wraps his arm around Jack and squeezes in between him and Savannah. Almost pushing her out of the way, he tries to one-up Johnny. "Your brother and I are fixing to be Hawks soon, you know?"

"So I've heard, over and over," Johnny responds.

"Well, then pay close attention to us this season. You could actually learn something."

Jack jokingly tries to wrestle with him to shut him up. Johnny can't help but roll his eyes at the gloater as he continues to ramble on, while Katie passes on the fifth to him. Jack sees this and promptly snags it from his brother's grasp. Before he knows it, Savannah leads Jack to the dance floor, just as the song "Remember When" by Alan Jackson begins. Jack takes a nip from the fifth himself and hands it to Eli, then pats his younger brother's shoulder for the nice try and heads out.

More students gather on the dance floor, especially those who don't dance to the fast-paced songs. Jack tries holding Savannah's hand, but she disappears into the throng of students. He ganders around dancing couples, searching for his girl before spotting her in the middle of the floor. A warm smile spreads across his face.

She coyly stares at Jack. One of the many decorative drop string lights brighten the back of her head like a halo, giving her the image of an angel. They meet and hold each other tight, gazing into each other's eyes.

"Last prom," Savannah says.

"Sure is," Jack replies.

"Are you gonna miss it?"

"I don't know. Maybe."

The nostalgia of their time left in high school that Savannah insinuates isn't getting through to him. The dreamer is more concerned for the moment and lost in a world of what could be, rather than what he's already done.

"To be honest, I'm nervous as hell for Tuesday," Jack reveals. "I'm finally eligible. All I can think about is making the roster for Opening Day."

There's a bit of pain behind Savannah's fake, cheerful expressions. She refrains herself from saying anything else, not wanting to ruin this dance- which is surely their last.

"I know, babe," she replies. "You'll make it. You deserve that."

Jack holds her tighter.

"Things are going to get crazy this summer," Savannah says. "Think you'll have time for me when you're a big shot around here?"

Jack joyfully smirks and touches foreheads with her. She closes her eyes to embrace him, and he jokes in a babyish voice, "Oh, I'll always have time for you, sweeetie."

"Seriously, Jack."

Jack's chuckle fades when he looks her in the eyes and earnestly tells her, "Listen, I get scouted by some pro teams, then we're flying high. We'll buy a big ol' house with some land. We'll be set."

"That's some plan. What about school? I still don't understand why you can't go to college and play. Scouts attend more college games than they do here anyway."

"You know I've wanted to be a Hawk since forever. We have the best baseball in the country. Why would I pass on that?"

"Come with me to Colorado, Jack. They have great schools there, great teams."

Jack distances his hold on her, a bit irritated by her words, "Let me do it my way. If I play my game, more scouts will find me. They'll have to . . . It's the Summer League, babe, come on."

Forcing that same fake cheerfulness back, Savannah nods and then buries her face in Jack's neck to end the conversation. In the midst of this, Jack redirects his attention towards Eli. He notices him in a small group of male students, discreetly accepting some cash. Eli thumbs through it, huddling close to the group. Once pleased, they all leave the gym together. Jack can only assume it's for a weed transaction. Eli has sold marijuana since he was fourteen. He doesn't make much money, but just enough to help support him and his mother.

Jack then spots Nick dancing with his tiny date. His giant arms wrap around her, and her feet barely touch the floor. Lou and his date are feet away from them. Suavely, he whispers sweet things into her ear. Kissing her cheek, she has fallen under his spell.

Jack then searches for his brother and spots him furthest across the dance floor. He's intensely making out with Katie. A nearby teacher chaperone immediately pulls them apart.

☞   ☞   ☞

Darkness envelops the wooded area around the Kosko family's lakefront hunting cottage. Next to it is a massive bonfire with a blaze that can be seen for miles across a lake called Big Pike. In and around the cottage high school students party hard. On this celebratory night, seniors and underclassmen populate every inch of the property. Most are still dressed in their prom attire, now loose and in disarray. Music, mostly country, blares throughout. Outside on the old, creaky wooden front porch freshmen are hazed into doing keg stands, which draws laughter and cheers. Across the yard, Nick is in his truck doing donuts in a muddy pit. He takes turns against other friends' beaters in a long-standing pastime they call Mudding.

Huddled around the bonfire made of broken pallets, scraps of wood and old tires are Jack, Savannah, Lou and several friends. Each fist an alcoholic beverage from the overage of coolers brought to the party. There are only three drink options here: Budweiser, Labatt Blue, and Jack Daniels, which is usually mixed with Coca Cola that's on hand.

Jack scans the yard. "Anyone seen Johnny around?"

Lou points near the cottage's fishing dock, where they spot Johnny, Eli, Katie, and a few friends playing horseshoes. Passed around them is a bottle of Wild Turkey, and between drinks, various students take Eli aside in hopes of scoring weed. Johnny loves his way. He loves the attention Eli garners. He clings to his every word and every action. The way the teen carries himself in this cool and careless way is admirable to him.

"We gotta reload," Eli says, pointing to the empty Wild Turkey that Johnny polished the last few drops from.

Johnny chucks the empty in the lake. "About that time, ain't it, bro?"

He, Eli and Katie make their way towards the cottage. Jack grabs his brother by the arm when he passes near the bonfire, breaking him from Katie's side. Johnny becomes defensive right away, "Oh, come on. Don't play big brother tonight."

"You've gotta game tomorrow," Jack reminds him.

"No shit."

"You gave up five runs your last start. Think this will help much?"

"Couldn't hurt. Surprised you even knew that, golden boy."

"Johnny, go home. Dad's gonna get on us both if you're out too late anyway."

Johnny jerks his arm from his grasp. "I'm sure the old man will be fine. He's gonna sit up there in those stands tomorrow like some wooden Indian with his arms crossed, all serious and shit." Johnny imitates. "Fish up an excuse for me, I'm sure he'll believe you."

Less than amused, Jack doesn't say a word, and Katie leads Johnny into the cottage.

"Watch him for me, Masterson. Would you?" Jack asks.

"Sure thing, boss," Eli replies and follows Johnny and Katie.

"Boy's got an attitude on him, huh?" Lou remarks.

"Yeah, something," Jack says, dropping his lips into his cup for another drink.

☞   ☞   ☞

Nick's truck sits in a visitors' lot facing a massive prison facility that's more like a brick rampart wrapped in barbwire than a prison. Inside the truck, Nick and Jack scarf greasy burgers to nurse their hangovers. They're still dressed in their tuxes from the night before, which are presently sloppy.

Jack can't help but notice Nick's foot nervously tap. He says, "Weird, isn't it?"

Nick swallows the largest of bites down fast to reply, "You have no idea." He finishes the rest of the burger and reveals, "I haven't made it down here once since he's been in. My grandma wouldn't let me. She said he never wanted me to see him like that. "

"Damn. "

"We gotta look for work for him now too, I guess. And he has to do all these programs and check-ins. Crazy shit."

"Are you bringing him back to the old place?"

"Yeah." Nick becomes lost in his overwhelming thoughts.

"You and the guys going in to get your physicals tomorrow?" Jack asks, changing the subject to calm his friend as best as he can.

"Yup," Nick replies, coming out of his trance. "You're not?"

"What, and have my nuts felt by Lou's dad? Nah-uh, I'm good, bro. I'll probably head to Dixon or something. Savannah wants to check out a few bookstores there anyway."

Nick chuckles, "Mr. Webb does keep his hand down there a little long, doesn't he?"

The two share a long, hard laugh. So hard that they can't even eat anymore.

"I swear he ices his fucking hands before he sees us too!" Nick states. "My shit gets totally shriveled, looking like I've been neutered or something."

The laughter comes to an abrupt halt when the prison's tall gates suddenly slide open. This triggers Nick to hide his burger wrappers behind his seat and exit to stand in front of his truck's bumper. Through the opened gates walks George. His long hair is in a ponytail, and his beard matches his tame flow of gray.

George doesn't even look at Nick first. Instead, he opts to breathe in the fresh air, raising his head back. Gazing at the blue skies as a free man, all he can think is that they are bluer than anything he's seen in years. Everything has special meaning today. He tightly clenches a plastic bag of his few belongings, and his other hand is balled into a fist that he opens and closes out of anxiousness. When his eyes finally set on his son, they soften, and his fist unclenches. He's amazed how much Nick has grown. He's even taller than him. His son has grown into a man. It's a long walk to Nick, but when he gets within a few feet of him, he stops to a Kosko standoff of silence.

"My Nicky-boy, look at you," George says proudly, spreading his gapped smile of the many teeth he's lost from both his meth addiction and too many fights on the inside.

Nick just stands expressionless, unsure of what to do next.

His father looks him over before he says, "Didn't have to get all dressed up for me."

Nick gathers the courage and with a simple gesture, extends his hand to him. George steps forward and gladly shakes it. The handshake turns into an uncomfortable and awkward hug initiated by George that doesn't last as long as it should.

Jack exits the truck to let George in on his side. While doing so, he glances in the truck's bed to check on Johnny, unconscious and lying on a couple of blankets. Alcohol has become victorious.

George eyes Jack and remarks, "It's good to see you, Dalton."

"Good to see you too, Mr. Kosko," Jack says, letting him in the truck.

"Let's celebrate, boys!" George says, situating himself between Nick and Jack.

"Sounds good to me," Jack says with a polite smirk.

Nick drops the extra food bag from the dash onto his father's lap.

"Karen's diner?" George asks hoping as he digs into the bag.

"Of course, Pops," Nick replies.

"Ooooh, it's been too long, my friend!" George says to the luscious burger before chowing down. "Too long."

By midafternoon, a high school baseball game is in progress between Rupland and Ippling. There is no lonelier place than the pitcher's mound. Johnny has gotten the start for his team, but is in rough shape, having not fully recovered from his hangover. Bent over and on the verge of puking from a splitting headache, his body cringes with pain. His latest pitch sails over the chain link fence for a two-run shot.

Every sound is drowned around him. He hears nothing but his own long, heavy breaths and the creaking of his aching muscles. Sweat pours profusely like a heavy rain, dropping on one of two gloves he's brought with him.

Johnny is the first and only ambidextrous pitcher the county has ever produced. He has more control with his right arm but has more velocity with his left. Some say he's the next coming of Hawks great Charlie Hylman. Regardless of the hype, the middle Dalton is a dual-threat on the mound and hopeful for a future on the Hawks pitching staff.

Behind him, the wooden black scoreboard reads: 3RD INNING — 6-0

The defeated hurler squints through the sting of sweat in his eyes to see his stout manager waddling towards him, signaling for a relief pitcher. He then catches a glimpse of his father beyond the foul lines of right field. Just arriving from work to watch his son's game, James heads back to his truck. By the way he struts in that flat-footed and heavy stride of his, Johnny knows he isn't pleased with his latest performance. The kid can only close his eyes and wish he wasn't here.

This night ends as badly as the 10-0 stomping his team suffered. Johnny isn't just scolded and grounded by his parents for drinking and coming home late with Jack that day, but James also uses this punishment to discuss everything Johnny did wrong during this afternoon's game. From the way he came off the rubber to his pitch selection and wild throws, his entire body of work is under a microscope until his next rotation start.

Johnny refuses to sit and hear this every night. He finds ways to escape the house to meet Katie and push his parents to harsher punishments. Punishments that involve him working at the store the majority of the time, or even helping James do maintenance and landscaping around the farm. James and Sandy try anything they can to keep their son out of trouble, but it doesn't help. Johnny finds ways to squirm out of everything.

☞   ☞   ☞

A couple of weeks pass. Senior graduation has come and gone and the high school baseball and softball seasons are nearing their end. On this Thursday, Jack is en route to Kenmore County by himself. Savannah isn't attending the trip. In fact, she doesn't even know about it.

Jack turns the radio off in his 1990 Ford Thunderbird to drive the rest of the trip in silence. The car is ugly as sin and in need of many repairs. It's a piece of shit for sure, but it's his piece of shit, and he earned it after saving what he made at the store last summer.

Rolling through the one-trick pony town of Dixon, he arrives at a nameless gym in a tiny, rundown strip-mall that sits between a Save-A-Lot grocery store and a laundromat.

When he enters the gym, it seems suspiciously empty, but the lights are on. The place is an absolute hole. Scattered throughout in no specific pattern is aged equipment, big box televisions that don't work and one dented water fountain. A thin layer of carpet masks the cold cement floor, which doesn't even cover the entire space and is full of past roof leak stains and rips.

"Hello?" Jack calls out.

A hulk of a man wearing hospital scrubs appears from a back room. Jack approaches with caution, unsure about this mysterious man.

"I'm Jack," he says, partially extending his hand.

The giant man's face turns upright, recognizing who he is talking to, and shakes his hand. "Right. Hi, Jack. Kelly. Come on back." His voice is high-pitched and lispy and doesn't quite match his muscular physique.

Kelly leads him into a dark back room that he uses as his personal office. It's about as bare and disorganized as the gym itself.

"Have a seat," Kelly tells him. "Sorry for the mess."

Obviously, Jack thinks to himself as he sweeps off a stack of empty boxes on a squeaky computer chair to sit. Kelly takes a seat at his oddly small desk. He opens a drawer and pulls out a shoebox-sized green tin with a lock and places it on his lap.

"Have you thought about this?" Kelly asks, facing Jack. "And I don't mean the pros and the cons. I mean the repercussions."

"Absolutely," Jack says without skipping a beat. "It's my only option."

Kelly acknowledges Jack's philosophical expression, "Okay. Because I have no problem taking your money, kid, but if anything goes wrong, this can't come back to me. Do you understand?"

"I promise it won't."

"Got the money?"

Jack digs in his pocket and reveals a good-sized clip of twenties. Kelly takes and thumbs through them before he spins the combination to the tin box. He takes a white plastic bag from it and hands it to Jack. Pills rattle from inside the bag.

"Thanks," Jack says and immediately leaves to return to his car.

He places the bag on his passenger seat. Realizing the stakes in the event he's pulled over by police, he opens his glove box and shovels his insurance and registration forms onto the floor and stuffs the plastic bag inside. The teen exhales in relief. Relief turns into guilt after a while, then rage. He starts furiously punching his steering wheel.

☞ ☞ ☞

Days later, the same high school field that Johnny played on hosts tryouts for the Rupland Hawks. Across the counties, this is considered the biggest day before the season starts. Dozens of teens and even former high school players attend these in every town to test their skills, dreaming of joining the famed league.

Parked vehicles sit to the left side of the diamond on a grassy knoll, overlooking the entire field. Many hopefuls prepare themselves to join the line checking in. Jack, Nick, and Lou are among them, getting dressed and stretching. Before long, Eli rolls in next to Nick's truck in his light blue 1973 Chevy Chevelle SS Coupe. He spent most of his teen years saving to buy the classic car, which he claims is his baby. When he exits the car, he stumbles, almost falling on his face. Sporting a Cleveland Indians cap that's lowered over his brows like some downtrodden cowboy, he tries to avoid any sunlight in his sensitive eyes. He's been wearing the same camouflage cutoff-tee and ripped jeans for three days now. And aside from looking like shit, he smells like a brewery.

"What do ya say, boys?" Eli says to the three in a scratchy voice.

Nick and Lou throw up a hand. Jack is the only one that doesn't greet their friend. He doesn't even pay attention to him. His cold, bothersome demeanor while clipping his catcher shin guard straps around his legs is clear.

Eli kicks his sticky trunk open. He grabs his gear that consists of his glove, pants and an old pair of cleats he's had for years and tosses them on the ground next to Jack where he plops himself.

"You're late," Jack says to Eli. "Gotta sign in still."

"Eh, I'll get to it," Eli replies. "My head is bumping."

Nick tosses Eli a beer from his cooler in his bed, "This will help, pard. Rough night?"

Eli ignores the question. He cracks open the beer and takes a hell of a swig as if he were dying of thirst. Jack turns his backwards cap forward and is the first of his friends to rise.

Nick joins him, and Jack lowers his hand to help Lou up. The three head to the field's entrance to see a line of thirty to forty hopefuls eagerly waiting to enter. Jack clings his chest protector and mitt in his hand tight, almost white-knuckling them with anticipation.

"Is everyone loose?" Jack asks and gets his answer with a nod from both. "Good. When we get on that field, no mistakes. No excuses. No regrets. Let's show them how we play."

"Amen," Nick says as he hits gloves with Jack and Lou before they descend the knoll to join the line.

Eli staggers behind, slipping on a cleat and tries to pull himself together. After check-in, Coach Roberts and Coach Sarah gather everyone at home plate. Jack takes a knee right away. He knows the routine. He's seen plenty of tryouts from the outside. The rest follow suit. Everyone eyeballs Manager MacIntyre as he takes his time walking from the opposite side of the field.

"Thanks for coming out," MacIntyre says after taking a minute to observe this year's crop of potentials.

"There's only three roster spots left, so lay it all on the field today." He lets that sink in for a second before continuing, "Gentlemen, being selected as a part of our team is a privilege. We only want the best. For those I choose, I ask one thing of you: keep making this game pure. Give our town a reason to smile during these summer days."

And with that, he lets Roberts and Sarah get the men situated. A round of claps for the manager start from the back of the group just as Coach Roberts steps into his place. He brings his thumb and index finger to his nose and rockets a wad of snot in front of a repulsed Lou.

"He didn't ask for a fuckin' applause!" Roberts surly remarks. The claps die as quick as they started. Roberts gets right to it and checks his clipboard, "Infielders on the left with Fred, outfielders on the right with Coach Sarah, and pitchers and catchers in the pen with me. Later, we'll test you shitheads with the 60-yard dash. Let's move!"

The hopefuls rise and spread to join their respected positional sections of the field. Now ready, Eli pokes his head around to find Jack to pitch to.

"Yo, Zoom, ready?" Eli asks his friend when he spots him.

Jack deliberately avoids him and walks next to another pitcher—Colton Ewen—a kid he played high school ball with. Colton wasn't all that great, but Jack knows how to catch him. Eli places his hand on Jack's shoulder to get his attention. Jack brushes off his hand without hesitation and leans into his former pitcher, almost in his face, and in an abrupt but quiet manner tells him, "Look at you man, you're wasted."

"It's nothing," Eli casually says with a shrug.

"No, it means something. Throw to somebody else. You're not ruining today for me." Jack backs away from Eli and rejoins Colton.

Insulted and disparaged, Eli stands back, at a loss for words.

☞   ☞   ☞

Two weeks pass, and Tryout Day seems like forever ago. For Jack, it's been an excruciating wait because it's just another step closer towards becoming a Hawk and playing in the league, and he'll be damned if he doesn't make the roster this season.

Today is Friday, and while most of his friends are preparing to be weekend warriors, he works at his family's grocery store; something he's done every weekend since he was eleven. He enters the kitchen from the back of the building after taking the garbage to the dumpster. Dipping into his mother's office, he grabs his bat bag.

On the store's main floor, many loyal customers shop throughout the colorful aisles full of product. Over the speakers, The Sweet's "Little Willy" plays lightly from Sandy's favorite classic rock station, 99.9 The Riff. Near the front Sandy rings up customers at the checkout counter with Joe bagging the items for her. The blemished-faced thirteen-year-old is about as tall as Jack is now and is "built like a brick shithouse," James tells him every so often. People say he'll make a better football player than he would a baseball player, but he has always followed his brothers' lead, and baseball is the path he wants most.

Sandy's once long hair is now chopped to her shoulders. One thing about this bright and bubbly mother is that she ages very well and still looks like she's in her early 30s. She's a master baker in the kitchen and works her store's floor like a used car salesman, up-selling even the smallest of deals. She's an affable owner, a skill she claims a person must possess in order to run a successful business. With the mine steadily cutting jobs and local businesses hit hard by the declining economy, the store hasn't been doing very well lately. Nevertheless, she still finds ways to bring in customers. Whether it's through holiday promotions or cute contests that dazzle old ladies and children, she always brings home the bacon. A one-woman show, the business is Sandy's domain. And she predominantly keeps it afloat, even more so than her husband.

When finished chatting with a customer, she sends Joe to the back to grab the broom so he can sweep the aisle floors. Joe continues towards the kitchen area. Meanwhile, in the office, Jack secretly chases a couple of blue pills down with some water. The sound of Joe rustling around in the kitchen makes him scurry to put everything back in order. He then swiftly exits the office, where he snags an apron from a hook to tie it around his waist.

"What are you looking for?" Jack asks Joe.

"The goddamn broom," an irked Joe replies. "I swear I sweep that floor ten times a day, and it's still not enough for her."

Jack chuckles to himself, understanding his brother's annoyance. He's been in that same place many times before. Knowing where the broom is, he grabs it from behind the meat cutter and hands it to him.

James is heard inside the store. His and Sandy's voices become louder as they make their way back towards Jack and Joe. Sandy explains to her husband, "I need help unloading the trucks today."

"Where's Johnny?" James asks. "He's supposed to be here anyway?"

As he enters the kitchen his eyes set on his eldest son, and he reminds him with a tone of annoyance, "And you're supposed to be at home waiting for a phone call."

"That's not today," Jack scoffs.

"It's the fifth; yes, it is. They call between nine and ten."

Jack checks the cloudy glass clock that hangs above the meat cooler: 8:51 a.m. An *oh shit* realization hits him, and he rips off his apron and snags his bat bag from the office. James sneaks a kiss to his wife before he leaves with him.

"Make sure to say your prayers, Jack!" Sandy says. "God will answer!" She puts her arm around Joe and comments, "Looks like it's just you and me today, kid."

"Guess so," replies Joe.

"This floor looks filthy. Let's get sweeping."

She walks back to the front. Joe rolls his eyes and begins to sweep.

☞   ☞   ☞

An eight foot tall, oak grandfather clock in the corner of the dining room ticks: 9:56 a.m. Next to it, a cord runs from the wall to a phone on the table. At the table sits Jack on one end and James at the other. Both watch the seconds and minutes tick by. They crack their knuckles, tap their feet and fidget in their seats. Jack plays with his plaid shirtsleeves, rolling them up, then rolling them back down, rolling them up, then rolling them down again.

He blurts, "I knew it! I should've bulked up more to drive the ball further. I promise I've been working on that, Dad."

"There's still four minutes left," James says.

"What if they don't call?" Jack asks with a ping of sadness.

"Then we'll try again next season."

Jack's eyes drop in disappointment as his hope deflates.

"Hey," says James, grabbing back his son's attention. "Next season . . . "

The last minute of the hour is upon them when the phone suddenly rings. Both perk up. But Jack's nerves kick in, preventing him from answering it.

"Dad?" Jack shudders, looking to his father like a child paralyzed with fear.

James reaches over the table and answers it for him, "Hello?"

Jack watches his father's expression for any sort of hint to his fate. The man is stone-faced in his responses to whoever he's speaking to. " . . . Thank you. Uh-huh, bye," James says and ends the call. He crosses his arms and sits back in his chair, exhaling deep and long.

Jack begins to take the hint, "Not my year, huh?"

James keeps his poker face for as long as he can before his jaw loosens and a grin stretches.

"I'm a Hawk?" Jack asks.

"First Dalton," James affirms proudly.

Jack doesn't know what to do. Something he's wanted for so long has come true. Every emotion sinks in at once. His overwhelming happiness begins to peek through, and he sits back in his chair, relieved.

☞　　☞　　☞

The Rupland softball team finishes their last practice of the season before their final game the next day. It's been an unsuccessful campaign for Manager Sarah MacIntyre and her high school girls. They're currently 6-18 overall, with a terrible 2-15 conference record. Many claim it's a rebuilding year. Eight seniors will be gone after tomorrow. But the talented sophomore and junior classes have shown some promise, giving their school an exciting preview of what the 2004 season holds.

Upon finishing some hitting techniques with Sarah, Savannah packs her bat bag and adjusts her black headband around her head before leaving the field level dugout. She spots Jack standing by the edge of the stands slightly grinning at her with a bite to his bottom lip.

"Good work today, Ricci," Jack says.

Savannah dismisses him as she keeps her stride, "You just got here; don't lie."

"I know, babe. I'm sorry. But—"

"This was our last practice of the season. My season. You made every single one but today? . . . Whatever."

She walks away from him. Jack follows behind to try to get her to stop. When she arrives at her silver Pontiac Sunfire, she notices Jack has already stopped following her. He just stands in place with that same mischievous grin.

"What the hell are you grinning about?" Savannah asks.

"I made it. "

Savannah places her bag on the seat and sighs a slight smile of her own, "God . . . You could've said something, instead of making me look like a bitch."

"I tried," Jack says, trying to hold back his smile.

She walks to him and hugs him tight, "Congratulations, baby."

He places his hands on her bare and sunburnt shoulders peeking from her neon cutoff-tee.

"I need you now more than ever," Jack mentions. "Shit just got real. It's gonna be a circus."

"You have me all summer until I go to school."

He kisses her softly.

Savannah gazes into his brown eyes and reiterates, "I'm proud of you. You know that, right? I'm very proud of you."

"Yes."

She glistens that radiant smile that Jack can't resist. He then wraps his arms around her body again, this time grabbing her shapely ass.

"I'm gonna miss you in these," Jack says, referring to her tight black baseball pants and neon green knee-high socks.

"Shush," She jokingly responds with a flattered simper.

☞　　☞　　☞

Three pairs of black and white Nike cleats step foot onto the greenest grass they can remember at Oren P. Rollins Field. Jack, Nick, and Lou stand tall as the Hawks rookies of 2003. This is their first practice. Each sport an official Hawks hat. Lou wears a black headband under his, and team baseball pants and a T-shirt. Nick made sure to break his practice gear in by removing the sleeves of his tee as soon as he got it in his possession.

They gaze into the outfield to see their new teammates playing catch and stretching. The friends stay close to each other as they inch past a group of seven media reporters that huddle around Cain McCloud, bombarding him with questions about the upcoming season. Cain also wears a cutoff but a size smaller with tight baseball pants that perfectly fit his god-like body and brand new Air Jordan XI—Jeter PE cleats that have his jersey #5 stitched on the tongues. His well-defined muscles gleam in the sun from the oil he rubs on himself before every practice. A little trick to get the media going, maybe even a few fan girls that hang around the field, if he's lucky.

Some of these reporters make their rounds leading to Opening Day, visiting every league team's facility for the inside scoop of potential starting lineups, new roster additions, and any injuries. Even the tiniest bit of gossip they get helps them breakdown predictions and update their power rankings. Last week they published the long-awaited preseason rankings. One of the most popular media sources throughout the counties is a bi-weekly paper called, *Through the Fence*. Everything that anyone needs to know about the league, teams, players, and coaches are in this paper. First published in 1980 by owner Hue Jensen, it has been a go-to source for the counties ever since. When the boom of the internet started, the publication branched into a website that gathers solid traffic daily. This is the only extent of publicity the towns are willing to allow their league to have. Aside from a small television and radio station coverage, the paper is considered a great advertising tool for each of the three counties.

Cain stands before the reporters now a thirty-one-year-old veteran. He's no longer that young, wet behind the ears up-and-comer, but someone who's between an icon and a legend in the prime of his career. Fielding questions, he's completely in his element. He answers them with poise and charisma, showcasing some humor in between, causing the media to melt in his hands. If there was a poster child for the league, he's it. Cain McCloud has blossomed into the real deal.

In the stands, a cluster of spectators watches the practice. Most are old men in their 60s, 70s and 80s who once played or coached in the league. Their lone purpose is to provide funds for the league. They're boosters. Among the counties, they're known as "The Committee." Besides the vanilla-flavored tobacco they smoke from their pipes, they share one thing in common, they've seen more games in this league than anyone. It's no surprise they're a respected bunch, almost Mafia Don status. In the offseason they'll meet at Rupland Family Foods or Huff's Hardware, giving their personal assessments of each town's team and players over eternal cups of coffee.

In the mix of the spectators is James. He stands away from the Committee, observing the practice by himself.

"It's that time again, James," says Cliff as he pulls a maple-carved pipe from his mouth.

"Sure is," James says.

Cliff is the Committee's longest standing member. He's established a solid friendship with James the past decade. His donations alone have helped the local Little League organization thrive. And he was instrumental in bringing James in as the coach of the Little Hawks during the years Jack, Johnny, and Joe played.

Standing in front of the dugout, away from the chaos, are coaches MacIntyre, Roberts and Sarah. They observe Cain handle the media like his own personal reality television show. Coach Roberts doesn't pay any attention to that, however. He's obsessed with the latest edition of *Through the Fence* that he flips through.

"Can you believe those sons of bitches ranked us behind Dixon?" Roberts says.

"That's cuz we're getting old, Lloyd," MacIntyre says.

"Pssh. Old," Roberts says. "I call it worldly experience."

"Worldly experience?" Sarah asks with a sarcastic chuckle.

"Mhmm."

MacIntyre shakes his head and shouts to Cain, having enough of his media antics, "Wrap it up, McCloud!"

"Okay everyone, we'll see you on Opening Day," Cain tells the reporters. "You're gonna see a good ball game, I promise you that."

He breaks away from them and heads into the outfield to join his teammates, where he sets his sights on the fresh meat stretching in the grass next to a few end of the road veterans. One of these vets is Charlie Hylman, now thirty-nine and in his 20th season of his famed-career. It takes him a little longer than most to stretch out the kinks in his aching muscles these days.

"We got new bat boys?" Cain quips about the rookies to one of his closest friends—Landon Steele, a thick-gutted workhorse in his late 20s and in his fourth season as a starting third baseman.

"He's joking," Charlie tells the rookies in his soft-spoken Texas-twanged accent. "Kinda . . . " He stands to bend his arms behind his back while telling Cain, "Take it easy on 'em now. Don't need to be scarin' off the rooks on the first day."

"Whatever you say, Char," Cain replies with a shit-eating grin on his face. He steps ahead and shakes hands with Jack, who stands to greet him. Cain's six-foot three-inch frame towers over the five-foot nine kid. "Cain McCloud. Catcher."

"Jack Dalton . . . Catcher." Jack projects with confidence, hoping to impress his idol enough to be taken under his wing.

"Catcher? You're a little small," Cain jabs. "Wait. Wait, yeah, you're that kid that stole home in the State Finals last year, right?"

Jack humbly nods once, neglecting to embellish on the feat.

"What do they call you again? Doom or Broom or something?"

"Zoom-Zoom," Nick chimes in with annoyance. He stands and grabs Jack's shoulder. "My boy will turn heads on this field, pard."

"Zoom-Zoom?" Cain chuckles at Jack's expense. "Okay. Yeah, I heard of you. Impressive. You won't get away with that kind of base running in this league though. Do that up here, you'll likely get a mouth full of leather."

He starts to play catch with Landon, in the same spot he runs his mouth, "Catchers get their asses kicked more than anyone. You gotta be ready for that. I can't tell you how many times I woke up the next morning after a game counting my bruises. Comes with the territory, I suppose. Right, Char?"

"Sure does," Charlie says.

"Base runners are lethal, man. Whether you're a catcher or fielder, they'll come at you. Hook slides that catch feet. Diggers that kick dirt in your face. They'll raise their hands to block your vision, take out slides galore. Shit, runners will even come spikes high if it means getting that safe call or protecting one of their own. Landon, show 'em your trophy!"

Landon hustles to them and pulls back the three-quarter sleeves of his practice shirt to show a jagged, lightning bolt scar on his forearm. He and Charlie admire it some.

"Had a bastard from Holton try to leg a triple a few years back," Landon recalls. "Came at me steel up, like daggers. Fucker dug deep. I held on to her though, still got the out."

Cain pats Landon's chest and sends him back to continue to play catch with him.

"Now that's *my* boy," he says with some competitiveness towards Nick as he catches a throw from Landon. "Pitchers? Pssh, they're a whole different story. Not a goddamn one of them is alike. Strike zones are a hell of a lot bigger in this league too, so these tricky moose knuckles will come at you with everything and anything they can. They'll throw ungodly stuff that you've never seen before. And they take more chances too. Throwing inside is not a problem. Don't dare crowd the plate, because they want to throw it at you! They do! Don't matter to them. Your older pitchers, like the antique model here—"

"Watch it," Charlie says.

"When their shit starts to dive, they have to get creative and add a few dirty pitches to the collection that doesn't wear and tear on their arms. You'll see all sorts of junk that comes in handy. Gotta be ready for it, rook. These aren't friendly to catch. Emery-balls, goop-balls, and even your good old-fashioned spitballs. Whatever does the trick."

"Umps don't give a shit," Charlie says, touching his toes.

"Nope. Free-for-all," Cain adds, tossing the ball back to Landon. "And would you believe it, coaches still treat these pricks like babies!"

"Fuck you," Charlie says to him. "Coddled is the last thing we are."

Cain laughs exaggeratedly loud.

"You trying to scare us or something?" Nick asks, unamused by Cain's theatrical description of the league.

"Just warning you greenhorns that our game is played a little different. It's fast. Fast as fuck. It'll take some getting used to. More than I can say for that Major League bitch-ball."

"We know," Jack comments back, not wanting his superiors to think they're soft. "We've been watching you guys play since we were kids. We'll be ready for what's coming."

"Yeah? Better be," Cain says. "Because it's something like a war."

Cain ends the conversation when he moseys to a different spot to throw to Landon.

Charlie waves the rookies to him so they can walk to the other side of the field together. "C'mon, I'll introduce ya'll to the others."

"Is he acting like a dick, or is that just what he is?" Lou asks Charlie.

"Oh, no doubt, McCloud is a dick," Charlie replies without skipping a beat, cleaning the lenses of his infamous thick-framed glasses. "You'll get used to him."

They come to a stop a way from the dugout where the reporters wait to interview Charlie.

"Them too," Charlie says, putting back on his glasses. "Follow me. It's better that they get to know ya'll."

Beyond the dugout, leaning against the barrier in the corner entrance to the park, smoking a cigarette, is Johnny. He, too, watches the practice. His father eventually spots him. Katie lays on the horn in the parking lot to let Johnny know his ride is here. James watches him crush his cigarette and leave.

☞   ☞   ☞

A lunch whistle screams like an oncoming train. Waves of miners flood the facility's cafeteria for lunch. James is among the mechanical group of fitters, welders, and boilermakers that populate the food line. After a short conversation with a coworker, he sits with his bag lunch at one of the long cafeteria tables. He pulls out a hefty meatloaf sandwich with sides of veggies that his wife made for him this morning. His eyes wander to the end of his table where he sees Eli sitting alone, slumped over his tray of an uneaten slop of spaghetti. A glazed look in his eyes intensifies his morose expression. Mining is Eli's life now. It's certainly not what he expected for himself.

James gathers his lunch and scoots on down to sit across from his former player.

"Masterson," he says to get his attention.

"Coach," Eli replies back, deadpanned, barely lifting his head to greet him.

"When did you start working here?"

"A couple weeks back. Part time. Started on third, but they moved me to first shift after a few days. Not a bad gig, I guess."

"Are you getting the hang of things? Guys treating you right?"

Used to his coach's concern for him, Eli breaks his first smile, "Yes, Coach."

"Opening Day this Saturday," James remarks. "Are you gonna be there?"

"I gotta see my boys' debut, of course."

James notices some pain behind Eli's response. Clearly, he understands, since three of his best friends made the cut, and he's the outsider.

"How's the arm?" James asks. "Have you been putting the work in?"

"To be honest, not lately, Coach. No."

"Next year could be your year. Keep busting your ass. You're more than welcome to train with us at the house anytime."

Eli politely nods and goes back to staring at his food.

"Spaghetti isn't too good here," James says.

"Kinda looks like shit."

James tears his meatloaf sandwich in half and shares a piece with Eli.

"Oh no, that's okay, Coach," Eli says.

"I ain't gonna eat this whole damn thing, Masterson."

Eli gladly takes the half from James and indulges.

Opening Day: May 31st, 2003
RUPLAND HAWKS VS. RANSVILLE REDS

This isn't just any Saturday, it's a county-wide holiday. Opening Day. And Rupland is celebrating in style on this humid night. Inside and outside Oren P. Rollins Field is a party of grand community spirit. Scattered throughout the parking lot are groups of tailgaters that cook, eat and drink. The smells of home cooking lure in more and more fans to partake in the event. This is the one time before the season starts where the home and away crowds can break bread and see eye-to-eye over good food and spirits.

The spread is delightfully massive. There's hamburgers, steaks, corn, pasta salads, buffalo wings, Ms. LaFord's famous ghost pepper fries, Mr. Manski's delicious Indian Summer Turkey chili, stuffed peppers, bowls and bowls of artichoke and cheese dips and assorted chips. County favorites such as turkey, Cajun and sausage pasties, cold cuts, nachos and of course, several varieties of punch and beer are also popular delicacies on the menu. These are fixings of most Super Bowl parties, but this is the biggest party of the year.

James drinks with a few friends from the mine, while Sandy makes her rounds with loyal customers. Near the Reds team bus, Joe and his Pony

League teammates join in on cornhole toss in one section of the parking lot. This section also has a Beer Pong table for the adults and a giant Bounce House for the kids.

Inside the park on the outfield, the Rupland High School marching band plays various fight songs before the fans that enter from the lot. Each fan picks their best spot to watch the game, almost as carefully as they would buying a new car. The feel has to be just right because this is the seat they will sit in the rest of the season, whether that be for comfort or superstition. No one wants to jinx their team. An hour later everyone fills the bleachers, anticipating the marquee match. This is it; the 2003 season begins. Summer begins.

A portly man in his late 40s tosses out the ceremonial first pitch of the game. He is Rupland's mayor Daniel Morrow. Throwing Opening Day pitches for each Summer League town's mayor is almost a rite of passage. It's a fifty-year tradition.

The Hawks players warm up on the field. Sitting in the dugout, dressed in their new threads, the rookies listen to the array of noises around the park. The only change from the uniforms of the 90s is the style. Gray, instead of white, is the main color with the same orange and black trim. Their caps are black and still showcase the orange Old English 'R' on the front. Jack wears his knee-high socks up to his knee-length short pants. Nick and Lou have embraced the Major League trend of baggier pants that lie over their cleats, just barely above the bottom of the back heel. Lou wears a black, tight-fitted compression sleeve on his right throwing arm, while Nick wears his uniform unintentionally sloppy. It's wrinkled and half tucked-in.

On the infield taking practice grounders, Ransville's players' uniforms are mainly white with red pinstripes and red belts. A white Varsity font 'R' stands out in the middle of their red hats, almost identical to the Cincinnati Reds uniforms.

Jack watches a brooding Nick stare into field he's about to take for the first time. The teen is lucky enough to have been named the only starter of his friends. He wears a first baseman's mitt with a wristband pulled to each forearm, and a good size dip of Skoal packed tight in his bottom lip.

"Nervous?" Jack asks.

"I'm ready," Nick replies with confidence.

Coach Roberts rushes into the dugout and begins to push players into the field. He's as excited as everyone else for tonight.

"Smells like Opening Day to me, men! Give 'er hell!" he shouts at the team.

Nick exits the dugout just as MacIntyre enters, observing the bench; someone is missing.

"Where's McCloud?" MacIntyre asks Landon Steele, who's got a foot on the bench, adjusting his own knee-high socks.

"No idea, Coach," he replies, also searching.

"Christ, he's missing on Opening Day?!" Roberts squawks.

MacIntyre's eyes float to the far end of the bench, where Jack currently sits by himself. With his catcher's mitt on, the rookie imitates caught balls being thrown by Ransville's starting pitcher Tyler Vegas, warming up across the field. He's making the most of his time on the bench, learning what he can so he's ready when his time comes.

"Dalton!" MacIntyre says loudly, getting Jack's attention. "Suit up. You're catching Hylman."

"Wha- what about McCloud?" he asks, caught off guard.

"Do you want to or not?" MacIntyre asks.

Jack slides his bat bag between his legs from under the bench as if he was prepared for this very moment, compared to the rest of his team, whose personal gear is either in the locker room or placed on the long wooden shelf above their heads. He starts to put on his personal catcher's gear. Snap after snap, he promptly straps his black shin guards with orange trim on and places his customized orange with black four corner trim TPX Pulse chest protector over his torso. After he inserts his cup, he tucks his Nokona mitt under his arm and exits the dugout.

MacIntyre blocks his way. He brings him in close, staring the rookie directly in his anxious eyes and says, "Call a good game."

Jack forces a nod through his nervousness, accidentally dropping his traditional style mask that's propped up on his reversed catcher's cap over his face. He pushes it back and gives his coach another reassuring nod, then hustles onto the field to join his teammates.

"Make me a genius, kid," MacIntyre says to himself under his breath.

The three rookies stand side-by-side before awed fans, their jersey numbers revealed:

Jack - #12

Nick - #40

Lou - #3

Not far from them, the umpire crew, Craig, Dale, and Aaron, in light blue shirts and gray pants, stand chatting with MacIntyre and Reds manager Steve

LaCroy. Both managers give copies of their lineup cards to Craig, then pin the originals up in each dugout. By the end of the games, every skipper has these scribbled on with subs, reliefs, stats and strategic notes that they will study for future situations.

Sounds of the park are music to the rookies' ears. The world from this view is new and exciting and far more spectacular than anything they've ever seen here.

"It's really something, isn't it?" Lou says to his friends.

Nick is too busy searching the stands for his own father to respond. A short while later, he concedes and joins his team on the right field foul lines. The Reds stand on the left field lines. In cadence, the marching band spreads into center field. A row of trumpets sound to begin the national anthem. Half way through the song, Cain makes his way from the dugout to join his team. He's half-dressed, tucking in his wrinkled jersey that still shows the captain's 'C' stitched to it. He joins the end of the line behind MacIntyre, where he finishes getting ready.

"Had a damn flat," Cain says to MacIntyre, buckling his belt.

"I'm going with the Dalton kid tonight," MacIntyre says.

Cain's eyes grow with surprise, and he crowds in closer behind MacIntyre, "You're kidding."

MacIntyre stands stone-faced, attention ahead, trying to lip out the anthem. An Army veteran himself, he takes great pride in the anthem every time it plays.

"It's Opening Day, Fred," Cain explains.

"And you'll enjoy it from the bench. You've been late for practices, team meetings, and frankly I've grown tired of your antics the last couple years."

"Come on! I can't help that I had a flat tire."

MacIntyre slightly nods towards the stands, asking his tardy player, "She help you change it?"

Cain glances back to see a voluptuous blonde with legs for miles, leaning on the gate next to the dugout. She holds his equipment bag that he forgot with her. Cain sighs resignedly.

"Now be quiet and show some respect," MacIntyre tells him as he lips the rest of the anthem.

Cain swallows his pride and steps back. He pulls his hat down off his head to place it over his heart like everyone else does.

Outside of the park is an entirely different atmosphere. The lighting is spotty, and there isn't a soul in sight. Sounds of the game trickle out and echo across the sea of vehicles in the lot. Sitting in his car in the middle of the emptiness is Eli and his cousin Cody Masterson.

Cody has a smarmy, grimacing face covered with acne and a slight head tremor from a dirt biking accident he suffered when he was fourteen. He's around the same age as Eli and originally from the Iron Lake area, 45 minutes west of Rupland.

The two have just come from the mine by the looks of their dirty faces and overalls. Peering at the field's lights with a fat joint dangling from his lips, Eli can only wonder what could've been.

"Hey . . . " Cody says to him, without a response back.

Eli is lost in the sounds of the game.

"Yo, cousin," Cody says again as he swipes the joint from Eli's mouth.

"Huh?" Eli says, breaking his trance. "Sorry . . . "

Two shadowy figures emerge from the east side of the lot. Their silhouettes couldn't be more different. An awkward duo; one is larger and the other very thin. As they approach the car, Eli recognizes the mysterious figures. One is an overweight, bald white man with rotted teeth and two missing fingers who the locals call Two-Stub. The other is Zeke who appears very different from six years ago. He now strides with purpose. No longer does he cower or sheepishly avoid confrontation. Since his father's death, he's taken over the county's drug operations. He wears a slick denim jacket with a sheepskin shearling collar. His once stringy hair is now full and overly gelled back like a good-fella, and he has a dragon tattoo sleeve that starts at his hand and journeys up around his neck in a choking animation.

"Not gonna see much out here," Zeke says to the teens, without stuttering.

Eli doesn't pay attention to the men much, instead luxuriating in his joint. There's an arrogance to him that noticeably bothers Zeke and Two-Stub.

"How'd we do?" Zeke asks.

Eli digs in his overalls and reveals a wad of crinkled bills that he hands to his boss saying, "Not bad. Mostly kids before the game."

Zeke admires the take and estimates the value of it by weighing it in his hand, then asks, "This everything?"

"Yes, sir," Cody replies without hesitation, a bit of fear towards Zeke in him. "Three thousand and some change."

Zeke slowly lifts his eyes to Cody, "I didn't ask you . . . "

Eli still doesn't give Zeke enough respect to even face him. But he does answer him when he's good and ready with a simple nod. Zeke then hands over the wad to his muscle.

Two-Stub puts his hands on Eli's back window and peeks through at a few boxes of cold medicine and remarks, "Quite a load you got in the back here."

"Don't touch my ride," Eli tells him.

"You barking orders now?" Two-Stub replies abrasively.

"Go on and take this load to my place," Zeke says, breaking the tension. "The shed is open."

Two-Stub begins to thumb through the bills, removing several of them and hands them to Eli and Cody for their cuts.

"Need a dime," Eli tells Zeke, handing back one of the bills.

"You're out already?" Zeke asks.

Eli's doesn't answer. Two-Stub digs in his pocket and gives him a dime bag of crystal meth that he hides in his overalls.

The starters for the Hawks take the field. Jack positions himself behind home plate and lightly kicks some dirt around to smooth his area in case of any diggers. Observing his office, he takes notice beyond the plate of the dirt in front. It's soft, almost muddy, and extends a dirt strip path to the mound to slow or stop movement of hard hit balls. This is a big advantage for a pitcher and catcher. Some league fields keep the dirt in front of their plates hard—cement-like—so any balls slapped down will have great bounce. Either way, it's a home team preference from game-to-game.

Jack squats to catch practice pitches from Charlie. Beyond the backstop in the radio announcer's booth, Frank Reese and Mel Grainger waste little time doing what they do best.

"It's Opening Day here in Rupland, and the fans are ready," Frank broadcasts. "Baseball season is upon us, Mel!"

"Can you tell these fans are hungry for a title run?" Mel says as he holds his mic out of the window to let listeners hear the roars from the home crowd.

"On the hill tonight is Charlie Hylman," Frank follows with. "Still one of the biggest threats in the league, despite his age."

"You betcha," Mel adds. "And he comes in leading the staff with that killer curveball of his. It's sure going to come in handy against these Ransville Reds."

The announcers scope across the bleachers to the Hawks dugout where they see Cain take a seat on the bench. He appears less than enthused.

"Cain McCloud . . . won't be starting tonight," Frank says, searching through stacks of research papers his staff brings him. "Might be an injury. There's no official word yet . . . "

"Who's behind the plate?" Mel asks.

" . . . Jack Dalton," Frank replies, grabbing a roster list to find his name. "He . . . is a rookie. I have some high school stats in front of me . . . "

In the stands, the Dalton family has spotted Jack behind the plate. James whispers quietly to the three of them, "Jack's starting."

"What?!" Sandy blurts aloud.

James tries to control his wife's excitement. Johnny takes this moment to slip out of the stands. On his way, he passes by Savannah. She sits with some of her teammates and girlfriends. When she notices him, she politely waves, and Johnny returns the gesture before disappearing into the shadows of the park.

On the mound, Charlie is as cool as ice, watching a Reds leadoff hitter step into the batter's box. The hitter is second baseman Hal Stanton, a four-year player who has started for Ransville since day one. He led his team in doubles and triples last season and is projected to keep the momentum going.

"Three up, three down, Char!" Nick yells to him from first base, to get the chatter started around the field.

"Rocket fire now!" another infielder says. "Rocket fire!"

Charlie goes into his no frills three-quarter style windup and delivers a pitch that's hit for a grounder to Landon at third. Landon backhands it near the outfield grass with ease, spins and lasers it across the diamond to Nick for the first out of the game.

"This first out brought to you by Norm's Excavating!" A deep-voiced public announcer broadcasts from the speakers.

Jack signals the field of the first out with one finger. The fielders set themselves for the next batter.

Zeke and Two-Stub leave Eli and Cody and journey to the other side of the lot. Around the same time, Johnny appears, trying to light a cigarette. He passes by Zeke and stops a few feet away, where he shakes his lighter to get any fluid left to ignite a flame. He glances at a few fifty dollar bills that lie on the ground. He then looks at Zeke and Two-Stub still in stride.

"Hey!" Johnny says to get their attention and retrieves the bills.
The two turn around.

"This is a lot of money to be dropping around here," Johnny says.

His honesty impresses Zeke. Two-Stub takes the bills from him and Zeke thanks the kid. With a flick of the wrist, he sparks his zippo to Johnny. Johnny hesitates at first but eventually leans in for the light.

"What's your name, boy?" Zeke asks.

"Johnny."

They shake hands. Johnny then puts his hand out to Two-Stub to introduce himself, but he doesn't show the same gratitude. The thug just stares at the hand with his bloodshot eyes.

"All right then," Johnny says. "Have a good night, guys."

"You as well," Zeke replies, watching him a while.

Johnny fist bumps Eli and leans against his car.

"How's your brother doing?" Eli asks

Johnny shrugs then asks, "Heading in?"

"Can't bring myself to."

The boxes in Eli's backseat catch Johnny's interest, and he asks, "Whatcha hauling there?"

"Things."

"That's a lot of things."

"Just another source of income, potentially," Cody says.

"Mine not paying well?" Johnny asks Eli.

"Not well enough . . . "

Charlie fires a pitch down the pipe that another hitter rips for a streaker to the outfield. It's caught by Hawks flamboyant center fielder Billy Hobbs for the second out like it was nothing. Hobbs is a black, five-foot eleven-inch, 180-pound fifth-year stud. His teammates nicknamed him Shoestring for the amazing catches he's known to make. And he's one of a few players in the last decade to master Rupland's outfield. Every edge, route, nook, and cranny. If there's wind, no wind, doesn't matter, he'll catch anything hit out there.

The next Reds player to enter the box is right-handed hitter RJ Gary. Gary has the best bat on his club. He has fast, strong hands with tremendous pop off his bat. His good-looking swing complements his knack for opposite field power. The past eight seasons in the league, Gary has had a solid record against Charlie. Last season alone he went 9-11 against the ace with a .818 batting average and a .766 average with runners in scoring position.

Charlie starts Gary with an exploding slider across the plate that the hitter leans back on for strike one. Gary didn't expect his adversary to start the count with that sort of pitch. Charlie's second pitch sails past without a swing for strike two. Gary knows Charlie isn't messing around. The ageless wonder has gone right to work on him to get ahead on the count.

Before every pitch, Jack eyes the batter and his knees are tight to his chest in his squat to prevent opposing first and third base coaches from stealing his signs to his pitcher. When it's clear, he throws down deuces to Charlie for a finisher and frames his mitt inside. Like a gunslinger ready to draw, Charlie dangles his throwing hand out before him and accepts the call. He fingers the ball and delivers a fireball of a curve that starts high inside and drops off the table to Jack, who shifts himself to the outside with the ball's movement.

Gary whiffs on it, almost breaking his wrists to not fully commit. The umpire behind Jack amuses the crowd with his kung fu style punches for the strikeout.

Cheers rise from the home crowd. The Hawks hustle into the dugout after the 1-2-3 inning. Jack bounces around Charlie in a kid-like way as if they just won the game. He's far more excited than Charlie is about their solid half inning, to which the veteran has to settle him.

MacIntyre waits for Charlie and then drapes a jacket on his golden boy's pitching arm. Charlie takes the gesture and sits next to Jack on the bench, who begins to strip his gear to get ready to bat.

"You're calling good pitches," Charlie says to Jack while cleaning his glasses with his jersey. "Way to earn your keep . . . Shoestring!"

On the other end of the bench, Billy Hobbs pokes his head out like a ground-hog.

"It's time to anoint the starting rooks!" Charlie tells him.

Shoestring digs in the cubbies above and snags some Wilson eye black paint from his bag. The rookies have no idea what's going on as they watch their teammates' excitement develop. Shoestring takes Jack's face and spreads eye black on both sides, creating a distinctive smeared Ultimate Warrior appearance that streams from his cheek bones down to the bottom of his cheeks in a fade. Shoestring stands back to observe his artwork.

"There!" Shoestring says with his gummy smile. "Your war paint. You got an official inning in, dawg. Your cherry's been popped!"

Shoestring then moves on to Nick to give him a thin cross under each eye. "Welcome to the team," Charlie says to Jack, patting him on the back.

A permanent smile stuck on his face, Jack can't help but enjoy every minute of this.

From the dugout's entrance, Roberts says, "Grab a bat, Dalton! Jesus Christ, you're leading off! Move! Move!"

Jack hops from the bench, rips off his chest protector and grabs a bat and helmet. Practically in the corner at the far end of the dugout, Cain sulks. His head hangs low, and his hands grip the edge of the bench. He couldn't care less, nor wants to take part in the team's antics.

At the plate, Jack digs in on the right side, gloveless; his preferred method of hitting. His batting stance is upright, keeping his front foot cocked back so he can drop it quicker to bring his momentum forward. This gives him an advantage of having a faster first step out of the box when the ball is hit—almost like a running hit. His bare, callused hands grip the wooden handle of his Louisville Slugger firmly, and his war paint is fierce as he stares down Reds ace southpaw Tyler Vegas who led the entire league with 10 wins during the 2002 campaign.

Jack watches the first pitch pass for a strike and realizes there's some funk on the hurler's backslide. Another flaw he's spotted, too—Vegas doesn't do a good job of hiding the ball properly before he delivers. Jack can see what's coming before anyone else can. It's surely due to the fact that Vegas focuses too much on his sluggish, exaggerated windup, reminiscent of an impact sprinkler.

When Vegas guns another ball in, Jack makes use of this pitch, laying out a surprising last second drag bunt. Jack has a great jump and runs like hell to first as the ball rolls beautifully along the third base line. The Reds corner guy grabs the ball barehanded and chucks it to first base where it skips off the ground and into the first basemen's mitt. But Jack has crossed the bag safely, beating the throw. He returns to the base and fist bumps first base coach Sarah.

Before Landon steps in the box, he looks to Coach Roberts at third. The coach signals a few signs that Jack watches also. Vegas comes from the stretch now but his windup is still sluggish, so Jack blazes ahead to steal second. Landon pulls back his bat to take a strike as the Reds catcher springs from his squat and throws a frozen rope to Hal Stanton covering the bag. Jack slides feet first away from the tag, kicking up as much dirt as he can into the face of

Stanton, blinding him. The second baseman loses the ball, and Jack gets the safe call. The two adversaries aggressively eye each other a bit while Stanton tries to wipe the excessive dirt from his face.

Before taking his lead off second, Jack targets another flaw, this time behind the plate. The Reds catcher is sloppy at hiding his signals to his pitcher. Jack sees him put down three fingers and tap the inside of his right thigh. The pitch is thrown, and it's a sinker outside that Landon swings and misses on.

Next time around, the catcher signs Vegas the same exact pitch and location he wants him to throw. Jack scoffs to himself in amusement. He has just stolen the signal that the catcher wants Vegas to throw an outside sinker. Jack stares at Roberts coaching third and flags him by putting his hands on his knees, and taps his right hand on his right knee with three fingers. Roberts deciphers this and signs Landon the same way of where the pitch placement will be and that it's a breaking ball. Landon then sets in his stance.

Vegas comes from the stretch again and rifles a sinker outside of the zone. Landon adjusts his inside-outside stroke of a swing and pulls for a shallow left field single. Jack is held up by Roberts at third base. The coach pats him on the ass for the earlier play. Vegas is wise to Jack's quickness on the base paths. He and his catcher make sure to keep a constant eye on the rookie as the ball returns to him on the mound.

From the dugout, MacIntyre reads the situation. He doesn't often take risks, but knowing Jack's history well, along with the fact that he got on base with a bunt and stole his way over, this is reason enough to test the waters early.

"Fuck it, it's Opening day." He says to himself and whistles at Roberts to give him a completely different sign than what was already given.

Roberts raises his browline. He then holds Shoestring at the plate and relays the sign from MacIntyre to him before the pitch clock can wind down. Cain reads the sign and darts off the bench, showing the most life he has all night.

"No way . . . " Cain says to himself in disbelief.

Shoestring sits back in his crane-like stance in the box. His elbow is high, and the bat drapes over his head as if he were perching or about to do the Karate Kid swan kick. Jack leads off third low, grazing his fingertips across the dirt. He lifts his feet to his tiptoes and holds his breath. Suddenly, he dashes away to steal home full tilt, just as Vegas goes into his windup.

Shoestring pulls back. The catcher receives the wide-pitched ball and lunges for the tag, but Jack hook slides, swiping the corner of the plate with his left hand. The umpire signals safe, extending his arms as wide as he can like he's a bird in flight.

Rupland's crowd goes nuts while Shoestring helps his teammate to his feet, leaving the Reds catcher to fend for himself in grief. When Jack returns to the dugout, he's greeted by the entire team, receiving celebrating arm hooks, high fives, and fist bumps. MacIntyre breathes a sigh of relief, thanking God he made the right call.

"Now that's 90-feet of beauty!" he tells Jack.

Jack responds with a slight smile.

In the stands, James begins to break away from his excited family.

"Already?" Sandy asks her husband.

"I'll be back in a few innings. Joe . . . "

Joe follows his father to the highest point of the bleachers where they stand, not sit. James crosses his arms to watch the game's every action. Joe mimics.

"There," James says, pointing to Vegas. "Your brother got to him. Risky call, but something like that, if done right, will affect a pitcher the entire game."

"It's a good momentum builder," Joe says.

"You damn right."

They watch Vegas walk Shoestring on three straight pitches. James was right, Jack rattled Vegas.

Batting cleanup, due to Cain's benching, Nick struts to the plate, wielding his big-barrelled 34-inch, 32-ounce Warstic-manufactured bat that has a white ring around it. In typical Kosko form, he hates every single pitcher he faces and mean mugs them all. The noticeable chip on his shoulder makes his eye black war paint look mean and crazy. His batting stance is back, and he holds the bat high with the inside of his left elbow covering his mouth. Fans dig this swag stance.

Nick sits on a couple wild throws that go by for balls. Looking for some light on a 2-0 count, Vegas' third pitch barely breaks, hanging over the heart of the plate. Nick licks his chops over this gimme and powers his arms forward like a catapult, with that long one-handed swing of his, and drives it deep center for a two-run bomb. The rookie has natural-born power.

"And Kosko goes yard to pull the Hawks ahead, three-to-zero!" Frank broadcasts.

Nick tips his helmet to the crowd, thanking them for the love as he trots home. There, he's congratulated by his teammates for his first career Summer League home run.

Top of the 5th inning. One out. Rupland is shutting out the Reds, 5-0. The infield shifts into double play depth; the corner infielders linger inward on the grass and shortstop and second closer to second base.

Ransville's Gary, who got on base earlier with a hot double down the first baseline, stands on third after moving over on a sac-fly. Charlie stretches his shoulder before he proceeds with his 57th pitch of the game. The next hitter lays down a bunt for a suicide squeeze. The ball trickles in front of the plate, spinning like a top. Jack swiftly snags it and tags Gary, who throws a wicked elbow to his temple when he rushes home. Then he fires off-balance to Nick at first, just in time for the bang-bang 2-3 double play.

Jack holds the side of his head. His ears ring with pain as he stumbles backwards. He glances at Gary returning to the dugout. With a spit and a shrewd smirk, the opposing player says to him, "Welcome to the league, fucker!"

The stands appear blurry to Jack now. The umpire lingers and rests his hand on the catcher's back, asking if he's okay. Jack shakes it off, picks his mask up from the ground, and returns to his team.

Top of the 9th inning. After Shoestring catches a monster shot in deep center, Jack signals the field for two outs from behind the plate. His breathing is considerably heavier than normal at this point in the game. Rightfully so, the kid has done it all tonight.

Charlie wipes a good amount of perspiration from his face as he stands behind the rubber. His hat is smudged with rosin bag residue. There's obvious exhaustion on him. Going this deep into games takes a toll on his aging body. He steps back onto the rubber with both feet and delivers some mediocre heat that the next hitter hits to the right field gap for a single.

MacIntyre calls time-out and jogs to the mound. Jack joins him. When they reach Charlie, MacIntyre grabs the ball from Jack's mitt and comments to his pitcher, "Tired, are we?"

"Fred, I got enough left," Charlie urges to his manager.

"How's he looking?" MacIntyre asks Jack.

Jack is hesitant. To avoid the confrontation, and maybe from nervousness, he rubs his lone double wide black wristband on his left forearm. The last thing he wants to do is throw his pitcher under the bus. Especially a veteran of Charlie's stature.

" . . . Uh, he's . . . he's battling good . . . " Jack stutters.

"Kid, you're my eyes out here," MacIntyre claims. "I expect honesty."

Jack looks from Charlie to his manager before spilling, "He's throwing dog shit. He's spent."

Charlie expels a disappointed sigh. "Just give me the next guy, Fred. If I throw one ball, yank me."

MacIntyre sits on the request. Again, *it's Opening Day,* he thinks. It could very well be the last one too for his longtime ace. And to go the distance could have special meaning.

"I'm in a giving mood tonight, Charlie," MacIntyre implies. "Finish it or I will."

He places the ball into Charlie's glove and leaves the mound. Jack stays behind to discuss strategy with his pitcher, covering his mouth with his mitt so the Reds can't read his lips.

"One more out," Jack explains. "Gotta guy on third."

"Calm down, rook," Charlie interrupts. "I ain't no virgin to this now. Get."

He shoos Jack back to the plate. Taking a moment to tuck his jersey in some more, his throwing hand dips down the back of his pants. After he adjusts, he steps back on the rubber, sets and throws a sick slider that the batter hits early on for a pop-up towards the visitors' dugout. Jack whips his mask from his face and jets for it. He closes in and slides on his ass to catch the out of reach ball, just missing a tumble into the dugout for the last out.

The Hawks players crowd the mound to congratulate their ace. Charlie kisses his throwing arm to mock the pain.

"What an end!" Frank announces. "A new era is upon us! The rookies have spoken!"

Jack rises from the ground to a thunderous barrage of cheers from the fans. The stadium begins their infamous singing of "Thunderstruck" by AC/DC. This time accompanied by music from the P.A. speakers. Many clap inflatable novelty thunder sticks together, a new addition brought on by fans the past few years.

Jack removes his catcher's cap to let his sticky hair breath in this breathless heat. An odd smell catches him funny, and he pulls the ball out of his mitt to take a whiff. He jerks himself back promptly. When he reaches the mound, he presents the ball in his mitt to show Charlie and gives him a *what the fuck?* reaction concerning the weird smell.

Charlie wraps his arm around Jack. An insinuating smile spreads through his bushy goatee, "Ass sweat makes for a good spitball, don't ya think? I call it the shit ball!"

Jack refrains from laughing and holds the ball to Charlie to have since he earned the game ball tonight.

"Keep it as a reminder," Charlie says.

"For what?" Jack asks.

"You can be honest about any other pitcher. But when it comes to me, you don't know shit. I'll tell you when I'm spent."

Jack acknowledges his words with a nod. Charlie keeps his arm around his catcher as they celebrate with the rest of the team. Alone in the dugout, Cain rises from the bench and moves towards the clubhouse entrance. He's not in the celebratory mood.

MacIntyre appears out of nowhere, blocking his way. "What's your problem?"

"Ten years I've played for you and haven't sat one Opening Day," Cain replies.

MacIntyre points to Jack celebrating with the team to make Cain take notice of him, "Heart. Remember that . . . Captain?"

"Are we done here?" Cain says and walks around him to descend into the clubhouse.

"Get it together," MacIntyre orders.

Jack squeezes away from his teammates and scans the crowd. He sets on his family making their way to the barrier next to the dugout. Stepping high on the brick, hanging on to the railing, he hugs and kisses his mom and shakes hands with his father. Frozen on James' face is a look of pride every father would understand.

"Hell of a game, Jack," James remarks. "Think I even saw some scouts in attendance."

Jack realizes someone is missing from the family, "Where's Johnny?"

"Around," James replies. "You know how he is."

"Honey, you played so good!" Sandy interjects.

"There's a few things I want to go over about the game tonight with you." James states.

"Can we later, Dad?" Jack asks. "The team is going out to celebrate. Opening Day win and all."

"Sure. First thing tomorrow though."

"First thing. Promise."

Savannah squeezes herself through the crowd to stand next to the family. Jack almost forgets about her entirely. She leans on the railing to grab his attention and plants a good kiss on him and then comments, "Baby, you played great! I'll wait for you by your car."

"Well... I was actually gonna do something with the team for a bit," Jack says ruefully. "I'll call you after though. Okay?"

"Oh ..." Savannah says, surprised by this. "Oh, okay. Sure. Have fun, babe..."

She forces a smile, and Jack returns to his teammates with contagious emotions that infect the whole group and encourage them to stay on the field a little while longer, thanking the fans.

☞   ☞   ☞

Across the hills that overlook the town and beyond the lights cast by the mine, lies a dark and dingy street on Rupland's north side. Most of the buildings here are abandoned storefronts and storage buildings that closed business long ago. A bar's illuminated sign in need of an upgrade provides the only light on this block: The Pickaxe

Jack, Nick, and Lou walk into the establishment without a care. Upon entering, they're bombarded with a haze of cigarette smoke. Decorated across the large mirror behind the bar is Hawks memorabilia next to artifacts of pickaxes and headgear from the mine. Flannel, plaid, jeans, scuffed boots, tobacco dips and loud country music populate the team's and miners' watering hole. On game days this place is always busy. And the later it gets, the rowdier it becomes.

"Are we even allowed in this place?" Lou asks, becoming concerned about being underage.

"Every Hawk comes here after home games," Nick explains. "It's tradition. We deserve to get fucked up tonight like every other bastard."

Nick leans against the bar to order himself and his friends drinks. Nonsense slurs are heard within spitting distance. He turns around to see his father nearly unconscious on his stool, inebriated. When the bartender approaches, Nick turns his attention to him and orders, "Three Labatt Blues."

The bartender eyeballs Nick for a moment, making his friends uneasy.

Jack says, "Maybe we shouldn't . . ." but pauses when the bartender reaches into his cooler and grabs three ice-cold ones for the trio.

Nick tosses some money on the bar. "Appreciate it."

The bartender slides the money back. "Courtesy of the Committee."

He points to the end of the bar where Cliff and two other elders of the Committee stand. They hold their beverages to the rookies. Nick returns the gesture and tells his friends, "We got fans."

Jack and Lou repeat the gesture as well. Nick departs from the bar with the two to join his other teammates, ignoring his father altogether. Many random eyes are on the teens, and they notice it too. They're on the radar of just about everybody in town after tonight's win. They aren't just faces in the crowd anymore.

Jack loses his footing and stumbles into Lou suddenly.

"You okay, Zoom?" Lou asks, holding him.

"Yeah," Jack replies. "My bad. I'm just a little dizzy after that dude rang my bell in the fifth."

"Are you sure?"

"Of course," Jack reassures him, then points to the pool tables to change the focus. "Let's get next game."

Before making a move to the tables, Lou raises his beer to his friends and toasts, "To great friends and baseball."

"Kinda cliché, but sure," Nick says with a grin, accompanying Lou and Jack with the cheers.

Cain's voice trails behind them, "Aw, that's cute."

Drinks in hand, Cain and Landon chuckle at their expense. Two easy women cling to their sides. The four are pretty lit, having had a head start tossing them back.

"I'm tickled," Landon says.

"That was quite a show tonight," Cain comments in his condescending way. "I haven't seen that much luck in all my years here, honestly. Real nice."

"A little more than luck, man," Nick responds. "Our team keeps this kind of play going, no one will touch us."

"Our team," Cain says with a chuckle. "Listen to you."

Nick's jaw tightens. He lowers his beer from his lips to ask Cain, "How's your ass feel?"

"What's that?"

"Your ass. You were sitting all night. It has to be sore."

Cain gets in Nick's face, "You've got some mouth on you for someone with only a game under their belt."

Jack gets in between the two, as does Landon to separate them. Cain strangely laughs at Nick, testing his patience.

"Let it go, fellas," Landon says. "Not here."

"Keep smiling," Nick says to Cain with a dead stare.

The rookies turn away to head to the pool tables. Cain raises his mug of local craft beer, patronizing loudly so the entire bar can hear him, "To our beloved baby Hawks! May God bless the bats they swing with!"

The patrons accompany his toast: "Here, here!"

Cain holds his spiteful gaze on the three longer.

Charlie plays pool with the rookies. They're quite a few drinks in at this point in the night. His right shoulder is a bulk of bandages wrapped in ice, but it doesn't affect his pool shooting. A tiny waitress with a squeaky voice serves him a shot of whiskey that he places on the edge of the corner pocket.

"Thank you, darlin'," Charlie tells her. "Doing anything after work? It's too good of a night to sleep."

"Says you," the waitress snickers. "I've been pulling a double today."

"Then that's plenty reason to join me. Sleep can wait."

His Southern charm seduces the young waitress.

"Aren't you married?" she asks pointing to the wedding band on his finger he puts on after his games.

"This? No, ma'am. My love died of cancer a while back.

"Charlie, oh no. I'm so sorry! I didn't even know—"

"Why would you?"

"See? My mind is even tired from working too much. I put my foot in my mouth."

"Don't worry yourself about that. I just keep the ring as a reminder to keep fighting the good fight in life. Gotta keep on living."

"That's a good attitude to have," she remarks. "Okay, Charlie. I'll talk to my boss."

"I like to hear that. Tell him I requested it. I'm sure he'll oblige, darlin'."

A permanent smile stays on her face as she serves another table.

"That true about your wife?" Nick asks. "We had no clue."

"Shit no," Charlie replies. "She left my ass. She didn't want to be a baseball wife no more. Good riddance."

He throws back the shot on the table, while the other three laugh.

"Horrible, man." Nick chuckles. "Wow . . . "

Jack also garners some female attention that no one else notices. He shares flirtatious looks with a stunning redhead that stands at the far end of the bar, sucking on the straw in her drink while dancing next to her three friends. She appears in her thirties and wears cowboy boots with the tightest dress Jack has ever seen. Her friends are nowhere near the looker she is.

Jack is having fun but remains cautious about treading this shady road. He has a girlfriend, but he pushes the envelope as much as he can with this woman without actually making a move.

"When I came here from Texas, I couldn't believe towns like this still existed," Charlie says. "My ex and I moved here for the work and for the baseball. It's changed some, but this place will always be home to me. I wouldn't want to live anywhere else, to be honest."

Using his left hand, he shoots a striped-ball into the corner pocket. He rises from the table, wincing in pain.

"How's the arm?" Jack asks, concerned.

"Keep worrying about your pitchers, catch," Charlie comments, eyeing his next shot. "That's good. Builds trust . . . Don't worry about me though. My arm will be ready by next start. Always is."

He winks at the boys and goes right back to running the table on them.

"You ain't half bad with your left," Lou tells him.

"Takes a lot of practice."

He lines his next shot and misses, then wisecracks to Lou, "Shit. Ya jinxed me."

Lou chalks the end of his pool cue and observes the potential shots left on the table to take advantage.

"Tell ya what, not much scares me on that bump, rooks," Charlie states. "But the day I have to leave her, hand her off to some young arm . . . now, that's a day I truly fear."

"Everyone meets their expiration date, I suppose," Nick says.

"A cruel fact of our profession," Charlie replies.

"There's always beer league softball," Nick jokes.

"Ugh. Softball is where ball players go to die," Charlie says.

Jack lets these words sink in as he watches Lou pocket a couple of shots of his own, then asks Charlie, "Ever get scouted? Do you know anybody that went on after playing here?"

"Sure. A few of us did. Others almost did. I mean that's the goal for you youngsters, ain't it?"

He points his pool cue at one of their teammates hunched over a table alone, drunk off his ass. Shawn Joski. He also goes by Jaws due to his giant buckteeth and the fact that his last name sounds similar. Jaws has been with the Hawks since 1998. The five-year veteran has a pointy nose and bushy brown hair.

"Jaws Joski," Charlie recalls. "Had a heck of a bat that caught the eye of a major league team or two. The bastard blew out his knee in the playoffs a while back. Now he drives transfer dumps at the mine in the offseason."

After nailing a couple of balls, Lou misses on an easy side pocket shot. Charlie takes control of the table again.

"Had the most level swing ever too, that one," Charlie comments.

"Picked the bottle up, hasn't been level since."

He glances at another player with scruff on his face and a bad comb over, trying to work his magic with the redhead woman's friends. Even though he feeds the girls compliments and drinks, he's undoubtedly striking out.

"Trevor Huff our closer; 'member him?" Charlie asks. "Best knuckle-baller in the whole league back in '94. Pro teams wanted him bad. The Major League strike kind of ruined his shot there. You wanna know his future now? He runs his dad's hardware store down the road . . . Shoestring too. Got kicked outta a D1 school for behavior problems, came here and the hype he used to have among scouts faded."

He knocks in his second to last striped ball. "I myself had a good enough arm to get people talking back in . . . well . . . Ha! Tore my rotator cuff in the '95 title game. No one would touch me after that. Too risky, scouts said . . . That was a means to an end with my old lady too."

"What are you saying?" Lou asks him.

"I'm saying ball players don't normally leave here, fellas. Haven't in years. And the ones that do end up coming back."

Jack remains quiet through this part of the conversation, opting to just listen. It might be disrespectful to contest the vet's meaningful words.

"There's no shame in that," Nick comments. "Playing ball, making money . . . "

Charlie smacks his last striped ball in a side pocket and then states, "Fellas, we are the official boys of summer. Rupland treats us like gods. Beyond this though, we ain't shit . . . We're fools to think otherwise."

He pockets the eight-ball to win the game and rises from the table to grab his shot waiting for him before he continues on. "So, I say while we're able to wear the orange and black, let's give this town the title they deserve . . . Let's touch heaven, boys . . . "

The rookies drink to that. Jack finishes the last swig of beer left in his bottle and heads to the bathroom. He walks into a stall and unzips to piss. A sway begins to overtake him as his dizziness returns. Touching his head, he falls unconscious.

☞ ☞ ☞

Two mysterious Marines lie face first in the blast hole of the Vietcong village. Before they're dragged away, a young James tries to turn them over to see their faces. When he touches the first body, he awakes from his dream when Daggett, the family dog, jumps on his lap in the chair that sits in front of a television.

"Get!" James commands Daggett, shooing him to the ground where the dog curls himself to sleep.

The Dalton house is still on this night. A replay of the Detroit Tigers versus the Oakland Athletics is on the television. James flips through the channels, finally settling on the CNN channel. A female journalist reports breaking news on America's war in Iraq:

"Good evening, everyone. As Larry said, we are now hearing reports that air-raid sirens are going off in Baghdad. We're also getting indications from our . . . "

Vehicle headlights shine into the windows, illuminating the living room. Outside, Eli's coupe brakes in front of the house. He walks around to his passenger side to open the door. Johnny's barely conscious body slumps, strapped in by a seatbelt. Eli undoes the belt and drags the intoxicated Dalton to the front door, knocks twice and runs back to his car where Cody and Katie wait in the backseat.

James opens the door to find his son sprawled before him. He then sees Eli's speeding car careen down the road.

"Jack?" James asks, not quite able to identify which son this is in the dark.

When he bends to lift him, he realizes it's Johnny. He heaves his child over his shoulder and carries him inside.

Johnny comes to, slurring his words, "I- I- coulda played better . . . "

Joe appears from his room when he hears the commotion. Spotting Johnny being carried in the hallway, he tries to help his father.

"What?!" Johnny slobbers abruptly to Joe. "Quit ugly-muggin' me!"

"Shhh. Go to bed," James whispers to Joe. "I got him."

Joe returns to his room, unable to fall asleep again, concerned for his brother's well-being. He's never seen his brother drunk before tonight.

James lays Johnny on his bed, removes his shoes and tucks him in. He shoos Daggett away again when he tries to lick at the teen's bare feet. Sitting on the edge of the bed with his back to his son, James hears him start to weep, " . . . I don't wanna be like him."

"Who?" James asks, turning his head.

Johnny mutters some incomprehensible nonsense before eventually drifting into unconsciousness. James can only watch his troubled son and wonder what's going on with him.

Outside of The Pickaxe, Nick and Lou help George into Nick's truck. Getting the heavy, drunken man into the cab is a struggle. They practically have to shove him in. Nick reaches for the seatbelt in his truck and tries to buckle in his father when he notices something protruding from George's top flannel shirt pocket. He grabs it and discovers it is the ticket he gave him for tonight's game.

Nick shakes his head and taps the ticket on his father's head, "Must've been busy filling out all those job apps, huh, Pop? . . . Yeah." He rips the ticket up.

"Hell of a game tonight," Sheriff Orson says behind the startled teens.

They turn around to see the sheriff has pulled in beside them. Both teens immediately are tense. They realize they might be caught for underage drinking. Or worse yet, if George is found in this condition, he'll likely be charged with a parole violation. Something of this magnitude would definitely send him back to prison.

The boys politely nod, not wanting to open their mouths for fear the sheriff will snag a whiff of their alcohol-infused breath.

"Keep up those big bats." Sheriff Orson tells them, observing the two.

Both boys nod.

"Kosko, you need to get that muffler fixed," the sheriff comments. "I can hear that thing clear across Main Street."

"Will do, sir," Nick replies, tight-lipped.

Sheriff Orson drives on. Relieved, both boys exhale.

"I damn near shit my pants!" Lou remarks to Nick as he squeezes into the cab.

"Think I already did," Nick replies, entering his side.

The three scrunch in the cab like sardines in a can. George rests his head on Nick's shoulder.

"Where'd Zoom disappear to?" Lou asks.

A sly smirk forms on Nick's face when replying, "He's, uh, getting congratulated for tonight's win."

☞　　☞　　☞

The rising orange sun presents a calming backdrop to the morning after last night's win. A boy on a bicycle delivers *Rupland Journal* newspapers to the town's south side. He hooks one sky high, and it drops on the steps of a white ranch-style house.

The front door opens, and Cain exits in a robe that barely covers his junk. He grabs and unfolds the morning paper to read about his game and other league games from the night before. Smack dab on the front page of the sports section is a photo of Jack Dalton sliding to catch the final out. The headline reads: *The Future of the Rupland Hawks.*

Cain's lips tighten with distaste. He flings the paper in his bushes and returns inside.

By the time the sun rises to its full light, the boy on the bicycle is delivering on the north side. He flings a paper at the door of The Pickaxe. A heavyset woman in a long Hawks t-shirt opens the door and grabs it, tucking it under her arm. She walks around back holding two full trash bags in each hand. She's beginning to prep the bar for the wave of third-shifters. As she puts the bags in the dumpster, she turns her focus to Jack's dew-covered car parked several yards away. Curious why a car is back here at all, she wonders if someone is sleeping one-off or if it was left there overnight. She decides to knock on the fogged window to see if anyone is inside. The window lowers slowly, and inside she finds a squinty-eyed Jack in the driver's seat. Next to him, naked, is the redheaded beauty from last night who hurries to dress herself.

"Take it elsewhere." The woman says, less than amused, and returns to the bar.

The teen puts his hand on his head. His hangover has kicked into overdrive. He asks the redhead, "Did we . . . ?"

"Oh yeah," she says with a chuckle and slides on her lacy thong. She then teases her messy hair.

Jack grabs his cell phone from the dash to find many missed calls from Savannah. Guilt hits him. He knows he fucked up.

"At any point was I in the bathroom?" Jack asks, that being the last thing he remembers.

"Yup. You came out looking for your friends after they left. Then you bumped into me . . . and . . . well . . . "

She pulls off Jack's old, worn Hawks hoodie and hands it back to him.

"Do you have any aspirin in here?" she asks.

Jack shrugs. She digs in her purse to no avail and then opens the glove box, which Jack slams shut on her, "There isn't any in there. Sorry . . . You need a ride somewhere?"

"My car is in front," she tells him, clearly turned off by his sudden erratic behavior.

Jack nods. All he wants is for her to leave so he can clean himself up to go see his girlfriend and hopefully put this mistake behind him.

"Anything you need, just call," she tells him with that alluring, flirtatious look on her face that first attracted him to her. "I put my number in your cell. I always take care of my Hawks."

She grabs Jack's face and gives him a hell of a kiss he'll remember. He's left in an unresponsive state, loving the kiss so much so that he feels his soul has left his body.

"Sure hope you can handle Delta tomorrow better than your booze, hon." she says.

Jack forces an awkward smile and watches her walk back around to the front of the bar. She holds her cowboy boots in one hand while pulling her blue dress down over her heart-shaped ass with the other.

Jack starts his ride. At the end of the alley, Savannah has driven in with her Sunfire. She's seen enough. She storms from the car, her hellish eyes set on her cheating boyfriend. Before he notices she's even there, she reaches through his window and punches him hard in the face. "Bastard!"

Jack recovers and chases her back to her car.

"Savannah, wait!" he pleads.

He snatches her by the arm, but she squirms from him. "You're disgusting! Leave me alone!"

"Baby, please don't do this!" He insists, trying to spit something out that makes sense. "I- I can explain what you saw!"

"You don't think I know what the players do?! I must be some kind of stupid for thinking I could be just as important as all of that. Congratulations, you made it. You're a full-on Hawk piece of shit."

"Sweetie—"

She becomes emotional and says, "You ruined us, Jack. You broke my heart."

"Okay, I fucked up," Jack admits. "I'm really sorry."

"Doesn't matter. We both knew this wouldn't last forever. You playing ball, me going to school in another state. Even lately when you're here, you're not actually here with me, Jack, so this doesn't matter anymore."

"But I need you . . . I don't want to do this without you."

"I'm not your fucking cheerleader!"

Jack hangs on to her door, not ready to let her go. Her face is a mix of emotions. Nothing more can be said between the two that will make things better.

"Let go!" she screams.

She drives on, leaving him behind. He makes the walk of shame back to his ride. Slamming his head back against the seat, he lets it sink in. A thought comes to mind, and he digs in his glove box for a pill bottle. He opens the lid and swallows a couple of pills.

"Friendships are forgotten when the game begins."
—Alvin Ralph Dark

A NOW FIFTEEN-YEAR-OLD JOE works a hot dog and hamburger booth that's sponsored by his family's store. The booth is an 8 x 10 stand that's wrapped in decorative Rupland Family Foods banners and houses a grill, buns galore, and a plethora of condiments and toppings that are on the front counter for customers to prepare their own food. His girlfriend Chloe keeps him company from outside the booth.

Not far from them, most of the locals and tourists gather in a large beer tent. Around this tent, other booths populate the scene. There are booths for sub sandwiches, snow cones, cotton candy, darts, Milk Bottle and shooting games, and raffle tickets. The area has turned into a carnival of sorts. All stand on a piece of land, usually used by the Sportsmen's Club that's in close proximity to downtown.

Joe serves a pair of chili dogs to two sixteen-year-old girls.

"Three bucks," Joe says to them.

"Is Jack working here later?" one of the starry-eyed girls asks.

"Eventually, yeah."

"We'll be back," the other girl says. "Tell him that, would you?"

Chloe says, "You know Joe here plays on the high school team. Could lead them to state this year."

The girls are at a loss for words.

"Um . . . Okay, I'll let Jack know," Joe says to them, and they walk away with their dogs. "Chloe, I don't know why you had to tell them that. They don't give a shit."

"They should. It doesn't always gotta be about Jack. "

"Yeah, I—"

A cellphone rings next to the grill. Joe answers it and listens.

"Right. But Johnny isn't here . . . I don't know where he is. Maybe getting ready for his float?" As soon as the call ends, he digs through his mother's purse to find a disposable camera.

"Can you watch the booth for me?" he asks Chloe. "I have to give this to my mom."

"Joe, I don't know how to—"

"Just watch the booth, you don't have to work it. Well, you can work it later for me but . . . " He winks at her, and she giggles.

"Oh, my God, just get out of here already! I'll watch the booth."

She shoos him, and he hops one of the sides. His jeans get caught on part of the booth, tearing them. Joe frees himself from the snag and waves at Chloe before he enters the busy downtown streets. These streets are a decorative exhibition of Memorial Day celebration. Waves of marching bands play throughout, setting the patriotic mood.

Joe squeezes through the crowds that have gathered along the sidewalks to watch the festive parade. He discovers his father talking among coworkers and members of the Committee. Finding an opening in the parade, Joe runs in between a Rupland Mine float that has employees waving on top. A souped-up '69 Dodge Charger with a few Vietnam veterans inside it throwing candy to the children pulls the float. It's buffed to a shine, making it impossible to take one's eyes off it. Joe is able reach the other side of the street and interrupts his father's in-depth discussion about this year's Hawks team compared to last year's. No one can forget the '04 Hawks run that ended with a heartbreaking loss to the Ellison Legends in extra innings in the first round of the playoffs.

"Aren't you supposed to be manning the booth?" James asks Joe.

"Mom wants her camera, so I had Chloe watch it while I brought it to her."

"Why isn't Johnny helping?"

"I think he needed to get ready for his class's graduation float."

"Well, give the camera to your mom and get your butt back to the booth."

"Where is she? I can't find her."

James points across the street, where Joe just came from. There stands Sandy with Denise Webb, watching the parade.

"Shit," Joe remarks, before heading back that way.

"Hey!" James shouts at his son.

"Sorry!" Joe apologizes, and he once again is dodging parade traffic in his quest.

Out of breath and frustrated from his strenuous journey to find his mother, he's finally able to hand that damn camera to her.

"Thanks, honey," Sandy says and starts to snap pictures of the parade. Observing the camera, something isn't right. She says, "Joe, this is the wrong one. This doesn't have as many pictures left on the film."

Joe is beyond devastated and annoyed. The last thing he wants to do is trek back for another camera.

"Never mind," Sandy says. "It's too late. This will have to do, I guess."

Minutes later the Rupland Hawks float rolls by their section of the street. It looks like someone puked orange and black all over it, with chunks of hokey-looking miniature Styrofoam Hawks and player numbers dangling from its sides. This dreadful showcase is far from complete. The only thing worth paying attention to—besides the players that ride atop and the gorgeous red and black '65 Dodge Power Wagon that tows it—are the banners hanging proudly from the sides.

2004 DIVISION CHAMPIONS

The Hawks wave and toss Hubba Bubba gum to kids whose faces have the numbers of their favorite players painted on them. Others have their faces painted in a style to replicate Jack's infamous warrior style eye black.

Jack, Nick, Lou, and Cain stand near the front of the float. The former rookies are two years older and two years wiser. Jack's long locks are gone, and he rocks a much shorter haircut now that he parts to one side, giving him more of a clean-cut, All-American appearance. Nick and Cain, on the other hand, have grown their scruff to beards. And Lou's Faux-hawk is a bushy afro.

When the float comes to a stop, groups of fans crowd around it to score autographs and slap hands with the players. Jack gathers an abundance of fanfare. Cain gathers none. There's been a shift in stardom. Nick and Lou have even become fan favorites, eclipsing Cain's number of fans by the float.

Upon the friends' arrival to the league, Cain's numbers have dived dramatically. In 2003, he ended his dismal year hitting a whopping .212 with three homers and 10 RBIs. Last season wasn't much better as he saw a noticeable dip in the lineup too. This in part after he sustained a quad injury to start the year. He batted in the sixth spot and didn't see the same pitches anymore. His role with the team declined. By now, most think Cain's play has plateaued, while others think he should be playing the best ball of his life since he's in his prime. Whatever the case, Cain's confidence is lacking, and Rupland's three newest stars overshadow him.

Sandy starts taking as many pictures as she can like she's a member of the paparazzi. Creeping down the street, a few floats behind the Hawks, roll six 2005 Rupland High School graduation floats being pulled by a series of hot rod trucks. Sandy directs her camera to these and starts snapping pictures again.

Dressed in black graduation caps and gowns, most students wave to the crowd, and others throw candy to them. Sandy realizes someone is missing on the floats. She lowers her camera and asks Joe, "Where's Johnny?"

Two men disguised in ski masks, hurdle a porch's flimsy wood railing and flee from a white-rusted 150 square foot trailer. Smoke billows from a rival meth lab that's located deep in the woods. Down a long, barren yard, the masked men run for their lives. One has a duffel bag clutched in his hand, the other a tire iron.

Without warning, a gun's blast rips past them, turning a tiny tree they pass into toothpicks. A grotesque and obese man with no teeth stands on the porch, his shotgun's barrel smoking. He bolts down the steps while reloading his weapon.

The masked men, almost like a cartoon, with their feet hanging back sideways and their torsos in front of them, turn a corner and dive into the backseat of an open car door. Katie and Eli sit anxiously in the front. Katie hollers at Eli to drive. Eli punches the gas, kicking up gravel from his tires, and they're gone in a split second, tearing along the two-track trail. The man with the shotgun escapes further into the woods from the trailer just as it suddenly explodes in a great inferno. He drops to his knees in bitter disappointment.

Turned on by the excitement, Katie hops on one of the thieves' lap. She unmasks him, revealing the bandit as Johnny. He's winded, and his adrenaline is through the roof.

"Holy shit! Holy shit!" he cries.

Katie grabs his face and kisses him wildly. She loves the thrill.

"Let me see what you have," Eli says to the other bandit, Cody, who unmasks and drops the duffel bag on the front seat.

Eli's teeth are at the beginning stages of meth mouth; a hint of brown and decay across the top row. And he's lost significant weight, which causes his Adam's apple to protrude noticeably from his skinny neck. Unzipping the duffel, he sneaks a peek inside to check his crew's take. He grabs a shiny, nickel-plated, snub-nose revolver that he had tucked in between his legs during the heist and stuffs the piece in his glove box. Everyone in the car is too caught up in the commotion to notice what he's doing.

By midafternoon, Eli drives to a lakefront property. Katie and Cody stay in the car while Johnny and Eli walk to the elegant lavender lake house. Zeke answers the door's knock with his muscle leering behind. Eli remains silent and just hands him the duffel. Zeke opens it to see a pile of loose cash inside.

"This it?" Zeke asks.

"Should be," Johnny replies.

"I took some for gas you owed me from the last job," Eli says.

Zeke looks at Eli with a sneer, "That's for me to dole out, wouldn't you think?"

"Sure thing, boss," Eli nonchalantly responds.

Their looks drag on each other some before Zeke hands the bag back to Two-Stub.

"Now that we've eliminated our competition, we got another job coming soon," Zeke says. "Payout is three times what you'd make for me in a month. I want you to sit tight until you hear back from me."

Eli accepts, and he and Johnny turn towards his car.

"Dalton," Zeke says, grabbing the teen's attention.

Eli stops too.

"Just Dalton," Zeke tells Eli, dismissing him.

Eli continues to his car.

"How you doing with this work?" Zeke asks Johnny.

"Not bad."

"Are you getting the hang of things?"

"Yes. The money is good, of course. Better than working at my parents' store, you know?"

Zeke chuckles a bit. "I bet." He glances past Johnny's shoulder at Eli waiting for him in the car. "I need people I can trust. People such as yourself."

"Me?"

"Everything I own—the cars, the toys, everything—I earned every piece by paying my dues."

Johnny nods, not quite knowing how to respond.

"Keep paying your dues, and I'll see you're taken care of."

"I appreciate that Zeke, really."

"I know Eli runs your crew, but I need you to look after him for me. Make sure he's doing things on the up and up. Do that for me, you'll be running your own crew, sooner than later."

Johnny nods and smiles.

"Congratulations on graduating, by the way," Zeke says. "I never had the luxury. Big accomplishment, finishing school."

"Thank you," Johnny says.

"Is college in your future?"

"I wanted to take a year to think about it. Baseball is coming up potentially. After that, I guess I haven't really thought about what I wanna do."

"Smart. Going to school, you'll be there four years, maybe more, and not a penny ahead. Debt hits you before you start making any real money. The type of money you'll make with me is no joke. I guarantee you'll make more than your parents could ever imagine. Think about that."

"Absolutely. Thank you, Zeke."

Johnny returns to the car, and Eli leaves.

"What'd Zeke want?" Eli asks.

"Just wanted to know if I liked working for him," Johnny says. "Nothing important."

"Some advice—take what he says with a grain of salt. I might work for him, but I don't trust that dude for a second."

"Why?"

"Do you think he got to where he is by being honest?"

Johnny considers this, having been a part of Eli's crew for the past two years. Eli has made a profound impression on the young man's susceptible mind.

☞   ☞   ☞

Jack hits Joe's pitches in the field at the farm. Both are beat. They've been practicing for hours. Jack breaks his stance when he sees a kink in Joe's release.

"Hey, man," Jack says. "You gotta tuck that elbow in some more. You're out, you're in. Tuck it. You'll have more control."

Joe nods, intently listening to his brother's coaching.

Next to the house's patio, James mans a charcoal grill, prepping steaks for tonight's dinner. Every time a breeze catches the meat, his boys can smell the mouth-watering aroma clear across the field, making them want to end today's session more than ever.

A car is heard approaching from the road. The brothers stop their play to take notice of Eli pulling in. Johnny peers at his father from the car. He sees James' angry stare.

"Shit," Johnny says lightly. "This should be fun."

"Tend to business, my man," Eli says. "Let's hook up at the beer tent tonight."

"I'm down."

Johnny leans back in his seat and kisses Katie, then slaps hands with Cody and exits. As he reverses, Eli waves to Jack when he spots him in the field. Jack doesn't return the gesture. There's obvious tension between them that's been brewing since Eli has taken Johnny under his wing.

When Johnny approaches the house, James blocks his way to prevent him from avoiding him by going right inside. "Where were you today?"

Johnny shrugs.

"Nothing to say?" James asks. "You had an obligation to be on those graduation floats today. And you were supposed to help your brother at the food booth before that. Mom was very disappointed. Is that how you show her respect?"

"Sorry," Johnny says, not looking his father in the eye.

"You're sorry? Isn't that something? Same old answer. Give me something else. Come on, I want to hear something different for a change. Say, I was out with my girlfriend, or it was tough, Dad, the fish were biting too good. Let's hear it."

"I don't know . . . I'm just . . . sorry. Sorry I didn't show."

"Look at me," James says. "You're at an age where you're growing into a man. There's certain responsibilities that come with that."

"I know."

"You don't know, Johnny."

"Okay, I don't know then . . . "

"Tomorrow's a big day, why aren't you out there with your brothers preparing?"

"I'll go get my glove."

"You'll go get your glove."

His son cautiously steps around him and enters the house. Inside, Johnny searches for his second glove in various rooms, chucking things around, angered by his father's confrontation.

"Mom," Johnny shouts from his room. "Where's my lefty glove?!"

"I don't know!" Sandy replies from the kitchen, prepping side dishes for dinner. "Just grab your father's in our room."

Johnny enters his parents' bedroom and digs in their closet. He finds the glove on top of a shoebox and tries to reach it. The shoebox falls on his head, scattering pictures everywhere on the floor.

"Shit," Johnny says, and he begins to put them back in the box.

Each photo he collects, he's never seen before. Some are black and white, and others are Polaroid. They're from his father's life. He sees pictures of his former baseball teams, including his play in high school and the year he spent in the minors. Some photos show a championship past and several accolades he received throughout his playing career. Accolades that are now stored away in a shed. Not that surprising, considering his father is a humble man, not one to boast of his accomplishments.

Johnny comes across baby pictures of himself, Jack and Joe. He stares a tad longer at particular photos of himself with James. There are ones of them playing and others of James feeding him when he was three-years-old. Joy overcomes. When he sorts to the bottom of the pile, he finds photos of his father in the military—mostly Vietnam. Some are of his platoon on base and in Vietnamese bars. When scouring through the rest of the non-military photos, he notices there's always the same person with him in every one. It's a younger, dark-haired man who looks almost identical to James but has a rounder face and actually smiles, as opposed to James who never does when posing for a picture.

"That's your Uncle Jacob," Sandy reveals, glancing over Johnny's shoulder for God knows how long.

Johnny turns around holding a photo of James and Jacob. Sandy takes it from him. A soft smile forms, remembering her brother-in-law.

"Your father adored Jacob," Sandy says.

"How come Dad never talks about him then?"

"He just never does. Jacob was born a few years after your dad, and those two were inseparable. When he got out of the service, he didn't want Jacob to enlist, but Jacob was stubborn and wanted to follow in the footsteps of his big brother. He actually did really good for himself. Even worked his way up the ranks. Your dad was real proud of him. We all were."

After a thoughtful pause, she adds, "And when he died, he was crushed. It took him a long, long time to get past that."

"How long?"

"Around the time you and your brothers were born. He's so proud of each of you, even if he doesn't show it, hon."

"Pssh. Right."

Sandy hands back the photo. " You're our miracle baby."

"What?"

"Those months were hard carrying you. Harder than your brothers. I was frequently in the hospital. Always told to consider our options that there might be complications with your birth. Your father and I prepared for the worst."

"Really?"

"Yes. When you were born, you weren't breathing, in fact. The doctors spent what seemed like forever to get you to breathe. Both of us thought we lost you, but then . . . We heard a cough . . . and then another, and you cried! Our baby boy survived."

"Man, I almost died?"

Sandy nods.

"Damn."

"Johnny, you and I are a lot alike. Do you remember when I told you how my mother, your grandma, died?

"A plane crash—sure."

"What I never actually told you is that she was pregnant with me at the time it happened."

Johnny's mouth drops a little.

"She and the rest perished in the wreck," Sandy says. "But I was the only survivor. When they extracted me from my mother, they found I was healthy. I was perfect weight and size. They called me a miracle."

Johnny is quiet, not knowing what to say.

"We're miracles, kid . . . Please know that you're special. You will always be special. Maybe your father has a different way of showing you that, but give him a break. He's hardest on you because you were almost lost. In his mind, he's fighting for your life every day. And you want to know something else? You remind him most of Jacob. Everything about you, right down to that contagious smile of yours."

She touches Johnny's face, and he cracks a warm smile.

Minutes later, Johnny, now dressed in Under Armor attire with both gloves tucked under his arm, joins Jack and Joe in the field at his usual leisurely pace.

"You good?" Jack asks him.

"I'm always good," Johnny responds when he steps on their man-made mound.

"The old man chewed your ass out pretty good this time," Joe says.

"Doesn't matter," Johnny says, digging his usual deep groove in front of the rubber. "I just keep quiet, and he talks himself tired eventually."

Jack wipes the pool of sweat from his face with his shirt, asking, "Why was Masterson giving you a lift home? You shouldn't be hanging out with him, man. I don't know how many times I gotta tell you that."

"Really, you're gonna get on my ass now too? Fuck off—let's go."

Jack steps to the plate with his bat in hand. Joe squats behind to catch Johnny. Johnny slips on his lefty glove, goes into his long and lackadaisical windup and tosses one in that Jack ropes far left. The three watch it sail.

"Still haven't figured how to get one by me," Jack says. "More practice might help that."

Johnny just shakes his head and digs the hole in front of him deeper. His inability to pitch successfully to his older brother has always tormented him.

"Just saying . . . " Jack says with his boyishly mischievous grin before he sets back into his stance.

Johnny chucks another down.

☞   ☞   ☞

George walks to the back entrance of the house, where Nick is chopping logs for their wood stove. On the side of him are stacks of kindling he's already cut, a daily chore neglected by his father. George opens the door and tosses Nick's truck keys on the coffee table and then makes his way into the kitchen to snag a couple of brews from the fridge and a box of Corn Flakes from atop. One after another, he places each bottle's top against the counter and slams his hand on them to pop off the caps.

"Hey, Ms. Susie Homemaker," George jokes to Nick through the open door as he plops himself in a chair at the kitchen table. "Take a break and have a brew with me."

Nick drops his axe and enters. George oddly pours the Corn Flakes in the bowl and dumps his beer in it like milk.

"Thanks for letting me borrow the truck," George says, eating his beer cereal without a care.

Nick sits across from his father to drink. He sets his sights on a stack of bills that lay before him.

"How's the job search going?" Nick asks.

"Could be better, Nicky-boy. There's not many people that wanna hire an ex-convict."

"Still though, there's other options; that's all I'm saying."

George chooses not to respond. Nick trickles the bills in the middle of the table so his father will pay attention.

"I'm not trying to get on you," Nick says. "But I could use some help around here. I'm playing ball and taking odd jobs here and there. Shit, by the end of the month we're always behind."

"What do you want me to do, get on my hands and knees and beg people for work?"

"The Daltons said they'd give you hours at the store."

"Look, I ain't no bag boy. And I sure as shit don't wanna work grocery. I was a miner in this town for chrissakes! A knuckle-dragging grease monkey! How'd that look?"

"Dad, the mine won't take you back, you know that. Doesn't matter anyway, they're letting go of more workers than they're hiring these days. We need to think of some realistic options here. I know MacIntyre told me the grounds crew could use some extra hands this season at the field. That's another option."

George springs from his chair and barks, "Who's the goddamn parent here?! I'll figure it out! Get off my fucking back!"

He then sweeps the bills onto the floor and leaves the kitchen in a huff. Nick chugs half his beer in one swallow before he picks the bills up from the floor.

☞   ☞   ☞

Jack anxiously waits in Karen's Diner at a tiny table near the front windows. The bell to the entrance rings, and in walks a middle-aged man with thin hair wearing a yellow polo shirt and khakis to match his clean, golf-pro appearance. Jack partially rises from his seat to greet him.

"Hi-ya doing, Jack?" the man asks and takes a seat at the table.

"You want coffee?" Jack asks.

"Sure. That would be great."

Jack gets an elderly server's attention.

"Let me know when you're ready to order," she says, pouring two fresh cups of coffee for them. She then leaves. The old wood floors of the establishment creak with every step she takes.

"Thanks for meeting with me," the man tells Jack.

"Are you kidding—the Pittsburgh Pirates," Jack titters with delight. "Why wouldn't I?"

Letting a hearty chuckle out as he stirs some cream and sugar into his black coffee, the scout says, "It's hard to visit here often. But I have been able to see a handful of your games the past couple years. I like what I see, Jack."

"Thank you, sir," Jack says, trying not to display any over-excitement, even though he's joyfully screaming inside.

"The way you play really caught my eye. Your style is unique, for sure. You play with such child-like enthusiasm like you're having more fun than anyone else out there. In the bigs, players are trained not to show emotion, but your passion just spills from every pore—I gotta tell you, kid. You're a lot of fun to watch. The Pirates organization could use more of that. Hell, our league could use more of that."

"Thank you, sir. It's how I've always played. Forgive me for saying this if you're a God-fearing man, but I love this goddamn game more than anything."

Jack's words bring an infectious smile to the scout, "One of those eat, sleep, and breathers, huh?"

"Absolutely, sir."

"With the kind of league you're playing in, I can see why. I love this crazy ass league," he snickers into his coffee cup while taking a sip before he continues. "Your game behind the plate is impressive. Real solid. Good instincts. I saw you catch veteran arms and newcomers, and you seem to really know how to work with each of them to get the most out of their innings. Fred and I spoke—"

"You know Coach?"

"Of course. Fred and I go back. He's one of the first managers I talk to every season before I travel this way. He gives me a breakdown of who I should be looking at on his team, what they bring to the table—that sort of thing."

"Wow, all right."

"He spoke very highly of you, Jack. Out of everything, he said your biggest strength is your leadership. And that's what we want at our level. Leadership. Maturity. Sometimes it's just as important as talent."

Jack listens closely to the scout. Much like his father, he's humble, so hearing compliments about himself is hard to listen to. But the fact that he's getting an opportunity to talk to a scout—his first one—is exciting.

"I got to be honest, your overall hitting power could develop some more. I like your quick hands, and judgement of pitches is very nice, but get the ball screaming off that bat more consistently. Drive it."

"Absolutely, sir. Definitely," Jack says without a breath. "If I can ask something though, what happens next?"

"Next?"

"What happens if the Pirates like me enough to sign me?"

"If we do take you on, then we'd send you to one of our farm teams to start, so—"

"No, I'm sorry. I mean the process, before you sign a player . . . "

"Like contract negotiations? Money."

"No, I mean physicals. That sorta thing."

"Oh. Yeah, okay," the scout says, apparently surprised by the question. "Let's compare it to buying a new car or horse for breeding. Other than cutting you open, we break down your whole chemistry. CT scans, X-Rays, MRI's, blood tests, urine tests. We question every scar, every bump, and every bruise. You would be an investment, so the club would make sure they're getting the most bang for their buck."

Jack doesn't react right away. He leaves the door open for the scout to continue, but he does not.

"Hello," the server interjects when she returns to their table. "Are you two ready to order?"

"That's fine, ma'am," the scout says with a smile. "Thank you. Coffee was great."

The server nods and leaves.

"Tell you what," the scout tells Jack. "Work on that power and keep playing the way you have. I'll be back here near the end of the season, and we can talk again. Sound good?"

"Absolutely, sir."

"Great. Very good stuff, Jack. Keep it up."

He puts a five-dollar bill on the table, shakes Jack's hand, and thanks the server again before leaving the diner. Left alone, Jack just stares at the table in a world of his own.

☞   ☞   ☞

Fifteen Hawks hopefuls showcase their talents on this smaller than usual Tryout Day on the high school's ball field. Most are recent high school graduates with a few players in their twenties taking part. On the pitching section where the portable mounds are, Coach Roberts monitors Johnny's pitching, while Coach Sarah radars his speed behind the tryout catcher. The tempestuous flame thrower's velocity and command impress today.

"Little Dalton!" Coach Roberts loudly says to him as he inches closer. "Yup. I heard of you, pitching this way and that."

Sulking at the term 'Little Dalton,' Johnny snaps his glove retrieving the throw from his catcher and gives Roberts acrimonious eyes. He sets again and shoots a bullet. Sarah's radar gun clocks: 89 MPH.

She nods. Roberts then hones in on the younger Dalton's anger. It appears to make him throw harder.

"Holy hell!" Roberts says. "Impressive. Show me again?"

Johnny repeats his hard fastball. The radar clocks: 87 MPH.

Sarah shakes her head, indicating to Roberts that the teen's velocity dropped.

"Let me see the other half of ya," Roberts says.

Johnny drops one glove and slips on his right-handed glove.

"I was a pitcher in the league once," Roberts reminisces to Johnny. "Had a . . . well . . . a golden arm . . . Not everyone can make it, unfortunately. To stand on my mound, you gotta be a pitcher, not a thrower. Now, you're a scrawny fuck, so I assume you're one of those that can't hack it here. Am I right?"

Johnny grunts when he throws more gas down the pipe: 91 MPH.

Sarah's eyebrows raise. Roberts lifts his hat from his head to run his hand back on his unmistakable receding hairline. He still can't let go of the shoulder length, stringy hair scraps that remain. He has Johnny right where he wants him. Now it's time to go for the kill to see just how high the kid's ceiling is.

"Your brother says you can easily get rattled at times," Roberts says, pushing the envelope further. "That true?"

Johnny's nostrils flare, and he kicks his leg high as if he's poking a hole in the clouds. He unleashes a hellish pitch that rides the radar and smacks the catcher's mitt so hard that he has to pull his hand from it to shake away the pain: 95 MPH.

Sarah's mouth turns upright.

"Best sound in the world, ain't it?" Roberts says to Johnny, slapping the kid on the back before he moves on to another tryout pitcher.

Jack, Nick, and Lou soak in rays while fishing on beach chairs on a dry, grassless spot the locals call Clay Banks of Rupland's rolling Gamme River. They've been fishing this spot since they were knee-high. Chaws pack tight in their bottom lips and they dress similarly with sweat-stained, frayed-brim Hawks hats that hover just above their eyes, cutoff shirts, basketball shorts, and flip-flops.

Beside the chairs lie fishing poles with lines cast into the water on one side, and beer cans—some full and some empty—on the other. The men haven't caught too many fish in the hour they've been here, but they couldn't care less. They're taking advantage of their vacation before the craziness of the season begins.

"Boys, it don't get much better than this," Nick says.

"Sure doesn't," Lou responds.

Nick notices Lou's line barely being tugged in the water every so often. "There's something on your line, pard."

Lou pushes the brim of his hat up from his eyes then back down, "Nah. Just a wannabe bait-stealer. I'll reel her in in a few."

"Bro, how'd the meeting with the scout go?" Lou asks Jack, who's remained quiet since they arrived.

Jack keeps his hat lowered without looking up and simply replies, "Good. We'll see . . . "

"We'll see?" Nick asks.

"We'll see . . . " Jack repeats, detached from the conversation his friends are trying to spark. He's in no mood today.

"A scout called my mom the other day," Lou says. "He wanted to know some particulars. Didn't amount to much. Shit, my parents couldn't care less about me playing ball anymore. They're on my ass about going to medical school like they did."

"Ouch," Nick says.

"Ain't that some bullshit though?" Lou says. "They said at my age they were working towards something real. Like what we're not working for isn't real. What the fuck?"

"Your folks are cold, pard," Nick says.

"No doubt," Lou replies. "How about you? Any scouts show interest?"

Nick chuckles, "I think y'all know where I stand with that. There's no future in baseball past this league for a shit kicker like me. Besides, I'd rather play here 'til I'm an old fuck anyway."

"Yuuuup," Lou says, burping.

"To hell with getting old," Jack says under his breath.

A motor revs behind the trio. Lou and Nick turn to glance at Eli riding in on his dirt bike. He parks next to the three four-wheelers the rest rode in on.

"How they biting fuckers?" Eli asks as he dismounts and unloads his fishing gear from the back of his bike.

"Nothing so far," Lou says. "Didn't think you were gonna show."

"For fishing? I'm always up for fishing."

For the first time since they've arrived, Jack shows some life, pushing his hat up to take notice of Eli. His eyes harden on him when he does.

Without a chair, Eli plants himself in the grass on the opposite side of Jack, next to Nick. It's not long after he casts his line in the water that he searches for a drink to quench his thirst.

"Who's got the brews?" Eli asks.

"Everyone brought their own," Jack coldly says.

"Nick, I'll hit you back," Eli says.

"No worries."

When Nick goes to grab a cold one from the cooler for Eli, his hand starts to shake slightly. He stops himself a moment to observe. Pumping his hand some, he ignores the tremor and grabs the can to hand it to his friend. Eli overly animates opening it and taking his first drink in spite of Jack.

"Keep it up, man," Jack warns Eli as he turns his hat backwards and leans forward to reel in and cast to another spot on the river.

"Easy," Nick says to ease the tension between them. "We haven't hung out in forever. Let's enjoy ourselves today, huh?"

Tobacco spitting, beer drinking, and re-casting pretty much details the next half-hour or so. Eli is the first to speak after a time, "You guys remember that huge fire in town when we were like ten? Started at this river, didn't it?"

Lou and Nick laugh when remembering.

"I'm pretty sure you started that," Lou wisecracks. "Kidding."

"No man, did you forget?" Eli asks. "Remember, we all rode our bikes to the tree fort to protect it?"

The memory comes back to them.

"That damn fort!" Lou says. "Yeah! Yeah, I remember. The fire was on the other side of town, and here we were acting like we needed to save it and shit."

"Half the town was searching for us, thinking we were caught in the fire," Nick adds.

"My ass got beat when I came back home," Lou says.

"All ours did," Nick chuckles. "My parents were tag teaming me."

"Crazy . . . What ever happened to that fort?" Lou asks.

"Got destroyed," Eli says.

"What?" Nick asks. "Why?"

"Why was that, Zoom?" Eli asks.

"Seems you're quite the storyteller today," Jack says. "You know why."

Eli quiets and refocuses on fishing.

"Sooo . . . one of you gonna spill what the hell happened to our sweet fort?" Lou asks.

"Jack was worried that some Black River boys would wreck it, being so close to their end of town, so he tore it down," Eli says. "Guess he didn't trust Nick and me."

"Seriously?" Nick asks Jack.

"Wrong," Jack claims. "I mentioned to you that I wanted to build a new fort and you just went there by yourself and did the deed."

"Not how I remember it," Eli says.

"You're a piece of work, Masterson," Jack says, shaking his head.

Eli sits upright annoyed. "Clearly you have a problem with me. Man the fuck up and say it to my face, instead of sitting there like an asshole."

Jack hooks his dip out of his mouth and stands to face him. Eli also rises to the confrontation. Nick and Lou immediately stand between them to try and calm the increasingly tense situation. Jack and Eli close in on each other, pressing their friends in the middle of them even more. Eli spits to the side, his mouth tight with anticipation to throw down any second.

"Guys, come on!" Lou shouts.

"Don't ruin the day," Nick says.

"Leave Johnny alone," Jack says to Eli.

"Johnny is a grown ass man," Eli remarks. "It's none of your concern."

"When my family is involved, it is my concern. I'm not fucking around. Stay away from my brother."

"Are you threatening me? What are you gonna do?"

Jack then reaches over Nick to try to get a hold of him. Eli does the same, but they are quickly separated.

"Fuck you, man!" Eli yells. "Fuck all of you!"

Lou and Nick are taken aback by Eli's turn on them.

"Back at ya, pal," Jack says.

"What the hell happened to you guys, man?" Eli asks. "Jack, I used to sleep over your house all the time when my mom was dating a long line of assholes. You used to give me some of your clothes, Lou, because we couldn't afford new outfits for school. Nick, we're Black River boys. We grew up in the same neighborhood. Our bond was tight . . . Us four . . . We were . . . We couldn't be torn apart . . . Now y'all are ghosts ever since you made that damn team!"

"It's not like that," Lou says, trying to calm Eli by putting his hand on his shoulder.

Eli shrugs him off, "Don't touch me! Just because you became something here, doesn't mean you're better than everyone!"

"Dude, what the fuck are you talking about?" Nick asks.

"Baseball was supposed to be our dream together! Remember that? Guess it's every man for himself these days."

"You weren't good enough!" Jack blurts.

"Jack—" Lou tries to stop his crude honesty.

"No!" Jack shouts at Lou. "He needs to hear this. What do you want us to say, Masterson? You didn't want it bad enough. The parties, the drugs, the booze, the women, that's what you cared about most. No one was stopping you from trying out each year to make the squad, but you didn't. Quit bitching that we changed and look in the mirror! We just grew up, so go cry somewhere else!"

"Know what? I'm over this. Y'all can have each other," Eli says and grabs his things and leaves on his dirt bike.

His friends don't stop him. They decide to call it quits as well and leave separately. The day is a bust.

☞   ☞   ☞

Johnny leans his head against Eli's passenger window while they cruise around town. He gazes at the empty shells of buildings on the south side. These structures were once long-running, successful establishments that have since closed in recent years. The decline of the local economy has been steady.

Fifteen years ago when the Daltons first arrived, Rupland was a flourishing example of what hard work and being proud of where you came from was rewarded. The town was even in the top 100 of "The Best Places to Live in America" by *Lively Magazine*. But this once-thriving town has since left several areas unkempt, abandoned and forgotten. It yearns for the tender love and care it had maintained.

Eli pulls into a small gas station on the edge of the Black River. Johnny and Katie enter the store while Eli fuels his car. A small, chubby, middle-aged woman reeking of cigarette smoke and unwashed clothes, sits behind the register and restocks packs of cigarettes. Katie heads to the bathroom located in the deepest part of the store.

Johnny grabs a Gatorade and heads to the counter. "A log of Skoal wintergreen, please. Long cut."

The clerk pulls down the Skoal and places it on the counter.

"That it?" she asks in the gravelly voice of a lifelong smoker.

Johnny nods and digs his wallet from his back pocket.

The woman simply slides the items forward to him and says, "Have a nice day."

Johnny becomes irritated with the woman. He doesn't want anything for free. This sort of thing has always bothered him, "Don't do that, I'll pay."

"No worries," she says. "You're Zoom-Zoom's little brother."

Johnny just throws a few bills on the counter anyway, snags his items, and exits the store. He gets back in the car where Eli now sits with a joint pinched between his lips. In his hands, Eli holds a recent paycheck from the mine and just stares at it. He drifts from the check to the Pontiac Grand Am in front of him that's being filled with gas. Orange and black bumper stickers of Jack, Nick, and Lou's jersey numbers cling to the back of it. He then notices other vehicles around the pumps showing similar Hawk pride.

"Dope," Johnny comments on the paycheck. "Pay day."

"Last one too," Cody reveals. "We got laid off today."

"Damn, man," Johnny says. "Sorry . . . "

"We'll live," Eli says, folding his check and tucking it into the pocket of his overalls.

He then passes the joint to Johnny, who gladly takes a few generous puffs. Katie exits the store with a bag of her own in hand. She enters the backseat next to Cody.

He razzes her some, trying to grab at the bag. "Whatcha get me, Kay?"

She slaps his hand, upset.

Johnny asks her, "You okay?"

"Sure am," she responds. "Just tired of being stuck in a car full of boys."

Eli leaves the station and turns onto a back road to joyride some more.

"Yo, why aren't you wearing it?" Eli asks.

"Nah-uh," Johnny replies humbly. "That's all right."

"Come on, baby," Katie urges. "If you won't wear it, I will!"

"Go ahead, try it on," Eli insists.

Johnny reluctantly picks a hat up from the floor and places it on his head. A perfect fit. It's an official Rupland Hawks hat. He's made the team.

"See," Eli says. "Now you're somebody."

"I don't know about that."

Johnny removes the hat and puts it on Katie's head instead. It's sort of big on her, so she turns it around to wear it backwards.

"Aw," Johnny says to her. "Beautiful . . . "

☞   ☞   ☞

Later in the afternoon, Eli arrives at his mother's house to visit. It's been about a year since he moved into his own apartment downtown. Nevertheless, he sees his mother daily; usually takes a quick shower at her place after work and to eat whatever she cooked the day before. With a flick of his near-finished cigarette, he enters. As usual, the place is dark and empty.

"Ma!" Eli calls for her, making his way into the tiny kitchen that's to the side of a guest bedroom.

Through the open window, above the sink, he finds her in the backyard. Many half-smoked cigarette butts lie on the ground around her. Eli reaches into the noticeably dark fridge and grabs some leftover lasagna. He decides to eat it cold from the pan since the electricity is seemingly out anyway.

"Ma, did you pay electric this month?" He projects loud enough for her to hear while grabbing a fork from a drawer. "I saw Mr. Allen today. He told me he's closing his tavern for good this time. When were you gonna tell me about that?"

Entering the backyard, he keeps his eyes on the leftovers he inhales. Alicia sits on a plastic patio chair smoking another cigarette, staring at the overgrown grass in the fire pit. One of the straps to her pink tank top hangs around her shoulder. Streaks of mascara run down her cheeks. A decent amount of dried blood surrounds her nose, and she has a few deep scrapes on her face to match. She's so distraught in her own life of hell that her son's words don't sink in.

"What are you gonna do for a job now?" Eli asks her. "The Pickaxe isn't hiring any help . . . " He plops on the chair next to her, still scarfing. "Have you been using the money I've been giving you?"

Eventually, he glances at his mother and sees the horror of her battered face. The pan of cold lasagna falls to the ground when he rises from his chair to be by her side.

"Mom?!" he says, grabbing her face and moving her once-thick, bleach-blonde hair from her eyes. "What happened?"

Alicia finally acknowledges him. More tears begin to flow. Her voice shrivels and cracks when muttering, "I'm so sorry . . . I should . . . shouldn't have provoked him. Bruce just gets kinda nuts sometimes . . . It's my fault . . . " She tries to compose herself, explaining more to him. "I asked him for some money to help around here . . . and he just went . . . "

"Where's the money I gave you?"

She doesn't answer.

Eli clenches his jaw with frustration, knowing Bruce is to blame.

"I sure know how to pick 'em, baby," she says. " . . . I don't know why I keep putting myself through this. You didn't have a father figure, so I tried being both. It didn't suit me; I know. I tried, I just . . . Your father . . . He was—"

"Please . . . " Eli interrupts. "Just don't. I've lived 21 years without knowing a thing about that man. Let's keep it that way."

Alicia bawls into her only child's shoulder, repeating how sorry she is.

"No, Ma," Eli says. "You . . . you don't always need a guy in your life. You're better than them. Hey . . . "

Alicia lifts her head from his shoulder and looks at him. Eli stretches a clean part of his overalls to her face to wipe away the mess of blood, makeup, and tears.

"You always got me. I'm the only guy you need—the hell with the others."

She smiles a bit and cups his face with both hands. "My baby boy, I love you." She hugs him tightly.

With his cheek rested on top of her head, Eli's face becomes visibly enraged. He's a volcano ready to explode.

Eli's coupe skids to a stop into the front yard of a dingy hole of a house deep in God's country that's built on a hillside. A bluff overlooks it. He exits in a hurry, forgetting to shut his door, and struts to the front porch. After a few hinge-shaking knocks, no one answers. He peeks through the windows and then walks around back to spot two haggard men, one of them Bruce. They look alike and are in their 50s with scraggly gray beards and puny bodies. They hover around an old Ford truck's engine they work on while sharing a bottle of whiskey.

"Hey!" the smaller man exclaims, jumping back when he sees Eli approaching with purpose.

"Stay out of it!" Eli barks, pointing at him.

He grabs Bruce by his flannel shirt and decks him to the ground, sending the man's stained trucker hat tumbling under the truck. Standing on top of him now, he pummels Bruce's face repeatedly. What seems like normal blows turns into a blood bath of fury. Bruce's buddy watches helplessly. Ending the beating from plain exhaustion, Eli steps off what's left of him. He then brandishes his nickel-plated, snub-nosed revolver that's tucked away in his overalls and points it at him.

"Whoa, whoa, whoa!" Bruce's friend pleads, holding his hands in front of him. "Please, Eli! He told me he didn't mean to do that to your ma!"

Eli ignores the friend and shoves the revolver into Bruce's mouth, "If you come near my mom again or so much as look her way, I will fucking end you, Bruce!"

He jams the piece further in Bruce's mouth and pulls back the hammer. His eyes are a twisted evil of hate. This surge of control brings him great satisfaction. "Nod if you understand me."

The battered man is coherent enough to give a slight nod. Eli removes the gun from his mouth and fires a round through his ear, blowing it almost completely off. Bruce holds the wound, groaning in agony as it gushes blood like an oil derrick. His buddy makes a move to see if he's okay, but Eli points the gun at him now and holds.

"No, p-p-please . . . " the friend begs.

Eli shoots another round past the friend's head to scare him, dropping the weakling to his knees. He pisses all over himself.

"I expect you to repay me the money you took from my mother too," Eli tells Bruce. "Thirty days."

And with that Eli leaves the property in a flash.

☞   ☞   ☞

A league game between the Dixon Vikings and Clarkston Black Sox plays at Dixon Park. Jack, Joe, Nick, and Lou attend to watch the competition since they're scheduled to play Clarkston in a few weeks. The stands are moderately full, and the aging wooden structured park itself is a nice complement to the respected heritage of Dixon. Dixon Park is one of the shorter fields in the league and is often considered a hitter's park that kills pitching careers. Their green and white scoreboard remains its oldest relic to date. Sitting on top of it is a vintage clock that still runs. Not one piece of new technology is anywhere near it. A local kid works the inside of this scoreboard during game days, updating the runs, hits, and errors.

Dixon's uniform designs are a throwback to the Chicago White Sox of the 1980s. They wear white, buttonless, V-neck jerseys with three maroon stripes across the front of them that bleed on the sleeves—the outside stripes a lighter maroon. On the middle stripe, "Dixon" is spread thick on the front in total white. The pants are white, too, with large maroon stripes along the sides of each pant leg. Their belts are maroon, and their caps are maroon with a white brush script-fonted 'V' on the front for Vikings. Most of the players wear maroon socks or mix it up with white socks and maroon stirrups.

On the other side of the spectrum, Clarkston wears black mesh jerseys with white lettering and no names on the back, only numbers. And they wear white pants with black pinstripes, complete with solid black socks and black belts. Some players choose to wear white stirrups with these as well. Their hats are entirely white with black brims and a single black, Tiffany-fonted 'C' for Clarkston stitched on the front. Their Gothic look fuels the fire of their bad boy image.

The home team's mascot is Mr. Viking. He roams the park dancing and taking pictures with kids and families on this *Star Wars*-themed day. Mr. Viking is one of seven-league mascots that remain. Rupland hasn't had a mascot in over 20 years.

At the plate, a right-handed Black Sox hitter with a high leg lift, reminiscent of a mule kick, hammers one far left for a stand-up double. A run scores.

"He hit the shit outta that," Lou remarks.

"Clarkston has some big bats," Jack says. "We can't just come at these guys hoping for strikeouts. Forcing them to hit grounders and pop-flys is our best plan of attack. Offensively—small ball—nothing flashy."

"Who is that?" Joe asks, pointing to the batter that just hit the two-bagger who's now adjusting his nutsack.

The six-foot inch, 222-pound slugger is a white twenty-three-year-old with monstrous hands that seem like they could crush a skull. He has a bald head and a long bushy ginger beard down to his chest that covers the "Black

Sox" name on the front. This rugged, muscular man is the Terminator version of a lumberjack.

Lou and Nick thumb through their game day programs to find his name on the roster.

Jack already knows who he is. "Tim Kanter. Usually hits cleanup. Sometimes they put him in the three spot so he can see better pitches. Even though his manager is a sabermetrics guy, he floats him in the same two spots in the lineup."

"Jesus, Zoom," Nick says, impressed with his scouting report.

"Maybe if y'all would come to these games with me more, you'd know that," Jack says.

"Pard, we have lives," Nick sneers back.

"The Black Sox are about the best in the league," Lou says.

"Eh, we can beat 'em," Nick boldly claims.

"These sorta teams we can't make mistakes against," Jack reminds them as a Black Sox hitter lines out to short, and his team takes the field to start the next inning.

Nick finishes his plastic cup of beer with one swallow. As he lowers his hand, it begins to shake again. Concerned, Nick clasps his hands together to try to stop the tremors.

"You all right?" Lou asks him.

"What?" Nick says, startled.

"You're sweating a lot."

Jack and Joe notice too. Nick wipes the perspiration from his head and checks his plaid shirt to see that it's wringing wet. He tries to laugh it off.

"It's not even hot out," Joe remarks.

"I ate some spicy food earlier," Nick says. "Guess I don't have the stomach for it like I used to."

Jack's cell phone suddenly vibrates, and he pulls it from his pocket to check a text. Shoving it back, he becomes anxious and rises from his seat. "Watch their starter Rizzo for me, guys. I'm gonna grab some more popcorn. Nick, I'll grab you some napkins . . . or something."

"Get me a Bud while you're at it," Lou says.

"Jesus, I'm taking orders now?" Jack asks, somewhat annoyed.

"Not even noon yet, guys," Joe remarks.

"You got up first, bro," Lou says. "Nick, you down for another?"

Nick tightens his hands again as the tremors subside, "Um . . . nah. I think I'm done."

"Well, I'm leaving before you change your mind," Jack says and leaves.

Joe's suspicions ignite. His brother has never left during play. He always does that in between innings. "I'll help him," he says to the two.

And he follows Jack outside the stadium, where he sees him approach a white Escalade parked in the deepest part of the lot. The owner of the fancy ride is Kelly. Dixon is in Kenmore County, so this location isn't a far drive for him.

When Jack is close enough, Kelly meets him at the back of the Escalade to open it. Joe witnesses the handoff of cash and Jack receiving a mysterious white plastic bag in return. They go their separate ways. Joe waits for Kelly to leave the lot before he starts to follow Jack again; this time to Jack's own vehicle. He trails at a safe distance and dodges in between cars like a spy. He plants himself behind Clarkston's team bus and spots his brother stuff the plastic bag under his driver's seat. Jack then returns to the park.

Joe decides to investigate what Jack paid for. Coming upon the locked car, he sees the driver side window is slightly opened. He grabs a broken branch in the grass and uses it to unlock Jack's car door from the inside. After fiddling with it for a couple minutes, he's able to pop it open.

He grabs the plastic bag and sees the various unmarked pills and paraphernalia inside. Concern washes over the youngest brother's face like a tidal wave. He's seen enough and plants the bag under the seat where he found it and locks the door again.

☞   ☞   ☞

July 24th, 2005
RUPLAND HAWKS AT HILLSDALE WOLVES

Top of the 3rd inning. A mid 70s, sunny afternoon brings many fans from both Hillsdale and Rupland to the game.

Hillsdale's home field is named Brickey Stadium after their late, great outfielder Dom Brickey. The grandstands located directly behind the backstop are in the Wolves' colors of baby blue and gold. Fanned metal bleachers stretch from it to the left and right field sides. The left field wall is 370 feet from home plate and is adjacent to the sideline of Hillsdale High School's football field. During football season, temporary bleachers from Brickey Stadium populate this side of the field, with the front of the bleachers placed along the left field wall facing the football field. The outfield wall is short and thick and gold with the depths of the field painted in baby blue.

Mack Moore, the game starter, sits inside the visitors' dugout, soaking his arm in a vat of ice. He's just pitched three and two-thirds innings, and the hard-throwing lefty has exited the game with a cranky elbow that's bothered him since the start of the season. Moore is a white, twenty-nine-year-old, freakish athlete, who stands six feet seven inches tall and weighs 180-pounds and has bleach-blonde hair that's cut to a Caesar-do. Aside from pitching, Moore plays the outfield when needed. He's one of many two-way players in the league. Or like most call them, hybrids.

One player's day might be ruined, but another's has just begun. Johnny gets the call for relief for the first time this season. His family attending the road game couldn't be happier. He wears his father's number from when he played—#8—and brings his right and left gloves with him to the mound. He'll need any help he can get today. The Hawks' road record is an abysmal 2-10 this season. Many have high hopes that the newest Dalton rookie can bring some life to their struggling pitching staff.

MacIntyre gathers the brothers on the hill after Johnny has finished getting warm. Jack still rocks the same warrior style eye paint he's worn since his debut. It's become his look, and fans often mimic it. The only thing that has changed on him, other than being an everyday starter behind the plate, is his jersey. The prestigious captain's 'C' is stitched over his heart, which was donned by Cain before MacIntyre relinquished the title at the start of last season.

The rest of the field has made some changes, too, these last two years. Lou has become a constant starter at shortstop. When Jack became the team's starting catcher, Cain moved to third base. Having still one of the best arms on the team, he makes few errors at the hot corner and devastates batters when the ball is hit in his general direction.

"Make him work the plate, Zoom," MacIntyre says. "Johnny, I want you to start out throwing left. Don't finesse your throws. Don't switch up arms yet. Just work your corners and get a feel for the hitters."

Johnny nods to his manager. MacIntyre pats his ass and leaves with Jack, one to the dugout, the other behind the plate. Per usual, Johnny starts to dig his deep hole in front of the rubber.

Wolves player, and top league rookie last year, Garrett Theus steps into the batter's box to lead off the third inning. He's a right-handed, streaky, middle of the lineup hitter, who keeps his hands in front of him and tilts his bat somewhat parallel to his shoulder like an old-time ball player. He wants so badly to introduce this Hawks newcomer into the league with a hit here.

"MacIntyre looks to the fireballing rookie Johnny Dalton to relieve an ailing Moore," Frank broadcasts. "This will be the younger Dalton's first appearance. Interesting enough, he's the only ambidextrous pitcher in Summer League's history."

Jack signs Johnny to bring what he's best at with his first pitch. Johnny shakes him off. He repeats the sign, but again, Johnny shakes him off. Miffed, Jack calls time and heads to the mound to talk to his pitcher.

Standing on the highest point of the bleachers to watch every angle of the game as they usually do are James and Joe. They're confused as to what the miscommunication is between the brothers. Much of the same confusion unsettles Rupland's coaches too.

"What are you doing?" Jack asks aggressively, removing his mask.

"Let me do the pitching, you just worry about catching it," Johnny says.

"That's not how we work here. I call the pitches. You're gonna swallow your pride and throw what I call, okay?"

"Jack, just get your ass back behind the plate."

Jack scowls at his arrogant brother and hustles back to avoid being called for a delay of game. He again throws down one finger for the fastball, but once again Johnny shakes him off. He then shrugs for him to bring whatever he wants. Johnny goes into his normal long and lazy windup and throws a mean slider, twirling off the mound in his momentum, as he does post throw. The ball smacks Jack's mitt hard for a strike. Jack tosses it back to Johnny, who now sports a smug smirk.

Jack signs him again for a fastball, which is once again shook off. Johnny then delivers another slider that Theus smacks to left for an easy double. When Johnny gets the ball back, he glares at Theus now on second. The hitter winks at him. Johnny takes this personally and spits in disgust, digging his hole before the rubber deeper.

Bottom of the 5th inning. Tied score 2-2. Johnny delivers another that a nine spot hitter sends through the middle for a base hit. Jack shifts his infielders into double play depth, retrieves the ball from the umpire, and heads back to the hill to talk to his brother.

"Had enough?" Jack asks in spite. "They're rapping you all over the damn field."

"Just give me the ball," Johnny sternly tells Jack, keeping his glove out for it.

Over Jack's shoulder, Johnny notices Theus is at bat again. Johnny wants this hitter more than anyone.

"We've got one on, one out," Jack explains. "Throw some breaking stuff to force grounders."

"I'm striking this dude out."

"He wants you to come at him. You're giving into his strength, Johnny. Let's play smart."

"Give me the fucking ball."

The umpire stands impatiently at the plate while the pitch clock counts down. He's about to penalize the team.

"What's going on?!" Roberts shouts to them from the dugout. "Let's go!"

Concerned, Lou hustles to the brothers and asks, "What's the matter?"

"Kick rocks, Lou," Johnny rudely says without looking at him. "Ball, Jack!"

The clock ticks zero, and the umpire calls ball one on Johnny, much to the dismay of the coaches and any Rupland fans.

"Get going!" MacIntyre screams at his players.

Jack stuffs the ball hard into Johnny's glove, then grabs him by the jersey to force him in close and says, "Make the goddamn thing break!"

He pushes him back and then walks away. Lou leaves as well. Johnny stands insulted and humiliated in front of everyone. His anger builds, and he removes his glove and whips it at the back of Jack's head, knocking his headgear off. Jack turns around and rushes at his brother, tackling him on top of the rubber. The two scrap, throwing violent punches.

Rupland's bench clears, and the fielders run over to break up the fight. Cain casually sits on third base, refusing to involve himself in the family skirmish. The Wolves, the fans, and the Dalton family are left bewildered as to what exactly is happening.

The scoreboard after the game reads: HILLSDALE 5 — VISITOR 2

Almost every fan has since vacated the stadium. Players from both teams begin to trickle out from the locker rooms after showering. Waiting in the van for Rupland's players to exit the clubhouse are James, Sandy, and Joe. James chain smokes nearly half a pack of cigarettes, his eyes fierce. He's impatient.

"Let's not make a scene," Sandy pleads with her husband. "Start the vehicle. We'll handle this at home . . . Start the vehicle, James. "

James darts a glance across the lot to see his sons emerge from the locker room with their teammates. They're about to board their team bus. James chucks his cigarette and exits the van, power walking towards them, tight-fisted.

"James!" Sandy shouts.

James steps in front of his sons to block their way on the bus.

"Well?" James asks, his face expressionless.

"Three-game suspension," Jack says.

Grabbing Jack with one arm, James slams him against the team's bus. At the same time, he grabs Johnny with the other hand by the scruff of his jean jacket. Teammates and coaches stop their stride to watch the spat.

"Both of you embarrassed our family!"

"Dad!" Jack yells, squirming.

"Jack, you're the leader out there! Captains don't act like that!" Then he shakes Johnny. "And you, shaking signs? The catcher is the general. He calls the shots. I taught you that! Boy, what's wrong with your head?!"

"Get off me!" Johnny projects to his father, escaping his hold with a push.

His son's actions surprise James. Johnny stands his ground, arguing and pointing at his father and brother. "I don't need you or him!"

He walks away from the two and hops in Katie's car, and they drive away.

"Johnny!" James screams. "Johnny!

Unhooked from his father's grasp, Jack boards the bus, "Just go home, Dad. I'll talk to you later."

James notices everyone's eyes in the lot are on him. Embarrassed and still enraged, he returns to the van.

☞   ☞   ☞

The Pickaxe is near empty tonight due to the Hawks playing on the road. Johnny enters the bar and takes a seat next to Cody, who has been there for a while. The teen's bruises are still fresh from the earlier fight with his brother.

"Hope Eli has a good reason for calling me in here this late," Johnny says.

"I think it's a job," Cody responds.

"The big one?"

"Possibly."

Eli enters the bar with a black hoodie covering his head that casts a shadow on his face. Sliding his cell phone on the bar, he sits in between both of them. "Boss man squashed it."

He dashes his crew's hopes.

"I need to start making money, Eli," Johnny says. "I'm not getting paid with my three-game suspension as is. Why isn't Zeke giving us work lately?"

"If I knew that, I'd tell you," Eli replies. "You're not the only one that needs cash. I need to get the hell outta Dodge for a few weeks 'til things blow over with the law."

From behind the bar, Nick serves them shots of whiskey. When Eli pulls back his hood, Nick can't believe his childhood friend is there, "Shit, Masterson. What are you doing here? Sheriff's been searching for you for that beating you handed your ma's boyfriend. You fucked him up pretty bad. They're talking brain damage fucked up."

By the blank expressions on Johnny and Cody's faces, it seems they're already aware of Eli's troubles.

"I've got it handled," Eli says. "What the hell are you doing on that side of the bar anyway?"

"Bills gotta get paid somehow," Nick replies.

"Your pops ain't pulling his weight still?"

"Something like that."

Eli places some cash on the bar, "Well, in that case, keep 'em coming."

Nick moves down the bar to tend to the usual bar flies.

"See, that's what I'm talking about," Eli says to Johnny and Cody. "This town isn't what it used to be. A Hawk, one of their own, can't even get ahead."

The other two indulge their shots, but Eli doesn't. He slaps both hands on the bar after a thought, "Know what? . . . screw it. I say we do the job and get some cash in our pockets tonight."

"Seriously? Are you kidding?" Cody asks.

"Shit. I don't know," Johnny says. "Going against Zeke's orders—"

"Yo, you said yourself you need cash," Eli interrupts. "Fuck we waiting for Zeke to give us work for?"

The three quiet when Nick arrives with their next round of shots.

"Thank you, kind sir," Eli says, and Nick leaves again. "Look, Johnny, let's just check it out. If it's too risky, we won't do shit."

Johnny mulls this over before agreeing. They throw back their shots.

☞   ☞   ☞

Eli stops near a dirt trail's entrance that twists and turns to a pristine red log cabin. Thick trees provide perfect camouflage for his coupe as it creeps further into the darkness of the night. Parked in front of the cabin, they see three newer Cadillacs.

"Some downstate, yuppie lawyers run a big poker game every other Saturday during the summer," Eli explains to Johnny and Cody, each dressed in black. "This is the job Zeke made us wait on. We'll just grab and go. Our take will be about two-to-three grand apiece, easy."

Cody whistles the impressive figure.

"How do you know all this?" Johnny asks. "I doubt Zeke tipped his hand."

"I've been doing some research on my own. Lately, I've been following him and his men. Outside of dealing meth, he's gonna have us start robbing these rich tourists. He figures with his drug clientele dwindling, this would bring in some steady revenue for a while. Let's beat him to it. We can use this as a side business when I get back into town."

"Cooking and selling is one thing, bro," Johnny says. "But . . . like, we don't even know who these guys are—if they're packing, or if they have friends in there or more coming . . . "

"Dude, I just told you what you need to know. I'm not gonna jam us up. Show some trust."

He reveals a glass pipe from his hoodie pockets and lights loose crystal rocks packed in it. He takes a toke, then offers it to the nervous Johnny. "Here. This will help the nerves."

There's some hesitation, but Johnny accepts. He wraps his lips around it and inhales a good-sized hit. What follows is repetitive coughing that takes him a minute to control.

Eli and Cody already begin to prepare. Johnny follows suit. Putting on his gloves, he slowly builds enough courage to carry on with the job. The mask is the last thing he has left to put on. But he can't find it anywhere. Searching the backseat, he comes across Katie's plastic bag she must've left behind. It's been under the passenger seat the entire time.

"Coming in hot," Eli says, handing Johnny a small, black 9MM.

"Whoa . . . " Johnny remarks, off-guard, shifting his eyes from the bag to the gun now lying in his lap.

"A buffer," Cody says.

"We never used guns before," Johnny says, dropping the gun back in the front seat. "What the hell?"

Cody and Eli look at each other with doubt.

"I always keep one on me," Eli says. "With this much cash, we gotta protect ourselves. You never know, man." Eli glares at Johnny in his rearview and urges again, "Take it."

"I'm not carrying a gun, bro."

Eli reaches around the seat and pins Johnny against his, "I'm not gonna hold your hand through this anymore. I've done a lot for you. Do not go tits up on me now!"

"Let go!" Johnny beseeches Eli. "I'm done. I'm out."

"Think you're better than me, huh? Gonna throw me aside like your brother did? Fuck you. You're a nobody, just like me. Playing for the Hawks or being a Dalton doesn't make you a better man. Ask Katie, bet she'd like the kind of man I am. She'd like what I could give her, rather than some boy."

Johnny lunges at Eli and wraps his hands around his neck. Eli raises his snub-nose and points it at him.

"I'll do it; I ain't above it," Eli says, those evil eyes piercing through Johnny again.

Johnny releases his hold and drops back into his seat.

"Grab the gun and get your ass ready," Eli orders and lowers his aim to finish preparing.

Johnny reluctantly grabs it from Cody. It's hit him—he realizes he made a wrong choice by coming with them. He looks back at the plastic bag on the seat. Inside he finds a pregnancy test with a pink plus sign. Positive. He's in awe of what he's discovered.

"Ready?" Eli asks, staring at him in the rearview again.

Johnny tucks the pregnancy test in his pocket, slides on his same ski mask, and opens the car door. The masked-three sneak to the cabin's entrance, avoiding detection through the lit windows. They bust through the door and enter with guns at the ready.

"On the floor!" Eli shouts, leading the charge.

"Down! Down!" Cody yells.

The three freeze in their tracks to find Zeke casually sitting against a lone card table. Next to him, stand Two-Stub and two rather large Native American men with long hair and knuckles the size of wheel lug nuts. Oddly enough they're not the least bit surprised to see Eli and his crew.

"What's this?" Eli asks Zeke as he lowers his 9MM.

Zeke rises from the table. "Remove the masks and drop the guns. Now!"

They each abide without hesitation, place their pieces on the ground and unmask. Standing directly behind the crew, Johnny spots Eli's snub-nose tucked in the back of his pants. Eli carefully drapes his shirt over the piece.

"You listen like shit, Masterson," Zeke says. "I thought I told you not to carry this one out."

"We needed the money, Zeke. We're tired of this bird feeding shit."

"I consider myself a fair man. Maybe even a patient man. See, I've accepted your lies. Even let you skim from the top now and then, knowing you needed to support that fine-ass woman you call a mother. Thought you'd change your ways after a while, but I'm starting to wonder if you really think I'm an idiot or something. "

One of the Native American men hands Zeke a sawed-off shotgun. Eli doesn't bat an eyelash. He just coldly mean-mugs Zeke the entire time.

"But I'm not the one that took the bait," Zeke remarks. "Come here, Dalton."

Johnny approaches his boss with caution. The uncertainty kills him inside. His focus drifts from Zeke to his muscle. When he positions himself in front of him, Zeke sits back against the table and places the shotgun across his lap.

"There used to be a boy who always failed," Zeke says to Johnny. "He didn't have very many friends. He was unsure of himself. His father didn't think much of him either. But no matter what anybody ever told this boy, he knew he was smarter and more capable of taking the world by the balls than anyone. So, there came a point in the boy's life when he was finally free from judgement . . . Ridicule . . . Read to me what my gun says."

Johnny stretches his head and squints to read the bronze inscription on the stock. "Ezekiel O'Bannon, Sr."

"That was my father's name," Zeke says. "And he killed himself with this very gun."

Johnny steps back, the wind gone from his lungs. He holds strong, not wanting to show any weakness towards his boss, but it's hard as hell not to when anticipating imminent murder.

"The minute his brains splattered on his bed was the moment I was in charge. Like a caterpillar becoming a butterfly, I suppose. Pretty, right?"

"I'm sorry, Zeke," Johnny says. "We fucked up bad."

Zeke nods oddly, "You didn't fuck up, kid. They fucked up."

He looks at Eli who keeps his hard and disgruntled stare on him. Then at Cody who's the complete opposite. He appears he's about to shit himself.

"You're one of the good ones, Dalton. I knew that the moment I met you. I didn't think you'd take the bait, but you did. Most are greedy and just walk away with the money, like your buddies, but not you. Nooo, you did the honest thing."

"You were working me?" Johnny asks, remembering that night at the park they first met.

"As long as I could. You're done now."

Johnny doesn't know what will happen next. *Is this it?* he wonders.

"Go home," Zeke tells him.

Johnny stands baffled, confused as to what's going on. He cautiously begins to back pedal to the door, still keeping his eyes on Zeke and his men.

When Johnny reaches the door, Zeke calls upon him once more, "Dalton ... You forgot something."

Johnny notices Zeke holding a roll of cash. There's a good distance between himself and the door. He could just flee and risk his chances, but the mood is calm at the moment. He decides to return to face his boss.

Zeke generously hands him the roll and winks, "This is a lot of money to be dropping around here."

Johnny walks to the door confused and tense. Before he exits, he glances back at Eli, then proceeds through the door untouched and continues to walk the trail into the dark.

Zeke and his men raise their guns at Eli and Cody. The two await their fate. Time has stood still in the room, but Eli won't go down without a fight. With the firing squad about to pull their triggers, Eli jerks his hand behind his back and draws his snub-nose.

Outside, Johnny continues walking. Behind him, gunfire lights the windows brighter than ever. The gunshots echo into the quiet night, lasting a few seconds. Terrified, Johnny doesn't look back and turns his walk into a run, leaving this life of crime behind for good.

An hour later, the sheriff responds to the reports of gunshots in the area. He speeds along the desolate dirt road. His headlights suddenly shine on Johnny, exhausted and walking in the dark. He's as white as a ghost. The sheriff slams on the brakes, whips his cruiser around and flips on his light bar to force Johnny to stop. He exits his car with a flashlight in hand.

"Dalton?" he asks, unsure. "What are you doing around here?"

Johnny is in a state of shock. Even if he wanted to say something he can't. Suspicious, the sheriff forces his hands on the hood while he frisks him. It doesn't take him long to come across Eli's pipe and the pregnancy test, both of which he places on top of the hood. The pipe is enough to slap the cuffs on the kid and place him under arrest.

None of it has sunk in with Johnny; mentally he's removed from everything.

☞   ☞   ☞

It is nine o'clock the next morning when James bails his son out of jail. When the Sheriff's Department called the Dalton household about Johnny being arrested, James and Sandy thought it best he sits in a cell the rest of the night to think about his actions.

James and Johnny arrive back home. Waiting at the table since before sunrise are Sandy, Jack, and Joe.

James puts pressure on the back of Johnny's neck to urge him into his chair at the kitchen table. Johnny slouches in his seat. His eyes are heavy from the sleepless night. His mother is visibly upset. So much so that she can't even look at him or defend his actions like she normally does. Silence hangs in the air for a time, while James pours himself a cup of coffee and then stands next to his wife.

"It's those people you associate yourself with," James says. "Like that trashy girlfriend of yours. She's no good for you, Johnny."

Anger builds in the exhausted teen. The last thing he wants to do is listen to this after what he went through. He tries to stand, but his father quickly forces him back in his seat with his sure, strong hands.

"No, you're gonna sit right there and listen for once," James says.

"To what?" Johnny fires back with attitude.

"Everything!" James screams, startling everyone in the room. "I mean what's wrong with you? You have a great opportunity in front of you, and it's like you're giving up. I didn't raise you to be a quitter. It's like you're making it your mission to not only piss your future away but the family name!"

"The family name?" Johnny scoffs. "Why do you keep saying that? The family name. What are we, royalty? Baseball royalty? Pssh, please."

James sets his coffee cup hard on the table, making it splash some. "Boy, you watch your mouth and show me some damn respect."

"The same respect you show me?"

"You don't just inherit respect, Johnny. You gotta earn it. "

"I'll never earn it in your eyes," Johnny says casually. "Oh, and that trashy girlfriend you mentioned is the mother of my child. "

Everyone freezes. Jack and Joe look to their parents for a reaction.

"Just so you know," Johnny adds.

"What?" Sandy asks, finally looking at her son.

"No," James says. "No. Don't say that to us."

Johnny sits straight and drops the pregnancy test on the table he digs from his pocket. Leaning over the test, he faces his father and says, "You gonna put me in my place now?"

James doesn't take this disrespect lightly and grabs his son by his jean jacket, pulling him from his chair. He kicks the table out of his way, and the family spreads around the two.

"You don't know the first damn thing about raising a child!" James exclaims, his face an inch from Johnny's.

"I do!" Johnny lashes back, keeping direct eye contact with him. "I'll take care of it!"

"With what?"

"I'll keep playing ball, get a second job, anything!"

"Not that easy, Johnny."

"I'll do whatever it takes."

"No."

"Listen, Katie needs me, and—"

"Nope, this—"

"And this is my decision."

James releases his grip on Johnny, dropping him back in his chair and hollers, "This isn't us! This isn't what I had planned for you!"

"What did you have planned for me, Dad? Follow in your footsteps?" He then points at Jack, "Follow in *his*? I'll live my life the way I want; it has nothing to do with you!"

"Boy, it has everything to do with me! You're my blood! You fail, I fail!"

"Day after day each of us bust our asses to please you. God forbid we fall out of line. Guess that makes me the fuck-up, huh? But you know, I'm too tired anymore, Dad. There's no point in pleasing a man who's never pleased."

James is taken aback by his stand. Johnny's words sit heavy on him. Trying to find some calmness in this turbulent situation, he responds with a lighter tone, "Let's just take a breath here and start thinking how we can get you back on good terms with MacIntyre after the suspension."

Johnny sighs in disbelief. "You're delusional."

He starts to leave. James grabs his arm and tries to force him back to his chair again, but Johnny has had enough and pushes him. James falls against the kitchen's island.

In an instant, Johnny realizes what he's done and extends his hand to help him to his feet, "Damnit, Dad. Sorry."

Unexpectedly, Jack punches him in the face to defend his father, knocking him over his chair, "Fucking punk!"

Sandy wedges herself in between them, and Joe wraps his big arms around Jack to try to contain him. Johnny recovers, and bull rushes Jack and slams him and Joe against the kitchen wall. Joe slumps to the side, leaving a gaping hole in the drywall.

James and Joe jump to their feet and try to separate the brothers. When the chaos settles, Johnny squirms from Joe's hold and wipes blood from his nose. He glares at his family one last time and leaves the house in a huff.

"Johnny!" Joe shouts.

"Let him go," James says.

Johnny walks down the road, away from the farm. Within an hour, he's sitting on the steps of Katie's apartment complex. He waits for her to find him, choosing not to knock so he can gather his thoughts.

Even though he's nearing nineteen-years-old, Johnny's mature enough to know that there are only a few options for him and his girlfriend. One, keep the baby and support it. This means no more being selfish; his youth gone. Two, an abortion. To him a life is precious, and as a Catholic, he knows an abortion is not an option. Adoption is the last option. But the thought of not ever knowing his kid and the certainty that his parents wouldn't let that option happen without a fight makes his situation much more complicated. So here he sits and begins to think of every and any way to convince Katie to keep the baby, no matter the struggle.

By the time Katie opens the door to leave her complex, she spots him to her surprise. Johnny is a mess. He's tired. He's dirty. He's confused. Everything hits him at this exact moment. The teen's eyes swell, and he embraces her tightly, crying into her petite body.

☞   ☞   ☞

A few dozen people dressed elegantly in black crowd inside the small Masterson household. Sandy and Mrs. Webb help serve guests and prepare food and drinks. Alicia also helps as much as she can, but her loss is far too great for her to act normal. It's a surprise to everyone that she's even functioning, considering. She has on a black dress, and the bruises on her face left from Bruce can barely be seen behind her heaps of makeup.

On the front steps of the house sit Jack, Nick, and Lou. Johnny couldn't bring himself to attend the wake. Plates of food sit on their laps, but no one is hungry. Thoughts of Eli and the regrets of what should have been hang over their heads. A centerpiece of their childhood has vanished.

Nick untucks his dress shirt and grabs Lou's wrist to check the time on his watch. "Damnit."

"I hate these things," Jack says, loosening his own thin black tie.

George then pulls in with Nick's truck, behind a line of parked cars that rest along the front yard. He's a mess. A flannel coat that hangs loose on his frame and torn jeans with filthy boots are what he chose to wear to the wake.

"Perfect, not only are you late but you look like shit," Nick says.

"No one's gonna care," George says, handing the keys to his son. "Any food left?"

"Plenty," Nick says and hands his uneaten plate to him.

George squeezes between the three to open the torn, barely hinged screen door that broke from a fight or two. "Is it dry?"

Nick shakes his head, and George enters the house. Jack and Lou let the quiet soak in. They know it's not their place to say anything.

"I had to flush his stash yesterday before his parole officer came," Nick discloses to them after a while.

"How does he piss clean?" Jack asks, packing a tin of Skoal with heavy finger taps.

"Let's just say I drink a lot of water before the tests."

Jack takes a pinch of his tobacco and fingers it in his bottom lip. The others help themselves to his tin when he offers. Nick shovels a three-finger dip in, leaving the biggest of bulges.

"Sometimes I wonder if he *wants* to go back to prison," Nick says, staring at nothing after a spit. "He's violated his parole I don't know how many times already. Maybe it'd be good for him to go back. I don't know."

James walks outside for a cigarette. Lighting up, he asks the trio, "How are you boys holding up?"

No one answers him.

" . . . Yeah . . . I hate these damn things . . . "

A roar of vehicles is suddenly heard tearing through the neighborhood streets. Some pass by the Masterson house. Curious, James flags a passing work truck that brakes when the driver recognizes him.

A white-bearded man in his 50s pokes his head out the window and says, "They're cutting 3,000 more employees, Jimmy! Word just came in to our Union Rep. We're striking!"

The man whisks away, leaving a cloud of exhaust behind. James notices his truck is blocked in the driveway. Behind him, Nick says, "I'll drive, Coach."

The four men board Nick's truck—Nick and Lou in the front seat and James and Jack in the bed. When they arrive at the Rupland Mine's entrance, they see thousands of furious miners flooding the chained and pad-locked gates. On the other side of the fence, corporate suits dodge garbage that's pelted at them. Sirens blare onto the chaotic scene. Deputies try to calm the bleak situation. Standing back, the four can only watch as the law fends off miners from climbing the gates and heaving flaming trash over it.

Years of a steady decline in Rupland has come to a head. These hardworking men and women that kept the town afloat are seeing their mine decline to nonexistence. The latest employee cuts are a transparent act. It's an indication that the Rupland Mine is slowly but surely closing. The union workers here are damned if they'll let the rug be pulled out from under their feet.

☞ ☞ ☞

Final game of the season: August 1st, 2005
RUPLAND HAWKS VS. GAMME GRAYS

Sheets of rain pour on Oren P. Rollins Field. Since the Summer League doesn't cancel or delay games on rainy days unless lightning strikes, they must play on. Competing in the rain makes for an interesting experience, to say the least. These are trench wars full of late game strategies, which forces teams to win these battles playing small ball. Ground crews do their best to maintain the field in between innings during heavy downpours, but it doesn't stop the ball from doing crazy things when it comes off the wood.

"The 14-13 Hawks need a win today to clinch a playoff berth," Frank Reese broadcasts. "If they can get their 15th win here against Gamme, they will surpass the 14-14 Dixon Vikings in the Wild Card standings to play top-seeded Crockerty, who are 25-3, in the first round as an eighth-seeding. Dixon has scored more runs on the year than Rupland, so if Rupland loses and finishes in a tie in the regular season standings, Dixon will automatically advance based on the tie-breaker."

A baseball from a grounder Lou fields and throws slices through the rain and into Nick's glove at first for an out. When the ball returns to the mound, Charlie circles his domain while peering into the stands to witness the sparse home crowd that attends today's game. The majority are in raincoats or even make-shift trash bag coats, and umbrellas populate throughout. With the mine's strike in full effect and the threat of closure looming, baseball seems like an afterthought to everyone here.

Charlie irreligiously packs mud on any new ball he receives as much as he can between pitches to dull the shine. The rain is treacherous for both teams, so getting any advantage they can is a must. Jack even helps his pitcher by trying to keep the same ball in play without the umpires switching it. He often drops it in the dirt that has turned to mud to get a nice coating on it before returning it back to Charlie. From there, Charlie rubs the mud in tight. This does two things: gives his pitches more action and him a better grip.

Jack sports neon yellow nail polish on four of his fingers on his right hand so Charlie can see his signs clearly through the weather. Rain isn't the only time Jack puts on the polish. Charlie's eyes aren't what they used to be. In order for the catcher-pitcher duo to communicate, they agreed that Jack will paint his nails on days Charlie starts.

Gamme's starting pitcher Carson Haynes digs into the muddy batter's box. Haynes is a two-way sensation who also plays shortstop and is one of the best overall hitters for the Grays. But not today. His mainly gray with navy blue trim uniform is soaked, adding unneeded weight that has surely affected his hitting for the worse. In two plate appearances, he's yet to get a hit in this bitch of an afternoon.

Charlie slings in a cutter that's slammed by Haynes for a hot roller down the right field line to the wall. Rounding second, Haynes goes full-throttle to try to stretch out a triple. Landon Steele gets to the ball and relays it to his cutoff who then lasers it to Cain at third. Haynes goes into a feet-first slide, slinking into the bag and springing up onto it, but Cain's tag is too late.

From the dugout, Coach Roberts stands, concerned for Charlie, seeing how he's starting to implode this last inning, and he says, "Should we pull him? Put Huff in?"

MacIntyre shakes his head, "He can't end it like this, Lloyd."

The innings that follow are a mess for Rupland. A series of runs in the middle of the game, a crucial run-scoring error that eats up Cain at third and Jack's 0-4 performance at the plate seals the loss. Lou is the only player to offer any glimmer of hope, hitting a two-bagger in the 8th to bring in Shoestring Hobbs for Rupland's only score against Haynes' dominance on the hill in their 10-1 defeat.

End of the game. The poor attendance has fled the park early in a hurry to escape the storm that just won't die. The Pittsburgh Pirates scout is among them. In a newly bought rain poncho, he flees into his Jeep and leaves Rupland, following the disappointing outing. Hawks players file into the locker room, marking the end of a mediocre 14-14 season that dashes any playoff hopes.

Cain glimpses back at the field, understanding that this may well be his last game. Trying not to dwell too much on what he already knows is inevitable, he holds back any emotion and continues into the locker room. The last player left in the dugout is Johnny. His eyes fix forward on Jack who remains on the field, standing at the plate with his bat clenched in hand. Jack fell victim to being the last player out, but the captain refuses to leave the field, even though the rain pours harder than ever on him. Mud is slowly turning into puddles of muck. It forms around his cleats and sinks him into his office where he made his name.

Observing Jack, there is a pang of anguish in Johnny. He's totally familiar with what Jack is going through—the inability to rally from defeat. But watching his older brother take this loss harder than anyone, *there's something behind it,* Johnny thinks to himself. *Why? It's just a game,* but he understands it means more to Jack. And a loss like this is surely devastating to him. *But why take it that hard? Why should I even care what he's going through? Why?*

At the same time, James sits in his truck, having just listened to the game's broadcast on the radio.

"The Hawks' season ends at the hands of the Gamme Grays," Reese announces. "While other towns prepare for the playoffs, it has to be tough to think about baseball right now."

James shuts off the truck and rejoins his union brothers. Shouting, marching, and picketing, the miners keep their strike alive, rain or shine. The strike came at a time when production plummeted to its worst in a decade. This was due to tumbling iron ore prices and falling revenues and stock shares that steadily plagued the Rupland Mine owners over the past five years. When the mine was at its peak of production, it had an annual-rated capacity of 10 million tons of iron ore pellets that it produced. The owners expected employees to continue this sort of production, forcing them to work longer hours for less pay and less production help, due to cutbacks. The latest cuts put the union in a bind, forcing them to strike while they negotiate for higher wages and labor expansion to continue to run mining operations.

The strike put the owners' backs against the wall. It cost them big money to keep the mine open daily. Without workers, there's no point in having operations run during negotiations with the union, since there is zero productivity.

These two months are very trying for the counties. Negotiations stall and production eventually stops completely. This creates a frenzy among shareholders, and they schedule a meeting for mid-August to redirect talks about the possibility of closing the mine indefinitely.

☞　　☞　　☞

Through the doors of Rupland High School, the entire town packs into the old gymnasium. There are so many people in the gym that it's reduced to standing room only. That in itself leaves little space, with many pouring into the halls. Eyes stare forward to the center of the floor where three long folding tables sit end-to-end. Behind them are twelve town council members, each dressed in business casual attire, like it's any normal work day. A town meeting is currently in progress.

Johnny stands in the thick of locals, while his family came early enough to get seats in the bleachers. His attention wanders towards two hometown Marines sitting in the front row on the other side of the gym. They're wearing their formal dress blues. Every accessory, including their shoes, are spit-shined to a glow. Their posture is straight with a certain respected air to their stature. Johnny realizes they're recruiters for the high school. He remembers during his junior and senior years a new pair of recruiters would come around to try to enlist as many students as possible. Every one of those Marines would speak of the Corps with praise and tell grand stories of their historical victories in the last century. Usually, a handful of students would enlist by meeting's end. This was something Johnny had always neglected, or just wouldn't take seriously. The last thing on his mind was following in his father's footsteps.

In the center of the town council, Mayor Morrow declares into his microphone box, reading many cutbacks from a list on a clipboard that's been placed before him, "All firearm societies, cancelled. All holiday festivities until further notice, cancelled. Tourism groups, fishing derby, Camp Kostas, the Festival Committee, all Rupland Theatre productions, holiday productions, Sportsman Club, and the Summer League . . . cancelled."

Gasps and chatter spread like wildfire. The council becomes the victim of the town's anger.

"Please understand, we hate this as much as everyone else," Mayor Morrow explains, trying to quiet everyone. "But for our town to survive, these cutbacks are inevitable."

Committee member Cliff stands and asks, "After 91 years it just ends, like that? Doesn't seem right."

Sporadic outbursts spread. Some agree, some don't. During the loud chatter, James stands and shares his concerns, "It doesn't matter how much money we save. By closing what you have there on that list, that's what makes us a town. You take away those, we're crippled. Our soul gone."

Many chant in agreement.

"The mine was our crutch, Mr. Dalton," Mayor Morrow says. "Our crutch is broke."

A female council member chimes in, "Listen, we're not the only ones hurting here. Barrix, Irons, Kenmore, all counties and towns who depend on this mine are affected. The losses have spread."

"What if we use the league for some sorta cash flow?" A female resident calls out.

"Unfortunately, besides park upkeep and player wages—" Mayor Morrow says before being cutoff.

"We'll decrease player and coach wages!" A man's voice pipes up, his face lost in the crowd.

"We need to save now to keep afloat," the mayor asserts. "With the strike and the mine's closure that looms, setbacks mean no money for bills, uniforms, and equipment. No families means no players, fans, sponsors, which means no teams. Do you understand what I'm saying?"

"We didn't make playoffs this year!" An irate man in the top section of the east side of the gym yells.

Another man sitting directly in front of him lashes out, "Screw the league! I live in Clarkston, and I'm more worried about the future of our communities than some damn sport."

"Easy for you to say, you won the title this season!" the irate man fires back. "What, you scared of us kicking your ass next summer?"

"Shut up!" The Clarkston resident screams, pushing the man.

The gym erupts into outrage. Shouting matches and side conversations overtake the meeting. Council members sit in hopelessness, unable to calm everyone and take control back. James, Sandy, and Jack share looks of disbelief, while Johnny squeezes his way out of the gym, amidst the uproar.

Around the days the Summer League postseason winds down, Johnny boards a greyhound bus at night with a small gym bag in hand. Katie stands on the station's platform waving him goodbye before the doors close. Her two-month pregnancy is starting to show.

A handful of riders board the bus, and it drives on. In his seat, Johnny gazes into the distance at the Oren P. Rollins Field lights that he can see for miles and miles outside of town. Ground crews prep it for the winter months that lie ahead. Just before crossing the county line past Big Bo, Johnny watches the lights shut off, leaving the area black.

CHAPTER 6 — WINTER OF '05

"There are only two seasons—winter and baseball."
—Bill Veeck Jr.

A TIMBER LORRY WITH A LOAD of freshly cut oak logs strapped to its flatbed barrels along a hardened dirt and snow-covered two-track. Its destination is the Rupland Sawmill. Winter season has arrived, leaving the once-vibrant colors of God's country a palace of cold white.

Working one of the many skidders that help load the lorries when they enter and exit this nearly clear-cut area of land is Jack. The former town star has since traded in his captain's uniform for flannel and Carhartt overalls. A forestry helmet system with a brush shield protector, a pair of steel toe boots, and grip gloves complete his woodsman transformation. He would almost blend in with the frosted beards and wind-burned lumberjacks he works with, if not for his own patchy beard he struggles to grow on his baby face.

After pulling, dragging, and loading his last haul of trees onto the flatbed, Jack hops in a lorry to catch a ride back to his car. From there, he drives to a place where familiarity and happiness overcome him, if only for a short time. To Jack this place is home, and this home is Oren P. Rollins Field.

Passing by a weathered, female groundskeeper whose shift has ended, she hands off the keys to Jack, having saved some work for him to finish the day. Jack opens the maintenance door to the outside of the park, grabs a snow shovel and enters the confines. When he arrives at the center of the walkway, where fans once flooded in, the snowy landmark reveals itself. He lays his eyes at the work that awaits him. A fresh blanket of white covers the field. The bleacher seats are barely recognizable in the mounds of snow that have fallen on them.

There's a moment where Jack closes his eyes and remembers all that was once great here. When he opens them, he's forced back to reality. It seems almost unjust and incomplete to him how his baseball career ended, but at least the precious memories remain. And he thinks this might be as close to the game than he'll ever be able to get for a while.

He moves on to shovel the bleachers. Afterwards, he drives the small John Deere plow that looks like a lawn mower on steroids and plows the entire field. While the park isn't used for baseball anymore, it's still home to several independent companies' holiday events, such as Christmas tree lighting shows, Pee Wee hockey, and the occasional livestock auctions that roll into town during the winter months.

When he finishes, Jack ends his two-hour shift with some hitting practice off the pitching machine and some running exercises that involve dry swinging and sprinting to first base, something he calls Hit-and-Runs. Twice a week he does some cardio on the diamond that involves hopscotch jumps around the bases and back to the plate. Then it's on to a series of backpedaling around the same path. He finishes the routine with more sprints and Wall Grounders, where he tosses the ball at one of the park's brick walls to field grounders with his baseball glove. 100 times he does this before he calls it quits. The strenuous workout hardly suggests he has given up the fight to keep playing.

Jack ends his work days at five o'clock, right when darkness falls. Quitting time means drinking time at The Pickaxe, where he shares suds with Nick if he isn't working, and whatever teammate that still lives in Rupland that happens to stroll by. With his days packed full, he usually misses family dinners, so most of the time he'll grab a hot meal at the bar. By night's end, he either returns to his apartment with a new bar hookup or a sixer to end the day. Then the following morning he does it all over again. Even though he doesn't work on the weekends, he still helps his family at the store and continues to train and work on his game whether it's worth it or not. There is still hope in Jack that something good will happen. To him this process is boring, but it's a living.

Loneliness is what kills him though. Jack has never been one to commit to any relationship of any kind since Savannah. His focus always remains on baseball. As long as anyone can remember it's been hard for him to give any girl his full self. He'll tell his mother he's just holding out for the right one and is picky, just to keep her off his back. His buddies think he likes to play the field and not be tied down with just one, but in all reality, Jack doesn't think he deserves a good woman. Committing is permanent, and that scares him worse than suffering an injury or losing a game. Although he is a very private person, Jack yearns for that companionship, but committing means the concern of possible failure. Much like he is with his father, Jack doesn't like to disappoint. The possibility of not succeeding in a game translates to the same with a relationship. However, in a game, Jack knows he can control what happens. In a relationship, he cannot. Failure is his biggest fear. Failure he tries to remove from his thoughts.

James' cut-up blue jeans protrude from under a vegetable cooler he's trying to repair in the store. He works at the family's business daily. On the side, he fixes locals' vehicles for some extra cash. Five months after the strike, the mine couldn't be saved and closed, leaving Rupland searching for stability for the first time in its history. Many families have begun to move away.

As she trains new employee Katie, who is now eight months pregnant, on the register, Sandy can't help but woefully eye her near-empty store. Even though the Daltons can barely afford to pay her, they know maintaining a relationship with her and the baby is of the utmost importance.

In the canned goods aisle, Joe stocks what he can, facing products to the edge of the bare shelves to mask the emptiness. The store's aisles were once a collage of color from cleaning supplies and baking goods to canned foods and frozen foods. For 15 years, customers filled this place regularly. Many came to shop, but some would stay to engage in conversation with Sandy and drink the free coffee she set out for the Committee for hours. Now they're lucky if they get three customers in three hours; night and day from 1997.

"This is ridiculous," Sandy says to her husband. "We have enough to call the guy."

"Well, the guy costs too much," James says from under the cooler. "No need to pay someone else when we're capable of doing it. Hand me a seven-eighths."

Sandy hands him a wrench from his toolbox. A loud metallic clunk is heard. James groans in pain. The bell to the front door rings. Sandy walks back to the register, eager to greet potential customers.

"There, I think I got it," James says. "Plug it in, Sandy."

No one responds to him.

"Sandy . . . Hey . . . "

After zero responses, he scoots out to see Katie, then his wife hugging Johnny tightly. The self-enlisted Marine dressed in his Service C uniform has a clean-cut appearance and gained a great deal of muscle mass to fill an impressive physique. An abrupt quiet falls when James and his middle son lock eyes on each other for the first time in six months since he left without a word for Parris Island boot camp. The stubborn Dalton men simply share a nod.

James redirects his attention back towards the cooler as he tries to think of something to say to soften the awkwardness, "We should plug this thing in, Sandy." He meanders back under the cooler.

Sandy breaks the tension by telling Johnny what every mother tells their child, "God, you're so thin! Did they even feed you?" Before Johnny can answer, she continues, "Tell you what, how about I make your favorite meal—pasties—tonight?"

"Sounds good, Mom," Johnny says. "There's actually some news I'd like to share with everyone tonight."

Joe approaches his brother and gives him a light push to greet him.

"What's up, ugly?" Johnny remarks, gripping Joe's shoulder to bring him in for a hug.

Joe has since grown taller than Johnny—over six feet. And he's not shy to poke some fun at his older brother in saying, "You shrunk, bro."

"No, you're getting too big!" Johnny says.

By evening, the Dalton household is a familiar breath of fresh air to Johnny. The smell of home cooking, the conversations, the house's decor, it brings a sort of calming comfort to him. Out of everything that has changed in the town these days and in his own life, being home is something that never does.

Katie helps Sandy prepare dinner while Johnny playfully toys with her. He reaches around her shoulder to sneak a taste with his finger, and constantly touches her baby belly. Every few minutes he looks at her in amazement at their own family life that awaits them. There is heavy pressure from both sides for the two to get married. While that is the plan, Johnny wants financial stability before Katie and the baby move with him.

Jack stumbles into the house closer to dinner time. Sandy and Katie take little notice. He's just come from the bar, a long day in the woods visible on him. Hooking his lipper from his mouth, he tosses it in the garbage and heads straight for the fridge, ignoring Johnny's presence. He grabs a cold one and cracks it open. Finally acknowledging him, he stops and firmly shakes his hand.

"Nice get up," Jack comments on Johnny's uniform, before taking a swig.

"They give it to you for free; can you believe it?" Johnny says.

Like his father, Jack makes little conversation. He slaps his brother's shoulder, "You look good."

And the greeting ends before it began. Jack retreats into the living room to join his father and Joe to watch a Detroit Red Wings hockey game.

The family gathers to eat dinner. The table has a plentiful spread of pasties made with potatoes, rutabaga, onions, carrots, and spiced ground chuck filled in a pie crust shaped in the form of a mini-meat pie. Cottage cheese with diced tomatoes, salad, and bread and butter also fill the table. Underneath, a bony, aged Daggett lies, licking his chops, waiting for scraps to fall.

Sandy can't eat the meal she helped make. She's too busy admiring the simple gathering of her family again. "It's been a while since we've eaten together. This is nice."

A few of the men's heads veer up but drop back to their plates after a while, eating the Dalton men way. There's barely any conversation. Every so often, their eyes wander from their plates to look at one another. Particularly James, who glimpses at Johnny's dog tags around his neck that fall from his shirt.

"You wear those a lot, eh?" James mumbles to Johnny with a mouthful of food.

This is the first real sentence his father has spoken to him since he's been home. Somewhat surprised, Johnny swallows hard and replies, "Yes. I like wearing them, I guess."

He stuffs them back in his shirt, and James refocuses back to his plate of half-eaten pasty. Johnny glances from his father to the rest of the table—his mother takes her time enjoying each bite, Joe shovels in his food and is ready to stand for seconds, and Jack sways in a drunken stupor, trying to eat enough to absorb the booze. Katie rubs her belly while she eats. When she sees his eyes on her, she gives him a knowing look to say his piece.

Johnny clears his throat and says, "I'm glad everyone is here tonight. Very glad."

"Us too, sweetie," Sandy says, chewing with a grin.

"Yeah," Johnny says. "A lot has happened since I left. I've had a lot of time to think about my choices and my future in the service . . . I just wanted to let all of you know that after my leave here I'm being deployed with my unit to Iraq."

He stops talking to let the words ruminate, unsure how his family will react to the news. Eating trickles to a stop, and their attention turns fully on Johnny.

"What?" Sandy asks, not quite registering what he announced.

"I'm going to Iraq, Ma. I volunteered, and it's something I wanted to do for a while now."

Sandy's eyes water as she rises from the table, "Keep eating . . . I'll be . . . I'll be right back." She leaves the room in a hurry. James slides his chair from the table and goes after her.

"Ma . . . " Johnny stands to try to stop her.

The Dalton brothers and Katie are left alone at the table. Johnny drops in his seat, disappointed in the reaction he's received.

"Nice, man," Jack says.

"Don't start," Johnny replies with irritation.

"Guys—" Joe says to halt a fight before it begins.

Johnny leaves the room.

Kneeling at her bedside, Sandy prays. Tears aren't falling anymore though. Oddly enough, she's kept strong and is resorting to prayer, as usual, to help guide her. Behind her, James stands at a loss for words. He kneels by her side and hugs her.

"Go talk to him," Sandy whispers in his ear.

James remains quiet.

Sandy leans back to face him, "Even though you choose to ignore it, that's you in that kitchen. I once remember a stubborn young man who did what he wanted no matter what anyone else said. Go."

James exhales with hesitation. Sandy grabs his face and brings him close, making him understand just how serious she is. "This nonsense between you two—swallow it. Your son needs his father now, more than ever. Only you can talk to him about what he's going to experience."

By the kitchen sink, Johnny indulges in a cigarette. Smoke filters out the window he's opened. Katie stays at the dining room table to avoid breathing it in.

"That went as well as a fart in church," Johnny jokes.

"Yeah, but they needed to know," Katie says.

Joe joins them, placing his dishes into the sink. Johnny offers him a cigarette, which he rejects with a hand gesture.

"Smart," Johnny says.

"So, Iraq?" Joe says.

"Yup."

"There's some serious shit going on over there. You've got brass ones for volunteering, I'll give you that."

Johnny smirks, finishing his smoke.

"Scared?"

"I'm ready. Gotta rid the world of these terrorists."

A constant smacking sound from outside shifts his attention. He sees Jack hitting baseballs from a tee next to the barn that's endured slightly more exterior damage this winter.

"He still trains?" Johnny asks Joe.

"Every day," Joe says, emptying the last of the dishes into the sink.

"Son of a bitch doesn't quit, does he?"

"Ha. Nope. You know Jack."

Johnny continues to watch his brother muscle hit after hit.

"Has he spoken to anymore scouts?" Johnny asks. "Any possibility playing for a school maybe?"

"Don't know. He doesn't tell us much of anything anymore. We don't see him too much, really. He works a lot. Drinks a lot now too. Tell you the truth, that's about all we know about him since the league went under."

Johnny continues to watch his older brother hit, somewhat impressed by his relentlessness.

☞   ☞   ☞

A week of being back in town has taken its toll on Johnny. He's exhausted from greeting and talking about his deployment with everyone, including his former teammates and coaches. This evening his mother has unexpectedly invited a handful of veterans to the store to have coffee with him. They share their old war stories of where they fought, who they fought, and why they fought. Knowing he's in need of an escape, Katie lends Johnny her car to joy ride around town to clear his head this evening.

Depression is everywhere. What used to be a prospering and busy downtown is currently an afterthought of what once was. Vehicles that travel these streets are far and few. *Where are the business owners? Where are the children playing? What happened to the smell of maple syrup from the paper mill?*

Across town, the bar scene is where it's at on Saturday nights. New and classic country songs play from the jukebox at The Pickaxe. Lumberjacks populate much of the place these days since miners are steadily leaving the town. Jack, Nick, and a few former teammates share pitchers of beer at two tables they pushed together in the center of the joint.

The redheaded beauty is also there. She flirts with just about everyone and hangs on the shoulders of former Hawks. Her once striking appearance has faded. Years of drinking have taken their toll.

The only one at the table not indulging is Nick. He's been sober a full year. Quitting cold turkey was something he forced himself to do for his health. Knowing that alcoholism runs deep in his family, he understood that if he didn't quit when he did, he would've followed the same dark path as his father.

"How's Lou doing in JC?" Nick asks Jack.

"Hates it," Jack laughs, causing Nick to belt out a breathless laugh of his own.

"He'd rather be back here than studying every day."

"I miss that motherfucker," Nick says.

"We all do!" Shoestring yells from the other end of the table.

"Zoom, you know, I hear State is looking to rebuild their program," Nick says with some hesitation. "You should try out for them."

Jack pours himself another mug full and wisecracks to his friend, "What, and leave this behind? Besides, who's gonna keep you in line, pal?"

"True, true," Nick says, not digging any deeper into Jack. "I figure I might as well settle down. Maybe have a few little Koskos running around after a while."

"There's a scary thought," Jack chuckles. "Who's gonna wanna marry you?"

Nick roars a belch after finishing his mug of ginger ale, "I've got my options."

"Who?"

"Mary Ann Lanski, for starters."

"Oh, no. No, no, no. She's no good for you, bro. Hell, she's been heels to Jesus with half the team. You need someone that'll turn you into a gentleman."

"Fuckin'-A, that's a challenge. Appreciate the warning though. If she slept with you assholes, I'm sure she's caught something."

Cain and Landon stroll into the bar; a normal Saturday for the friends. They're early. Usually, they start at a few other hole-in-the-walls before coming to The Pickaxe for last call. Cain ignores his former teammates' table and heads straight to the bar. Landon doesn't. He greets his former teammates.

After Cain orders his drink, he erratically begins to sing, "Taaake me out to the ball gaaame. Take me out with the crooowd."

"It's been fun boys," Cain says to the table of teammates after he's handed his IPA. "Keep it pure."

"You're moving on too?" Shoestring asks him.

"Louisiana's the place. My uncle owns a fishing boat. Pays pretty good, so I'm getting the fuck outta Dodge while I can."

"Will you come back if the league reinstates?" backup midfielder JoJo Torres asks. "Talk around town is there's some ideas to keep it alive."

Cain scoffs. He takes a hearty drink from his mug and shoots down Torres' comment, "Man, the league's not coming back. It's gone. Y'all should make peace with it already. I have."

He chugs his IPA as he and Landon pick a couple stools at the bar, away from their teammates. Cain's opinion doesn't sit well with Jack. The last captain keeps his eyes on his mug in his lap, playing with the condensation that streams with his dirty, sticky tree sap fingers.

The words flow from his mouth lightly, "Stand there and act like you don't miss it, but you're lying."

"What'd you say?" Cain snaps, spinning around in his stool.

"You're a ball player. The game is all you know."

Cain inches closer to him and says, "For years I've bled the orange and black, and for what? Look at all of us now. It's done us no favors. I don't miss shit; so don't preach to me about the goddamn game, boy."

He puts one hand on the table and pushes it back into Jack's chest, undoing a couple of buttons on his plaid shirt. Many glasses and pitchers on the table clink and spill a bit. Jack sits straight in his chair, angry.

"Mind backing away?" Nick says.

"I do," Cain replies. "I'm about tired of that mouth."

Cain continues to agitate Nick and kicks a chair at his legs. Nick tosses it aside and stands face-to-face with him.

"What are you gonna do?" Cain asks Nick, egging him on.

Jack rises from his seat and squeezes in a punch that sends Cain against the bar. Landon then grabs Jack, but Nick punches him into a tall lumberjack that begins a melee of punches. A bar brawl erupts between locals and former teammates.

Cain recovers from Jack's punch and throws a powerful haymaker at Jack, sending him to the floor. A battered Landon hops next to Cain, and the two begin to work Jack over. From nowhere, Johnny appears and peels Landon off, then throws a floor rocking right hook to Cain's jaw. He then helps his older brother to his feet, and the two go back-to-back to fight with the rest. Each give and receive a fury of punches, kicks, and headlocks. The Pickaxe becomes absolutely trashed.

"Cops!" The angered bartender shouts from the back, slamming down the phone he called authorities from.

Sirens howl and lights flash blue and red through the windows.

"We gotta go!" Johnny says to Jack and hurries to the exit.

Patrons pour out of the bar. Like something from a *Dukes of Hazzard* episode, the Dalton boys hop into Johnny's ride and burn onto the road for the getaway, before a barrage of Rupland's finest can detain them.

A chilly wind haunts the surroundings of Oren P. Rollins Field, onto which Johnny drives. A deputy car whizzes by on its way to The Pickaxe.

"Think they saw us?" Jack asks, glancing back as the cruiser sped past.

"Doubt it," Johnny calmly says.

The brothers exit the car to check the few wounds they have in the side mirrors. When they realize their clothes are a mess and their boots are filthy with beer and debris, they simultaneously burst in laughter. Their breaths are visible in the cold air.

"Ouch," Jack laughs, holding his sore gut. "Oh, man . . . Thanks, Johnny."

Johnny lights a cigarette and leans against the car next to Jack who asks him, "Where'd you come from anyway?"

"I was driving around looking for you, actually. Joe said you'd probably be at The Pickaxe."

"For me? Why?"

"Don't know. See how you've been holding up, I guess. You don't seem right lately. And we don't talk, so . . . "

Jack sheds a *what the fuck* expression, followed by an unsure chuckle, before realizing his brother is serious. "Don't ask me that."

"Why?"

"'Cuz it's bullshit. We don't do this." Jack opens his door to leave and comments, "Marines Corps making you soft or something? Let's go."

Johnny ignores him while he opens the backseat door to grab his glove. He puts out his cigarette on his boot, buttons his pea coat, and heads towards the field.

"You got ten pitches," Johnny says, walking away from his perplexed brother. "Field is cleared, yeah?"

Jack nods.

"Then, let's go," Johnny urges.

Jack gives a warm, closed smile. From the maintenance room where he keeps his own equipment, he grabs a bucket of baseballs, a bat, and his catcher's mitt. Johnny takes the bucket from him and strips his pea coat at the mound. They play catch. No words are exchanged—only throws, each one hitting their gloves harder than the last.

"Things good at the mill?" Johnny asks first.

"Oh, living the dream," Jack says.

Johnny releases a hard enough throw that sparks Jack's interest. Jack, too, returns it hard. Their competitiveness awakens.

Johnny gestures to Jack to grab his bat from the ground. He does and positions himself in the frosted batter's box. Johnny starts to dig his usual gaping hole in front of the rubber, then slides his right hand's fingers across the seams of the baseball to grip a four-seamer. The familiarity brings him comfort. He winds up and delivers a hell of a pitch that Jack connects on, deflecting the ball foul to the backstop.

"Did you learn a new one?" Jack asks him, a little surprised by his brother bringing on the cheese, instead of the usual junk he tosses.

"Can't handle it, Captain?" a brash Johnny jabs.

"I can handle anything you throw, Nancy."

Snowflakes begin to fall, starting light and eventually turning thick. A light dusting of snow covers their heads and shoulders. Johnny pitches a couple more that Jack knocks into the outfield before he removes his glove and steps off the mound to grab his coat.

"What's the matter?" Jack asks.

"Guess," Johnny says, indicating the winter weather as he blows warm breaths into his clenched hands.

Jack pats the snow from his flannel fleece. "Pssh, figures."

Johnny's frustration develops, and he approaches Jack, "What's your problem, man?! You're always riding me!"

"You really wanna know?"

"Let's hear it."

"Johnny, you have talent. Real, natural fucking talent. You can throw with both arms. A switch hitter. You know how many colleges or pro teams would kill for that sort of player? I bust my ass every day to keep myself relevant. Everything I have, everything I am gets left on this fucking field to stay relevant. You'll never understand that because it comes easy to you, and the bitch of it is that you take it for granted. Jesus."

Johnny remains silent.

"All the years we spent preparing for the league, you just threw it away like it was nothing. You threw the team away. You threw *me* away!"

"I don't care about the game as much as you, all right?!" Johnny shouts.

"See, I don't buy that. Baseball is the one thing that we've always shared. You grew up in the same household, same rules as I did."

"That is not true."

"Come on—"

"We grew up in separate households. The old man didn't push you like he pushed me. You did everything right all the time, and I disappointed him all the time. It went beyond baseball, Jack."

"He had his reasons for pushing us."

"I can't live like that anymore. I'm sick of living in your shadow, man."

"Who asked you to? If your stubborn ass would've just listened to him for once—"

"To what? How to get scouted? Look how well that turned out for you—" Johnny catches his words, knowing he went too far, "Sorry . . . "

Jack gets right in Johnny's face and looks up at his taller brother. "Do not do that! Never pity me!"

"Okay. Whatever. Goddamn, dude."

Johnny quits the argument altogether. Jack blocks his way as he tries to leave the field. "Pitch to me."

"Not when you're hyped-up like this. It leads to no good between us."

"Hey, you started something here. You've got seven more pitches still. Finish it." Jack remains persistent, putting the ball in his brother's glove and then returns to the plate.

"I'll make you eat this damn thing," Johnny mutters, digging his hole again.

He then sets on the hill and runs a split-finger fastball up and in that Jack lines to deep center.

"Fuck!" Johnny hollers, upset with himself.

"Try left!" Jack says.

Johnny loses the only glove he's brought and continues without it. He throws six more pitches, each showing great command and movement. Some curve and others are just greasy fast with some life. But Jack is keen on every one and connects on all of them, driving each pitch to separate parts of the field.

Johnny's frustration explodes, and his face contorts as he comes down with lucky number seven—an off-speed pitch that's waist high. He slips off the mound and into the snow as he watches the ball in flight, sailing past Jack who whiffs on it. Jack's bat frees from his hands and sticks into the backstop fencing. A look of shock crosses the eldest's face.

Johnny stays on the ground in a sitting position. Jack walks to him to help him up, but he refuses. Snow begins to accumulate on Johnny. Everything has hit him at once. This is more than finally getting a strike past Jack. The reality of his own future is coming so fast.

"I'm gonna be a father, Jack," Johnny says.

Jack hovers over his brother. "I know."

"My kid's gonna have a life different from this place. He's gonna have the world . . . "

Jack remains stiff and quiet.

"Joe asked me last week if I'm scared to fight overseas, you know? Yeah man, I really am. But it's fine. I'm okay with that. And I don't even know if I should be. But I do know that I want this. Let me have this, Jack. Just let me have something of my own for once."

"War? That's what you want then?"

"Maybe . . . Man, see, I've always looked up to you as much as I tried to fight it. Heck, I still do. I was jealous that the old man always gave you his full attention."

"Johnny—"

"No, hear me out. Before I enlisted, I was fucking lost. I did a lot of stupid things. A lot of bad things. When Eli died, it sorta made me look at myself finally, like, what the fuck am I doing? The only thing that made sense to me was realizing that playing ball was not what I'm meant to do. You know? And if being a father and a soldier is, then I'll accept it with a full heart. I'll accept this life because I chose it. *Me.* Because I feel it's a second chance. I deserve that."

Jack pauses a moment, reflecting on what Johnny has said. He extends his hand to help Johnny to his feet, which this time, he takes and shockingly turns it into a hard hug. When they separate, Jack returns to the backstop to retrieve his bat.

"You can leave here, too, you know," Johnny says. "Plenty of schools and teams outside of this godforsaken town. The game doesn't have to end here, Jack."

Jack yanks and frees his bat from the fencing and turns to him. Any conflict from his expression is gone and is now replaced with peace. "I've gotta be around it, brother. I've gotta . . . But I'll never leave Rupland."

Johnny knows he must accept this response. The subject is far too sore for him to dig any further. *Maybe some things are better left unsaid*, he thinks to himself. He knows if questions aren't answered over time, then he has to bury and forget them. It's his family's way. Maybe that's okay this time because Jack has always gotten by. Being the eldest son, he's forced to lead by example from his parents. Luckily for James and Sandy, Jack was born a natural leader. *He'll survive*, Johnny assumes.

Jack grabs the baseball that he missed on and tosses his brother's victory back to him.

"Another ten?" Johnny asks.

Jack's face brightens as he steps back into the box. The brothers continue to play on in the snow.

☞   ☞   ☞

It's too early. No one is awake at this hour. James explores the halls of the hospital, holding two paper cups of hot coffee. He enters the waiting room and hands one to Sandy. Both sit anxiously waiting with Katie's father. Mr. Purnell is a slight, austere man with a great beak of a nose.

Before long, Jack and Joe also arrive to wait with them.

"Any updates?" Jack asks.

"Not in a while," Sandy replies.

Both brothers sit in the vinyl upholstered chairs across from their parents and Mr. Purnell. Over the next few hours, they read every outdated magazine that's on hand. Every nurse and doctor that passes through the emergency doors they bombard with questions and continue to grill the receptionist every half-hour for updates.

By six-thirty in the morning, Johnny arrives in the waiting room, dressed head-to-toe in surgery scrubs. A Cheshire Cat smile stretches across his face when he proudly tells the family members, "It's a boy."

Handshakes and hugs are given to the new father.

"How's Katie?" her father asks.

"Very good, Mr. Purnell," Johnny replies. "She's ready to see everyone."

Johnny leads them back. When they reach the room, they see Katie holding the dark-haired, eight-pound, six-ounce newborn. The new dad covers the baby in his blanket some more. "Meet Jacob John Dalton."

The family stands back in awe of this little miracle.

"How are you feeling, hon?" Sandy asks Katie, resting her hand on her forehead.

"Tired," Katie replies, her eyes drooping.

Sometime later, the nurses take baby Jacob to the nursery so Katie can rest. The family watches him in his hospital bassinet from the outside window. Hours later, the family returns home to grab some much-needed shuteye, leaving James and Johnny alone.

"I can't take my eyes off him," Johnny says, peering through the glass.

James watches his own son. "It's quite a feeling, isn't it?" He hints that he wants to say more but struggles to find the right words. He digs in his Rupland Mine company coat to reveal a flask he was saving for the special occasion. "Almost forgot."

"Are you sure?" Johnny asks.

"If you're old enough to fight for your country, you're old enough to drink." He presents the flask with the unknown elixir to his son, "Today we're celebrating!"

"Here?" Johnny asks.

"Are you gonna take it or not?"

"All right, all right," Johnny says, accepting the flask.

Both take nips from it and watch baby Jacob together.

"You haven't asked me yet," Johnny says to his father while staring ahead.

"Asked what?"

"Why I did what I did without telling you guys."

"I've got a pretty good idea."

"You do?"

"I did the same thing to my folks."

They share a joyful laugh.

"Sometimes a man has to do what's best for him," James says. "Bet it was hell those thirteen weeks."

"Boot camp?" Johnny asks after a drink he almost chokes on because of its bite. "The worst."

James laughs, knowing what Johnny had to go through.

"It was worth it," Johnny says. "I made Scout Sniper School, top of my class."

James smiles warmly and says, "Sharp shooter."

"And a lance corporal."

"Damn good, Johnny. Damn good."

"I'm ready, Dad. I'm ready to fight for my country, just like you did."

"I know. You've always been a tough kid. That's something you can't teach, son." James brings the flask to his lips. "Fear nothing." He grins and takes a drink.

"Ooh-rah," Johnny says, taking a swig after his father.

"I do have a question though," James says. "Why the name Jacob? I never spoke much about your uncle to you boys."

"Ma did. A lot. I just wish we could've met him."

This touches James a certain way. He's thought of his younger brother every day of his life.

"Your mother's quite a woman," James says with a grin of his own. "She ever tell you how you boys got your names?"

"From the Bible, she said," Johnny replies.

James chuckles, "Hmmm, yes and no. Your mother likes to believe that anyway.

"We're not?"

"There is some truth to that. Jack meaning 'God is Gracious,' John the Apostle, and yeah, Joseph of Joseph and Mary. But it just so happens those three names are names of my all-time favorite ball players: Jackie Robinson, Johnny Bench, and Joe DiMaggio."

"No shit?" Johnny laughs. "I should've guessed."

James winks and says to him, "Don't tell her I told you that."

"Our secret."

James grips his son's shoulder proudly and continues to admire his grandson with him.

"Today is a good day," James says.

☞   ☞   ☞

The entire state was hit with one of the worst blizzards it had seen in some time. Snow didn't stop falling for five days straight. When it finally did, it had accumulated to almost four feet. Plowing is an art form in these parts, but this sort of job has taken the county workers an extended period to catch up on every main and back road and side street.

Locals have been contributing to help each other. Anyone who owns a four-wheel drive has attached a plow to the front of it by now to help businesses and residential homes clear the excess heaps of snow from their driveways, parking lots, and personal access roads. The plummeting temperatures have forced most inside, leaving the ones with plows and snowblowers the only people outside. Unfortunately, every county team is scheduled to meet today to discuss any last to-do's to prepare for the official closing of the league.

Manager MacIntyre drives his rusty 1995 Ford Ranger on a road of thick white and black ice. The wind rocks his truck around, making it hard for him to keep it straight. As he drives around a long, curved part of the road, he loses control and spins several times before crashing into a large embankment.

"Of all the days," MacIntyre says to himself.

He takes a cell phone from his snow pants, removes his leather gloves, and calls his daughter. Luckily, he's able to reach her in time before she ventures out with friends to ride the trails on her snowmobile.

Twenty minutes later, Sarah arrives and tries to help her father get his truck unstuck from the bank but to no avail. His tires just spin in place, creating ice with no grip to move the vehicle forward. She agrees to take him to the meeting in downtown Rupland by snowmobile. When they arrive at the tiny town hall, MacIntyre asks Sarah to join him inside where the rest await.

In this conference room, every town's mayor or commissioner is there as well as the managers of every league team. Also in attendance are several members of the Committee that run the meeting. It's a room full of testosterone. This isn't a place for the youth. Some of the wisest baseball minds are here. Usually, these meetings happen once a year before every season to go over what lies ahead in the new year. Some say it's an excuse for the men to have a day to carouse and break bread with each other before they become enemies again. Sometimes the Committee hosts these get-togethers outside of the counties at casinos or lavish destinations for the managers to let their hair down and kick their feet up. But due to the bad weather and the reason for this meeting, no one is in the mood to celebrate.

"Bad roads get ya?" Mayor Morrow asks MacIntyre, presenting a seat next to him.

MacIntyre grunts, not wanting to divulge any details of his journey. Some snicker, others carry on with their earlier banter. MacIntyre and Sarah remove their coats and place them on one of many racks full of thick winter coats, hats, and scarves.

"Sorry, darlin' this is a private meeting," Clarkston Black Sox manager Hoyt Perkins tells Sarah from the other end of the long conference table. "Managers and league officials only."

"Darlin'?" Sarah says, annoyed by his comment.

"Shut up, Hoyt," MacIntyre says, ignoring him and slides a chair out for his daughter to sit next to him.

Seated at the head of the table is Cliff. He quiets everyone when he stands to begin the meeting. "I look forward to these meetings every year. This is the first time where I really didn't want to attend."

The room quickly quiets. No one wants to attend this last meeting. The fate of something as treasured as the league has brought tears to these proud men's eyes throughout these hard months.

"But we must move on," Cliff adds and hands a stack of folders to the manager of the Ottawa Deltas, Otto Fallon, to hand to everyone. "Per usual, inside these folders are emails shared with us Committee members this season, including revenue breakdowns for ticket and vending sales. You'll find details in here of the next steps for equipment sales and stadium stripping."

"Stadium stripping?" the manager of the Holton Bolts asks.

"Correct," Cliff answers. "We spoke to each town's official, which you will see in the email printouts there. Each park has many valuable pieces the towns could sell to generate funds for their respected communities."

"A fire sale . . . " Hoyt says.

"For lack of a better term, yes," Cliff replies.

The room isn't too pleased as they examine the contents of their folders. Sarah grabs a few email printouts from her father's folder and reads them also.

"Christ, Cliff," Steve LaCroy, manager of the Ransville Reds says. "These are monuments. You expect people to go along with this shit?"

"They're going to have to," Nelson Gerber, the mayor of Hillsdale says.

"I have to agree," Morrow adds. "We need every cent we can generate. We have good equipment and great fixtures in these stadiums that we can sell immediately and give the proceeds to our towns."

"That's bullshit," LaCroy declares. "Those are good parks. We can use them to host our high school team sports and other offseason events. What the fuck do we wanna destroy them for? To make a little money that'll be dried up in less than a year? Come on."

Managers around the room add their opinion in agreement with LaCroy. During the commotion, Sarah discovers something of interest and shows it to her father, who is just sitting back quietly observing the arguments between the managers and town officials.

"Did you see those roads outside?" Morrow asks LaCroy. "Our counties don't have the manpower to clear them in a timely manner. We've got frickin' residents volunteering all hours of the day. Using any source of funds will help our communities right now."

"Yeah, we don't expect you lawmakers to understand," Hoyt says with a sigh. "Every politician born on third base thinks he hit a triple."

"We care about the league just as much as you guys," Morrow states. "Don't act like we don't."

"We're doing what's best for the counties," Gerber adds. "The league is dead. Why should our towns have to die with it, huh?"

"Cliff, you played and coached in this league," LaCroy says to him. "You agree with this bullshit? Hell, the Committee—do you agree?"

"Absolutely hate it, to tell you the truth," Cliff replies. "But we do understand the circumstances."

LaCroy scoffs.

"Our money has always gone towards the league," Cliff adds. "We need to redirect that focus and find solutions to help our counties with the league and the mine done."

"Cliff . . . " MacIntyre pipes up from the end of the table, holding the email printout Sarah handed him.

Everyone stops talking to look at him. MacIntyre doesn't speak a lot, but when he does, it's something of purpose.

"This email back in April of this year—" he says, "who is Picwick? Is that downstate?"

"Mmhm," Cliff says.

"And Macklon?"

"They're a town from Tennessee."

MacIntyre studies the paper more, taking his time. "I see Craftley here. They're downstate, I know. Got some family in those parts. And Morway?"

"Iowa. Fred, what are you getting at?"

"Each of these towns have emailed you Committee members and . . ." He takes another few papers from Sarah. "They are asking the league to play them in exhibition matches. They've emailed the same requests several times throughout the offseason and even during the season. Who are they?"

Each of the managers dig through their folders to find what MacIntyre is referring to.

"They're independent league teams," Cliff says. "Frontier and Atlantic, I believe. We ignored them because it has nothing to do with us or our league."

"Macklon," Randall Figgs, manager of the Dixon Vikings says. "I've heard of Macklon. My cousin played for them a decade ago. They call themselves the Bulls. Boys can play some serious ball."

"Why weren't these taken into consideration?" Sarah asks Cliff and the rest of the Committee members. "They clearly want to challenge us."

"They're exhibition matches," Cliff says. "What would they bring to the table—one and done games?"

"Yeah," says MacIntyre. "That's exactly what they would bring."

Lights start to turn on in the heads of everyone in the room. Each ponder.

☞   ☞   ☞

The day eventually comes when Johnny's leave has ended. He's going to ride the bus downstate to join his unit. From there they deploy for Iraq. Dressed in his Service C's and his military sea bag flung over his shoulder, he stands on the platform of the bus station surrounded by his family.

Sandy gives Johnny a final hug before joining the rest of the family. They stand reserved.

Johnny takes his son from Katie's arms and touches noses with him, "Don't cry too much. Give your ma a break now and then, okay?"

"An engagement ring too!" Sandy chimes in, poking fun at her son in reference to his and Katie's marriage delay.

"Of course," Johnny says, shaking his head.

With that, he kisses his child and hands him back to Katie. He gives her a final kiss and promises to walk her down the aisle when he returns.

For the last goodbye, Johnny simply extends a hand to his father and shakes it.

"I'll call and write when I can," Johnny tells everyone before making his way to the bus door.

Sandy and Katie cry while watching him walk away.

"Hey!" James suddenly yells to his son, approaching him.

"Dad?" Johnny says. "Everything all right?"

James tries to say the right words, his guard shed now, and says, "Yeah . . . You be safe over there."

"I will."

"This is a damn good thing you're doing for your country."

He then hugs his son tightly. Johnny doesn't know what to think of his father's unexpected approval but gladly welcomes this surprise. He can't remember the last time he hugged his father.

"You're a . . . a good man," James says. "I love you . . . "

He let's go and stands back, not wanting to overemphasize the emotional moment. Johnny adjusts his bag over his back and boards the bus.

"Semper Fi!" James shouts.

When Johnny sits in his window seat, James clicks his heels and stands erect. His posture is straight, and he salutes his son out of respect. Johnny salutes back and watches his family, with his father not breaking stance in front of them until they're not visible anymore.

☞ ☞ ☞

An early spring in March has graced the counties. The snow melted days ago, bringing the dreaded winter to an unusually early end. Today is a *where were you when* kind of day. Mel Grainger begins his radio show different than usual. A heavy bass drum in the background sounds louder and louder.

"It's official; we're back to playing baseball!" Mel proclaims.

"Whoo!" Mel's co-host Eric Tinker cheers.

Cain loads his remaining belongings into a U-Haul and starts his long trek to Louisiana to begin a new life. Flipping on the radio, he hears the good news.

"This has been under wraps for about a month now, while negotiations and structure were being figured . . . " Mel announces.

As Cain drives through his neighborhood street, he can't help but notice clusters of *For Sale* signs that litter most front yards on the block. Waves of locals leaving Rupland is at a high.

"After a big push from league coaches and a number of fundraisers . . . "

Near the county line, Jack and Nick appear from the woods after the last day of small game hunting season. Both wear dull brown and green coats with bright orange vests strapped to them. Their pants are thick with khaki, and large Red Wing boots cover their feet. Cradled in their arms are twenty gauge shotguns loaded with bird shot. Stringed to Jack's side from a rope are a couple of dead partridges they were able to nab. They walk to Nick's truck parked on the side of the road and drop the tailgate. Both unarm themselves and place their game on it.

Nick ejects the slugs from his shotgun and retrieves them from the ground while Jack unsheathes his buck knife and gets ready to clean the partridges. Across the street, two county workers have parked. They fidget with a massive white sign about 60 feet by 40 feet, connected to Big Bo by ropes. Both Jack and Nick watch the men shimmy up the hydraulic ladder from their work truck that will only go so high, and begin to bolt the sign to the giant miner. Nick catches a glimpse of what the sign reads first:

2006 SUMMER LEAGUE TOURNAMENT

"What the mother-fuck?" Nick says.

Jack also reads the sign, and he and Nick look at each with anticipation. Jack asks, "Mel Grainger's show still on, yeah?"

"Go, go!" Nick says, flipping him the keys.

Jack swings the door open, lunges forward in the cab and puts the key in the ignition. He tunes into the show on the truck radio.

"The counties, with the help of downstate and out-of-state town boosters, have pooled enough funds together for one final Summer League tournament to end this historic league right . . . " Mel says.

Jack scoots out of the cab and the two look back at the sign, being able to read the 16-seeded bracket of all 12 Summer League teams, with two teams from downstate and two from out-of-state added:

ROUND 1
JULY 1: #1 CLARKSTON BLACK SOX V.S. #16 CRAFTLEY LAKERS*
JULY 1: #8 RANSVILLE REDS V.S. #9 IRON LAKE STARS
JULY 2: #5 PICWICK SPARTANS V.S. #12 MACKLON BULLS*
JULY 2: #4 ELLISON LEGENDS V.S. #13 MORWAY WILD*
JULY 2: #6 GAMME GRAYS V.S. #11 HOLTON BOLTS
JULY 4: #3 HILLSDALE WOLVES V.S. #14 IPPLING MINERS
JULY 4: #2 CROCKERTY CROWNS V.S. #15 DELTA OTTAWAS
JULY 4: #7 RUPLAND HAWKS V.S. #10 DIXON VIKINGS

"This July we'll have sixteen teams, four rounds, and one forever champion," Mel says. "Oren P. Rollins Field will be host to the biggest event of the league's 91-year history!"

"It's gonna be a summer for the ages!" Eric hollers in excitement.

☞   ☞   ☞

Almost a month later on the high school field, Joe pitches to Jack. Tournament training has begun early for the Daltons. Jack is clean-shaven and back to his All-American boy appearance. Joe's pitches are already a mess. His throws are up, wide, and in the dirt. Even worse, they're slow.

Jack drops his knees, blocking the latest digger that drops in front of him. He retrieves it and says, "Try digging a hole in front of the rubber."

"What for?" Joe asks.

Jack hustles to the mound and shows him, "Johnny used to do that. He dug a hole in front of the rubber so he had more power coming off it. Might help you. Your throws are losing velocity."

He notices Joe is tense. The forthcoming tournament is the biggest competition he's ever had to prepare for.

"Listen, I know you're nervous," Jack explains to Joe. "Tell you what, I know a gorgeous redhead, who I promise will fuck that right outta you if you show me some more oomph with your throws."

Joe laughs, "Seriously?"

"Seriously." Jack chuckles. "She helps every newcomer. Might be just the trick for you."

Both cease their training when seeing Nick's truck tear on to the grassy hill. His broken muffler still screams louder than ever.

"Who we got?!" Jack asks.

Nick snags a bucket of balls and his glove from his bed, "I spread the word. We'll see. Oh, and I was able to find another player. Better than nothing, I guess."

To Jack's surprise Lou exits the truck, his cleats draped around his neck.

"Aw, shit," Jack jokes, lit up with impish glee. "That's the best you could find, Nick?"

Lou meets him on the mound, where he and Jack share a hug.

"Don't tell me the littlest Dalton is on the roster now," Lou says upon seeing Joe.

Jack grips his brother's shoulder. "Boys, meet the latest addition to our bullpen."

"Either you're bullshitting me, or we're getting old," Lou says.

"Seventeen in a month," Jack says. "Just makes the cut. Plus, he can play the field too. It'll be good to have a good utility guy to back up our short roster."

"Fuck," Nick says. "So we *are* getting old. "

"The folks know you're back for the summer?" Jack asks Lou.

"Not yet," Lou replies, hiding a smile.

"That should be a fun conversation."

"Anyone hear from McCloud?" Joe asks.

"He left a month ago," Nick says. "Long gone."

"We're gonna miss his bat," Jack says.

Sounds of engines are heard in the distance approaching the area. One by one, vehicles park on the hill around Nick's ride.

"Here comes the cavalry!" Lou says.

Several teammates exit the vehicles, dressed in their gear or clung to their sides. The intact starting pitching rotation of Charlie Hylman, Mack Moore, and Finn Hood make their way down the hill. Not far behind is midinfielder JoJo Torres, infielder/outfielder Landon Steele and the back-end pitching of AJ Meers and knuckleball closer Trevor Huff. Sometime later center fielder Billy 'Shoestring' Hobbs, infielder Les Worley, outfielders Shawn Jaws Joski, Cyrus Evers, and Bucky Hogan arrive to begin their tournament journey.

Jack, Nick, and Lou join and stand before their team gathered on the mound. Jack eyes this ragtag bunch of diehards, knowing he must say something as their captain. The team's original 25-man roster is reduced to 16 since the mine's closure. Many other Hawks have moved on for work, and only five players from the original 2005 starting lineup remain—Jack, Nick, Lou, Landon, and Shoestring.

Finn Hood is a superstitious right-handed anchor of the starting rotation that likes to talk to the baseball. He is a pale-skinned, thin-faced, twenty-five-year-old with big ears that protrude from his dark, shoulder-length, matted hair.

Long relief pitcher AJ Meers is a tall man with a weak and exhausted appearance, whose body is in the shape of a Coca-Cola bottle. His hair is a wiry brown and brushed back from his temples. Neglecting to ever grow a beard, he has kept his Tom Selleck style mustache that has garnered pornstar status among teammates.

Torres is now the team's starting second baseman for the tournament. He is a five foot six-inch, agile athlete with good makeup, short arms, and a body that's built like a tank. His head looks like a peanut, and he has chipmunk cheeks to go along with his copper-colored eyes. With the muscle he's packed on in the offseason, he's hoping to improve his bat. Originally from the Dominican Republic, Torres' family moved to Rupland from Houston in 2000. And he graduated high school the same year as Jack, Nick, and Lou

Jaws Joski will be Rupland's starting left fielder. A career outfielder, MacIntyre loves to platoon the thirty-year-old late in games, when the offense needs a spark. At one time, he was a solid starter, but injuries and alcoholism have taken their toll on the once promising Major League prospect, succumbing him to an exclusive backup role.

Outfielder Bucky Hogan will take the start in right field. He stands at six feet tall, 200 pounds and has a small, muscular frame. His trapezoids are large, which buries his face, making it seem like he doesn't have a chin. After a few blown starts in his rookie season of 2000, Roberts was able to work with him to develop an effective throwing style, rather than the submarine technique he became accustomed to throughout high school. Accepting he didn't have the stuff to be a pitcher, MacIntyre molded Hogan into a competent utility player, and he has remained in that role ever since.

Cyrus Evers is a whisker-faced, big-boned, former Navy steelworker. And his buddy Les Worley is a bright blue-eyed, out of shape player who resembles anything but a ball player. The pair were walk-ons from the 2005 tryouts. Having stud high school years, they decided to give baseball another shot in their late 20s. They were strong backups for the team when starters needed to rest or injuries occurred. Their skill sets are similar, and they have proven their worth on more than one occasion when opportunity knocks.

"It is great to see your ugly faces again," Jack says, scanning his team. A few grins and laughs and inside jokes shout at him. "This everyone?"

"Yup," Nick replies. "Coaches are coming later."

"All right then, we'll win with what we have. I appreciate everyone showing up today. Four non-league teams with a shit ton of money have joined in on the fun to expand the bracket to 16 total teams. Word is they're stacked with prospect potentials. League teams who have lost players are stacking the deck too, which means there's a lot of work to do in these three months before the tourney begins. I don't care how many players we're missing, I'm proud to take the field with this bunch. Let's kick the dust off the tires and show these sons of bitches how we play Rupland baseball."

CHAPTER 7 — SUMMER OF '06

"A life is not important except in the impact it has on other lives."
—Jackie Robinson

HABBANIYAH AIRBASE, also called Camp Manhattan, is in central Iraq, about 50 miles west of Baghdad, just south of the town of Al Habbaniyah. A single 7,800-foot runway serves the airbase. Around it are eight hardened aircraft shelters—not all in use. Last time they were was during the Gulf War.

Across this camp clearing bounded by barracks and rows of identical aluminum trailers, sits Johnny at a card table in front of three bunks that inhabit a darkened and near-empty standard-issue military trailer. Shirtless, with just his camo-pants and his combat boots on, he has two letters in front of him. One is for Katie and the other for the rest of the family. He works each one side by side, writing about his experiences. The door to his trailer flaps inward, bleeding in the bright light from the outside. A lean, freckled Marine with auburn high-and-tight hair steps inside.

"Are you the new boot?" he asks with a New England accent rolling from his tongue.

"Boot?"

"New guy."

"Oh . . . Johnny." He shakes hands with the Marine.

"Rusty . . . First tour, I take it?"

Johnny nods.

"Best thing I can tell you, boot, is to get used to this god-awful heat. Oh, and your gun is your best friend . . . Oh yeah, and of course, don't trust any Hadjis. Rest should be nothing."

Johnny cracks a brotherly smile. Rusty's smooth-talking and pushy ways reminds him a lot of Eli. From behind Rusty, they notice their lieutenant talking to a unit member across the way. He's a scrappy version of Captain America himself but rougher around the edges. He has big biceps, a square, cleft chin, and shrapnel scars from IED's on his face and arms that could intimidate even the greatest of war heroes.

"Know much about the lieutenant?" Johnny asks.

"Matthews? Yeah, he's a prick. A real friggin' GI Joe, this guy. He's seen a lot of action, that's for sure."

"Big war hero, eh?"

"Uh-huh."

Rusty turns back to Johnny. "Got a girl back home?"

"And a baby. You?"

Without skipping a beat, Rusty reveals a faded picture from his pocket that has a number of creases and brags, "Sure do. Gorgeous, right?"

The picture is of a girl who appears way out of his league. Catching on to his bragging manner and accounting for the condition of the picture, Johnny assumes Rusty probably showboats a lot to others. Possibly a real shit-talker. The picture might not even be his real girlfriend, Johnny thinks.

"Good job," Johnny says politely.

Rusty smacks a kiss on the picture. Behind them, they hear Lieutenant Matthews approaching.

"Oop," Johnny sounds.

Rusty hurriedly tucks the picture into his pocket and turns to the doorway to greet his lieutenant with a salute.

"Enough of that shit, Cushing."

"Lance Corporal Dalton, I take it?" Lieutenant Matthews asks, his chest puffed and his hands crossed proper behind his back.

"Yes, sir," Johnny says.

The lieutenant takes a moment to observe his new guy. "Glad to have you aboard. Get your shit in check, and both of you meet in the P.L.O. at 1800."

"Yes, sir," both reply.

The lieutenant struts to the next trailer to greet another fresh-faced member of the unit.

"Welcome to Kilo Company, boot," Rusty says, climbing to the top bunk above Johnny's bed.

☞   ☞   ☞

Round 1: July 4th, 2006
#7 RUPLAND HAWKS VS. #10 DIXON VIKINGS.

A warm Tuesday night brings throngs of fans that pack into the host's park— Oren P. Rollins Field. It's the 4th of July, so many former and current locals have returned to populate this festive lot once more. There are tailgaters barbecuing, side games of cornhole toss, and beer pong with sparklers galore.

Neighborhoods celebrating around the area give remembrance to a community that was once perfect. No one is inside on this holiday. Porches, driveways, rooftops of houses and buildings, and in the streets kids and adults are either lighting fireworks or marveling at the colorful displays exploding in the star-filled sky.

The parking lot of the field is even more packed than usual. Since there are four teams who aren't in the league, they have brought with them hundreds of their own fans. Each of these teams have players looking to showcase their talents before the many scouts that pepper the stands with radar guns and note pads, picking them apart with a fine-tooth comb. The sudden surge of summer tourists has also brought an abundance of much-needed business to the town and the surrounding counties during their time of desperation. It's a damn fine day in Rupland.

On the other hand, if someone were to talk to the Committee, they'd tell you that they love the fan bases uniting like the old days, but aren't exactly thrilled about their secret league receiving abundant attention. But most of the counties love the influx of money the tournament brings, which expects to help tourism increase for many years to follow. Selling the picturesque small town and country life is the key, so the last few months each town spent many weeks cleaning, fixing, and decorating in preparation.

This past Saturday on July 1st, the tournament launched with the #1 Clarkston Black Sox absolutely destroying the downstate #16 Craftley Lakers 12-2. The Craftley squad consists of former high school and college stars, most of which played in the Big Ten Conference the past decade. But they were no match for the league's version of *Murderers' Row* that roam the middle of

Clarkston's lineup. Tim Kanter, Michael Harrow Jr., and Kyle Kennedy are a talented group of sluggers that punish opposing pitchers. Each hold OPS stats over .980 and had a combined 35 home runs and 75 RBIs in the 2005 regular season.

Clarkston also has an arsenal of crafty rotation starters that bring brilliant performances week in and week out. They had a combined ERA of 2.42 in 201.1 innings pitched. And since Clarkston won the 2005 Summer League championship, they were unanimously given the number one seed during league meetings.

Saturday's second game featured the #8 Ransville Reds against their long-standing rival, the #9 Iron Lake Stars. When it was over, it was the Reds snatching away the seesaw battle 15-14. Each team had to dig deep into their bullpens to counter the magnificent hitting display of both lineups that had 21 hits apiece.

The first game on Sunday was during the morning hours, which showcased one downstate team, the #5 Picwick Spartans, and one out-of-state team, the #12 Macklon Bulls from Tennessee. This was a highly touted matchup that brought many wealthy sponsors along with them. The Spartans easily eliminated the Bulls 6-1. Spartans starting right-hander CJ Adams was solid in his first Summer League start, pitching a no-no through seven innings. His manager pulled him after eight after a solo home run put a score on the board for the Bulls. He ended his start with 11 strikeouts, zero walks, and one run on two hits to get him the W. Two errors by the Bulls and lackluster hitting prevented them from getting any sort of momentum.

Later that afternoon, the first upset of the tournament came at the hands of #13 Morway Wild from Iowa. They defeated the #4 Ellison Legends 8-5.

The last game of the weekend was a tight and low scoring affair that saw the #6 Gamme Grays victorious 1-0, against the #11 Holton Bolts.

Earlier today, the sterling defense of the #3 Hillsdale Wolves edged the #14 Ippling Miners 3-2. Wolves center fielder Grayson Westerman's big play led the way. His two-run shot in the 6th lifted the Wolves a score ahead, and they never looked back.

About an hour ago, the #2 Crockerty Crowns bested the #15 Delta Ottawas 7-2, in a game that saw players clash with two bench clearings and several players on both sides ejected. By the last out, both sides were bloody and pissed enough to not shake hands, mostly because the umpires thought it'd be best to separate them from any further altercations. Much like the Black Sox, playing dirty often is Crockerty's reputation. This game was no different. Now they'll await the winner of the Rupland/Dixon game to reveal their second round matchup.

James, Sandy, and Katie with baby Jake take to the stands, eagerly anticipating the final game of the first round. Katie has turned into a die-hard fan since spending more time with the Daltons. She used to just sit back and listen to James talk about the sport, and now she adds to debates and conversations, challenging him every step. Both teams have a handful of players sporting tournament beards, some nice and manicured, others bushy like a hippy Jesus and some patchy. There are others that should probably shave what little they have.

Dixon is a solid squad that makes few mistakes. They're impressive up the middle and have been known to stage a comeback from any scoring deficit. Today they're being led by a top Major League Baseball and Japan's Nippon Professional Baseball pitching prospect—Akio Hara.

Dixon was clever by venturing out and using the newfound publicity of the Summer League tournament to acquire outside talent. League rules state that any team can have up to two non-local players on the roster, so they nabbed the premiere foreign talent and paid for his and his family's entire travel and lodging costs.

Akio is a right-handed, five foot ten inch, slight pitcher with an extremely high leg kick, which helps him come from the mound violently. He impresses scouts with his supply of pitches, most notably the Shuuto. In America, it's called the shootball—a pitch that breaks down to prevent the batter from making solid contact.

Although Akio is a heavily wanted arm who will have a nice career ahead of him, some see him joining the tournament as a risk. He and his family see it as an opportunity to raise his current late first-round draft stock to a top ten potential pick in next year's Major League draft. For the Haras, having Akio play in the league is one of great honor towards their heritage as well. His great-great grandfather played a season in the Summer League for Dixon when he moved to America to work. The mine provided him with enough money to bring his family over for a decade before moving back to Japan.

MacIntyre and Dixon's manager Randall Figgs meet Craig, the umpire, near the backstop and hand him their penciled-in lineup cards.

HAWKS	B/T #	VIKINGS	B/T #
Jack Dalton	R/R #12 (C)	Justin Heikki	L/L #21 (2B)
Lou Webb	R/R #3 (SS)	Dusty Barnes	L/L #2 (LF)
Nick Kosko	R/R #40 (1B)	Vince Simon	R/R #32 (1B)
Landon Steele	L/L #11 (3B)	Andy Crawford	R/R #7 (CF)
Billy Hobbs	S/L #6 (CF)	Franco Guzman	R/R #61 (3B)
JoJo Torres	S/R #17 (2B)	Joshua Healy	R/R #24 (RF)
Shawn Joski	L/L #27 (LF)	Chance Joki	L/R #18 (C)
Bucky Hogan	R/R #44 (RF)	Marcus Divine	S/R #15 (SS)
Charlie Hylman	R/R #1 (P)	Akio Hara	R/R #9 (P)

Coach Roberts and Sarah lead the Hawks out of the clubhouse and into the dugout early per MacIntyre's request. Nervousness overcomes this patch-work of a roster. On the bench, Joe admires himself in his new threads. He's a Hawk—the last Dalton to wear the colors.

"Wear it with pride," Lou tells him as he sits next to him to mess with his compression sleeve.

Jack can't sit. He's too anxious. Pacing the lengths of the dugout with his shin guards on, his war paint savage, and that orange captain's 'C' stitched on his chest, every defensive scenario plays in his mind: *Who in Dixon's lineup has had the best success against Hylman? They're an aggressive hitting team that normally swings at first pitches, so having him throw high and outside or high and inside might be best to tease them.*

Jack ends his meditated pace when he spots his nervous little brother and asks him, "Ready?"

Joe nods.

"Watch every hitter closely tonight to get a feel for them."

"Okay."

Jack's eyes then float to the middle of the bench, where Nick sits in his normal wrinkled uniform. He's just staring at the ground with his hands clasped together between his legs. Jack sits next to him.

Nick says without raising his head, "We're missing a lot of guys."

"Yeah," Jack replies. "We'll get by."

"It's gonna be hard to leave it all. This is my family, Zoom."

Jack puts a comforting hand on Nick's shoulder. "And that's never gonna change, man. Never."

MacIntyre enters. The entire team, even the assistant coaches, sit quietly with their attention towards him. The manager points to the dugout's ceiling, making them acknowledge the sounds of the beloved crowd—their town.

After some thought MacIntyre speaks, a bit of emotion strained in his voice, "Hear that? Enjoy it. Don't take one minute of it for granted. I never thought . . . " He stops to clear the emotion from his throat. "I ain't much for religion, so I'm not gonna make you recite the Our Father. Hell, go pray among yourselves. I look at this team and I start to think of all the players I've coached in here, all the games I've played out there as one of you, and I start to realize that maybe I took it for granted. Everything . . . You know since losing the mine and now that we're here for the last hoorah of our league, there's talk that the game seems to have lost that flair, that feeling of being pure . . . But you know what? That's bullshit. Don't listen to it. The Summer League is pure; always has been. This team is pure. And if we play with enough heart—our way—we will give this town the hope they need to pull through these tough times. We will change their lives forever . . . Because they will always speak of this moment. This time, this tournament, it will live on in them and all of you . . . Now, I've never once asked a player of mine for anything. Maybe I'm a selfish son of a bitch today; I don't know. But I'm asking you, right now, to play this tournament for your town. Play for your family . . . Your friends . . . Play it for each other . . . They need this. We need this. Sure, okay, we're down some players, but today, against all odds, we are back, gentlemen. We are kings of the game today, and no one can take that away from us!"

The team becomes riled more and more from the skipper's speech.

MacIntyre points to the field that awaits them. "Go out there and give them hope. Give them a reason to believe in the Hawks one more time! Let's go!"

Fired up, the team stands to step on the field. MacIntyre nudges Jack, and the captain leads his excited squad out of the dugout running. Their hometown greets them with a standing ovation.

"What a great day to end round one!" Frank Reese broadcasts. "Oren P. Rollins Field is host to the tournament to end all tournaments. Teams—including four additions—have gathered together to crown one last champion of this historic league. It's one and done here in Rupland."

"The Hawks face the number ten seed Dixon Vikings," Mel Grainger says. "Who, may I add, have one heck of a pitching staff."

Akio warms in the foul line bullpen.

"They're led by their number one guy—Akio Hara," Frank continues on. "A top ten big league pitching prospect with a big arm. This kid has a lot of hype going into the draft, and he's joined the Vikings to help them claim that title. Dixon has a good feeling coming into today knowing he can do the job."

Charlie starts the game behind the count on lefty leadoff hitter Justin Heikki, throwing two outside balls. The third pitch he just squeezes down and away, and the hitter smacks it up the middle. Lou flashes some fancy leather, backhanding it on the hop, crow hops, and sends the ball in flight. Nick snags it from the air for the first out.

The second batter is also left-handed—Dusty Barnes. He pokes at Charlie's stealth curveball, forcing the weak tapper in front of the plate. Jack easily scoops up the ball and finishes the runner with a toss to first for the second out.

A white, long-faced behemoth farm boy steps to the plate with a chaw in his cheek the size of the baseball Charlie is about to throw. Vince Simon is Dixon's menacing three spot hitter. Although he's six foot five, he walks short. More top-heavy. Simon isn't the smartest of players, shedding truth to that dumb hick stereotype, but can hit the ball a country mile given the opportunity.

He takes a moment to tighten his batting shin guard. A stream of Beech-Nut tobacco spits from his mouth when he rises, and it smacks on the plate before Jack, who has just finished signaling the second out to his fielders. Jack gives Simon a glaring look. Simon crowds the plate a bit to force Charlie to throw him outside. What this second year player doesn't know is that Charlie is one of the few pitchers that loves to throw inside. Jack puts down one finger and wags it to his left inner thigh for an inside fastball. Charlie accepts and throws, brushing the ignorant hitter back.

Simon grins a brown, sticky smile before adjusting his nutsack in his tight pants and comes back to the plate for some more. He inches even closer to test Hylman. Jack calls for the same pitch and Charlie serves it up—higher and tighter—almost taking Simon's head off. Simon ducks and stumbles out of the batter's box, almost falling on his ass. Jack slickly catches the ball and scoffs at the brute.

"Whoa!" Manager Figgs hollers from Dixon's dugout to the umpire. "He almost decapitated him, blue!"

The umpire ignores his cries. Simon whips a worrisome glimpse at Jack returning the ball back, then looks to Charlie again. The aging veteran gives him the death stare, which begins to take its effect during this atbat. Cautious, Simon returns to the box but now keeps a respectful distance from the plate.

Charlie doesn't mess around with the 2-0 count and quickly buries two immaculate breaking pitches that Simon neglects to take a hack at. Charlie realizes he's in the hitter's head; fear has taken his opponent. Jack signs him an inside fastball once more for the kill shot. With the count 2-2, Simon realizes he has to get the stick off his shoulder and look alive. Charlie winds up and rockets the pitch. Dreading the inside heat, Simon violently swings at it while leaning back, his eyes blinking rapidly almost stepping out of the box again. Jack catches the ball, and the umpire punches a final strike for the third out. Simon tosses his head back in disappointment. He shatters his bat across his knee in rage and begins his frustrated walk back to his dugout.

"Yo!" Jack yells to him as the other Hawks hustle in to bat. "Clean my fucking plate!" He points down to the tobacco juice that has browned the white plate since Simon disrespectfully hawked it there. He stands his ground, insisting Simon abides. The brute reluctantly returns and cleans the juice with his batting glove.

"The Hawks head in to bat as Zoom-Zoom Dalton will leadoff for his Hawks against the formidable Akio," Frank broadcasts.

On deck, Jack times Akio's warm-up throws, slicing smooth cuts through the air with his Warstic bat. Behind him, MacIntyre stands, also observing the future draft pick.

"Thoughts?" MacIntyre asks his captain.

"He's totally hype, Coach," Jack says. "Saw a lot of YouTube footage on this guy. He tips his pitches more than anyone I know. Starts with a two-seamer downtown always, then throws junk the rest of the time. If he's behind the count, he usually throws off-speed to the corners to get the chase. He relies on those first-pitch strikes because his walk-to-strike ratio isn't very good."

"Well, shit," MacIntyre says, proudly satisfied, before he returns to the dugout. "Go to it."

Jack steps to the dish, tightening the grip on his bat with his strong hands. Akio goes into his crane high kick windup and pitches a mean two-seamer that Jack lets go by for a strike. The next pitch is as expected. The righty delivers a so-so curve that Jack gets good wood on and tattoos with his two-handed swing of fury for a leadoff home run. Rupland fans cheer for Jack as he rounds the bags for the Hawks' first score.

Lou is up next. When he steps in to face the best arm he's possibly ever seen, he's unfazed. Cold as ice. This isn't surprising, seeing as how he was a nightmare for road pitchers last season. The shortstop's laid back stance is straight with little bend to his knees. He squares his left foot in line with the plate and his bat in front of him, leaning back. When he swings, he has an unorthodox follow-through, with a low pendulum-like kick to his leg, which shifts his weight forward with the ball.

Akio throws much of the same, which Lou is on to and takes yard past the center field wall for back-to-back shots. Hearing the hit itself, Akio didn't even turn around to watch the ball. He knew it was gone the moment it left the bat.

Rupland's hitters smell blood in the water now, and in the blink of an eye, three spot hitter Nick and the cleanup Landon also crush back-to-back dingers that were in their wheelhouses. Each on first pitches. With just five pitches, the first four hitters of Rupland's lineup make Summer League history, delivering four back-to-back-to-back-to-back home runs for the first time ever. This beats the '83 Gamme Gray's record of three in a row. Kids rush to grab the home run balls as souvenirs.

"Back-to-back-to-back-to-back shots!" Frank announces. "I don't think I've ever seen something like this."

Even before Landon crosses home plate, Manager Figgs emerges from the dugout, signaling for some merciful relief for Akio. Started by the Rupland Rowdies and spreading, the home crowd chants, "Sit down! Sit down!" Over and over again.

"That's how we do in Rupland, bonus baby!" Landon says to a defeated Akio leaving the mound, doing the baseball equivalent of a perp walk.

The rest of the game is more of an opening statement by Rupland. They keep the rhythm going and never look back, killing Dixon's chances of advancing to the next round in the 15-0 slaughter. Charlie lasts six innings before he's pulled by MacIntyre with a 10-0 lead. This is to preserve him for the possible games that lie ahead. In his six innings of work, he tosses seven K's, walks two, and gives up four hits.

The offensive studs are Jack and Lou. Each go 5-for-6 with four hits and draw a walk a piece. The bottom of the lineup is successful with getting on base as well, which helps Lou hit five RBIs and Jack four. Three of Jack's four come in the sixth when he hits a bases-clearing triple. Lou, otherwise, adds one more home run that comes in the bottom of the eighth, thus sealing the victory.

After the last out, a few scouts surround the Dalton and Webb families to inquire about their sons. Leaving the field after that win was like nothing else this Hawks bunch has ever experienced. Hometown fans make sure they feel every ounce of appreciation on this opening night.

☞ ☞ ☞

Johnny jogs around the camp. When he enters his trailer, he learns a Texas Hold 'Em poker game is taking place between Rusty and two other bunkmates, Private Tate and Lance Corporal Burke. Tate is a California skater that is all bones. Burke is a black man with slabs of muscles, a shaved head, and beady eyes. A lone light bulb hangs from a wire and sways above the table, splashing slivers of light to both sides of the trailer. Cigar smoke hazes around the mindless banter exchanges between the Marines. On one of the bunks, Eminem's "'Til I Collapse" plays on an iPod.

"Throw on some deodorant and grab a chair," Rusty tells Johnny.

Johnny removes his shirt. His chiseled six-pack of abs gleams in the dim light. Above his right bicep is a tattoo of an Old English letter 'D' in the form of brass knuckles. He dabs his sweaty face with his shirt then grabs a folded chair to join in on the game. His dog tags that hang from his neck clang on the table when he leans forth.

Artillery fire is heard in the distance. It doesn't concern these Marines of Kilo Company. Rusty puffs his stogie, dealing a new hand. In the middle of the table, crinkled dollar bills bunch together with no specific organization.

"Not my day, cocksuckers," he says. "Not even . . . "

A closer artillery blast rumbles their trailer some. Everyone but Rusty shows concern.

Rusty chuckles, "Yes, yes, my mates. That there is an M198 Howitzer . . . Shit, I can't even cheat and get a good hand." He throws a couple of cards on the table.

"That sound is gonna be our problem soon enough," Burke says.

"But not tonight," Rusty declares without a care.

"I've got another few months left," Burke says. "Last thing I need is to come home to my babies in pieces."

"Jesus Christ, Burke," Rusty says. "We came here for the action. How much have you seen already?"

"Fuck the action," Burke says, ignoring the question.

"How much have you seen?"

"Enough."

"Enough isn't enough," Rusty says, laying his cards on the table.

"There he goes again," Tate says. "Talking in riddles."

"That sound out there," Rusty says. "Yeah, it's coming to our doorstep. We're gonna have to be ready. There's no choice. Don't fight it, man, embrace it."

"Aren't you fucking cavalier!" Tate says with a snicker.

"My father was in Vietnam. My grandfather World War II," Rusty says. "They killed their fair share. Action is in my blood." He pounds his chest and howls.

The rest laugh, while Burke is the only Marine not amused.

"Boot, your father was in Nam, right?" Rusty asks.

"Damn straight," Johnny says.

"There you go. In. Our. Blood." He bumps fists with Johnny.

"I've got what, a year on you, Rust?" Burke asks.

"I guess."

"My first tour wasn't fun. We trained forever . . . All the bullshit we went through . . . One suicidal Hadji takes out half my unit. How the fuck can someone train for that? That's not fair by my standards."

Rusty scoffs, "Fair? When was war fair? Show me the handbook where it says that."

Johnny chuckles.

"War is unnatural," Burke says. "No one is meant to kill."

"We are. We're Marines, brother," Rusty says.

"You act like we're going to some carnival where you need to ride every ride. This isn't fun, Rust," Burke says.

Rusty sits with a grin on his face. The table is quiet, watching Burke and Rusty stare at each other.

"All right, guys," Johnny interjects when he realizes things could turn ugly. "What does everyone else got for hands?"

"What the fuck you grinning about?" Burke asks Rusty.

Rusty stands and removes his shirt and turns around to reveal a mural of tattoos on his back. Between his shoulder blades is an old insignia for the 3rd

Battalion 1st Marines. It's a bull with steam and lightning bolts snorting from its nose. Below the insignia is the title from a Billy Joel song: *Only the Good Die Young.*

Below are the dates of a bloody battle that took place in 2004 and twelve names that scale his spine:

11/7/04 - 12/23/04
Pvt. Howard, Pvt. Silva, Cpl. Hogland, SSgt. Lopez,
Pvt. Simmons, Pvt. Johnson, SSgt. Chavez,
Pvt. Pederson, LCpl. Horace,
Pvt. Antos, 1st Wave. Burroughs, LCpl. Pearson

The men in the trailer stare in awe.

"You were there?!" Burke asks. "Fallujah?"

Rusty nods when he's seated again, still without his shirt. "95 gone. 560 wounded," Rusty says. "I don't have a goddamn friend left from my unit anymore."

Johnny scoots his chair next to Rusty. "Shit, I'm sticking with this good luck charm."

"Won't help you much with poker though," Rusty says, puffing on his cigar again. "I'm a shit player."

The mood lightens, and the four play the next hand. Artillery sounds continue to haunt their surroundings, but the Marines don't pay attention to it anymore.

☞   ☞   ☞

Sandy hangs state and local newspaper clippings of Jack and the Hawks and tourney results near the store's entryway. On the massive cork board that she hangs them on, there are other clippings of real estate ads, vehicles, and miscellaneous items for sale that customers ask to post. More importantly to her, pictures of Johnny and his unit that he mailed home also cover the board.

Sandy walks on the store's floor. They've been busy since the start of the tournament. Unfortunately, she can only order a few months' worth of items, because the reality is while business is currently booming, once the tournament ends the store will go back to its lackluster sales until next spring and summer when tourists return.

In the back of the store, Jack stands in the meat cooler and chases a couple of pills with water. Joe opens the cooler simultaneously when Jack is about to exit and they nearly run into each other. Joe has known for some time that Jack is hiding something. The youngest Dalton just stands there in his way, looking down at Jack like he's the one that's caught in a lie.

"What?" Jack asks.

"Um . . . Dad has the DVD loaded." Joe uncomfortably says.

"Right on," Jack says, scoots around him and heads into the office.

"Lights," James says, sitting on one of three old and duct-taped chairs, trying to work an old DVD player remote.

Jack flicks the lights and grabs a seat next to his father. Joe trails in after, and James gestures him to sit as well.

An uneasy Joe sits next to Jack. James pushes the play button to start the DVD to one of last week's first round matchups—the Crockerty Crowns versus the Delta Ottawas.

"Rozner is on the hill this weekend, right?" Joe asks.

Jack nods.

"He's a good number two in the rotation," James says while he watches the game. "Boy, their catcher Whitley can call a hell of a game."

Jeremy Whitley is the last of two player/managers remaining in the league, a job he's held for six seasons. They watch as the chubby and tattooed Whitley works his pitchers with ease, almost always picking their pitches for them.

The three Dalton men study the game tape intensively. They watch bullpen arms. They watch every hitter's swing and take notes of any flaws they detect. Film study is a process James has had his boys do since they were children.

"That's nothing compared to how they steal bases," Sandy says, her voice trailing from outside of the office.

"Say what?" James asks, turning to her.

"Crockerty. They're the best base running team in the entire tournament." She steps further into the dark office to explain. "Last year they stole 38 bases, and that was just during the regular season. Their entire team has returned. Seeing how they spanked Delta last week, I'm guessing they haven't skipped a beat since last year's title game appearance. You guys have your work cut out for you, Jack."

The Dalton men sit dumbfounded, wondering from where her sudden burst of knowledge accrued. Of every single exhausted baseball conversation her husband and sons have had over the years, she's never joined in on any—not once. James sits back in his chair, a joyous smile spreading across his face.

"I keep box scores sometimes," she explains.

"That so?" Jack asks with a smirk.

Sandy hands him a piece of paper, "This is the guy you have to watch."

The paper is a flier that's in the style of a 'Most Wanted' poster. Pictured on it is a Crockerty Player raising his batting gloved-hands high after stealing a base:

MOST WANTED

FRANKIE MINOSO

REWARD—FREE STEAK DINNER AT KAREN'S DINER

Jack laughs heartily. "Is this for real?" He passes the flier to the others.

"Since last week these have been passed around town," Sandy says. "Minoso is their best runner. He stole 22 bases for them last year. Year before that 25."

"He's about the fastest in the league," James adds.

"I know who he is," Jack says. "I've never been able to throw him out."

"Lou's mother came in a short while ago," Sandy says. "She said every catcher in the tournament is gunning for this guy."

"Yeah?" Jack asks, gaining more interest, and he takes back the flier from his father to read it again.

"Then it's no secret they're gonna rely heavily on stealing to advance runners," James says. "Either that or this is a decoy they spread to see if anyone will bite."

☞   ☞   ☞

Round 2: July 15, 2006
#2 CROCKERTY CROWNS VS. #7 RUPLAND HAWKS

Good weather, a nice breeze, and vibrant fans. Saturday afternoon is the perfect setting for baseball. After this weekend, the final four teams will be set.

Yesterday's games saw four teams play under the Friday night lights. The first matchup was the #5 Picwick Spartans versus the #13 Morway Wild. They battled hard through nine innings of play. The Wild killed the heavily favored Spartans' momentum, upsetting them 5-4. Morway's Link Weathers came up big again, going 3-for-5 with a double and three ribbies. Starting righty Stanley Hope picked up the win for his Wild. He went seven, striking out eight and allowing four runs on eight hits. Both Weathers and Hope are strong prospects, who will get their chance at greatness with a legitimate school now that they've advanced to the final four.

The last game of the Friday night doubleheader was the #1 Clarkston Black Sox versus the #8 Ransville Reds. Harry Bloom pitched a gem for the Black Sox, garnering the complete game in the 4-1 win on a two-hitter. Offensively they were sound, making little to no mistakes. Richie Leigh went into beast mode and hit a monstrous three-run shot early on in the second inning. From there, the Black Sox sped into cruise control, eventually eliminating the Reds for good. The Reds, one of the oldest teams in the Summer League, had a hard time saying goodbye. They remained on the field for an extra twenty minutes after the loss, taking on a standing ovation from Ransville, Clarkston, and Rupland fans alike. The players left the center stage with a handful of the field's dirt as a memento.

HAWKS	B/T #	CROWNS	B/T #
Jack Dalton	R/R #12 (C)	Frankie Minoso	L/L #11 (CF)
Lou Webb	R/R #3 (SS)	Tom Koon	R/L #8 (3B)
Nick Kosko	R/R #40 (1B)	Sawyer Nunn	R/R #27 (LF)
Landon Steele	L/L #11 (3B)	Jeremy Whitley	L/R #13 (C)
Billy Hobbs	S/L #6 (CF)	Oscar Griffin	R/R #46 (SS)
JoJo Torres	S/R #17 (2B)	Terry Rozner	R/R #00 (P)
Shawn Joski	L/L #27 (LF)	Christopher Grant	R/R #50 (RF)
Bucky Hogan	R/R #44 (RF)	Logan Harrell	R/R #7 (2B)
Mack Moore	L/L #68 (P)	Warren Smith	R/R #22 (1B)

This afternoon's game is flying by already, now entering the fifth inning. Both teams have yet to score a run, leaving goose eggs on the scoreboard. Hawks starting lefty Mack Moore has been solid up until now. His command is on point, and he's getting in front of his hitters early, finishing them with cutters that have insane tail whips. There wasn't a single walk given until he flirted too much with low and in throws to the Crowns' leadoff left-handed hitter and Most Wanted base-stealer, Frankie Minoso. He walked him on five pitches. Currently, there's a runner on first with no outs.

Crockerty fans can't contain their excitement, and they rock the park with their chants, "Minooooo-so! Minooooo-so! Minooooo-so!"

The next Crowns player at the plate is a right-handed hitter—Tom Koon. Moore is very much aware of the threat that is Minoso on base presently. The entire field shifts. Jack keeps a steady eye on him, like an eagle scouting its prey. When he squats, he taps the inside of his right thigh, signaling Moore that Minoso is taking too big a lead from the bag. Jack knows if this runner gets to second, he's in scoring position and increases his chance of crossing the plate. Moore and he are on the same page. They must hold Minoso at first to take their chances for a double play, or even hitter mistakes by swinging at shit pitches.

Moore religiously glances to first. Nick leaves the bag this time, staying between it and the runner to create an illusion. After Moore sets, he's like Houdini with his pickoff move to Nick who nearly leaps on the bag. Minoso is on to him though and easily moves back to take on Nick's late tag to his calf. The umpire signals safe.

Minoso isn't the master of base-stealing for no reason. Obsessive studying has helped him learn Moore's patterns. He knows the mechanics of his pickoff moves and the number of seconds it takes him to throw so he can get a good jump.

Moore receives the ball back and sets on the mound again before he's called for a delay of game. The runner takes a generous lead, his hands spread to both sides, feeling the air through his batting gloves. Obviously, the throw back from Moore didn't faze him any. Jack repeats the tap on the inside of his thigh in between signs. Moore throws over to Nick once more, but not in time. The southpaw is visibly agitated, hurrying Nick to give him the ball back.

Minoso takes signs from his third base coach and once again takes an incredible lead. Jack knows now that, per league rules, he only has one more pickoff attempt left this inning and signals Moore to bring on the heat instead, so if Minoso does steal he'll be able to catch the ball faster. Before the pitch, Jack pays close attention to the third base coach and then to one particular flinch Minoso hasn't done until now. His left heel is slightly raised all of a sudden.

Moore loses his wide leg windup and throws from the stretch that Jack leaps from his squat to reach to his right for. Minoso has already sprinted away, digging hard to get his sixth steal of the tournament. Jack snags the overthrown ball and on one foot slingshots it down to Lou hovering on second base. Minoso does a Pete Rose slide, hugging the bag with both arms, while Lou catches the great throw and tags him too late. Jack adjusts his crooked mask, while he watches Minoso dust himself when standing.

Jack squats back down. Watching Minoso take the sign from his coach and short lead from second, it's no surprise to him that this might be a hit-and-run. Jack signs Moore for an inside changeup. If Tom Koon doesn't hit it, Minoso could be a sitting duck for Jack. As Moore begins his delivery, Minoso speeds off. The pitch is then hit by Koon to the opposite field, where Bucky Hogan can't get to it in time. Instead, he grabs the ball from one hop and immediately relays it to his cutoff man Torres. Runners are on the corners, and there are no outs. Odds are against the Hawks. Sacrifice flies and any hit that gets through the infield could give the Crowns the first run of the game.

Next batter up is Sawyer Nunn. He's the Crowns best all-around player and has been known as a southpaw killer. His career average of .689 against left-handed pitching ranks the best of any current Summer League player. Most Valuable Player in 2001 and 2003, he is your typical ball player. Standing clean in his nice-fitted threads, Nunn appears as if he was born to wear a baseball uniform.

Nunn brings his bat around on a bad pitch from Moore and fists a hot grounder between first and second. Torres dives to grab the out of reach ball and in one move, whips around to throw it across his body back to Lou at second. The runner comes at Lou with his hands raised high to block his line of sight of first base. Lou grazes the bag with his right foot and zips the ball to first for the 4-6-3 double play. Unfortunately, Minoso has scored to put the Crowns on the board first. Minoso's brilliance on the bases has given his team the upper hand yet again.

It's another two innings before Jack can get another chance at Minoso. Before that, Moore gives up a second run, which seals his fate after 6 2/3 innings, giving right hand reliever AJ Meers a chance to save the game. Meers is a reliable pitcher with a giddy-up windup and a thunderous four-seamer that frustrates the opposition. Before he faces Minoso, Meers already has two strikeouts and zero walks under his belt. And the bases are empty.

Minoso only connects on one hittable pitch that nicks the tip of his bat foul. He watches four more too high and too low pitches miss the zone to give him an easy and crucial walk. Minoso gladly trots to first base to do what he does best. Crockerty's fans are already at it with the "Minoooo-so!" chants to fuck with Rupland's head.

Relentlessly watching the slender speedster take his gaping lead, Jack is determined not to let him make a fool of his team a second time. Meers takes the sign from Jack and delivers the ball, which Koon takes a cut at for a strike. Jack pops up from his squat as Minoso cockily fakes him out like he's going to run but doesn't. A knowing smirk from Jack is hidden behind his mask as he throws back to Meers. Before he squats again, he adjusts his fielders some more to make sure they're in the right spots. He then glances at the Crowns third base coach signing Minoso. He's touching the brim of his hat three times in between earlobe pinches, just as before. Jack shifts his eyes to first to see Minoso take his big lead. Again, that left heel inches from the ground. The *ah-ha!* moment washes over Jack. Not only does he know that Minoso is going to steal again, but he's also deciphered their stealing sign from the third base coach.

Jack signs Meers with a fist between his legs. Meers agrees, sets, and side-eyes Minoso before throwing away a pitchout outside the batter's box and wide. Minoso is already elbows, assholes, and shoe-soles to second base. Jack springs in advance to catch the ball and guns it to Lou, beating the runner. Lou catches and applies the tag to a head-first sliding Minoso, tagging him on the head for the out that the umpire brings his fist down like a hammer for.

Rupland fans jump to their feet with praise. Jack has just picked off the Flash himself, nabbing the Most Wanted bounty.

Minoso returns to the dugout, tipping his helmet to Jack respectfully, "Enjoy your steak!"

Jack gladly takes the compliment from his adversary.

Top of the 8th inning. The Hawks' backs are against the wall, facing a 2-0 deficit. After an unfortunate ground out by Meers, Jack attacks a splitter, roaring it to right field for a double. This sets up his team in scoring position with only one out.

Lou takes to the box next. After an 0-1 count, he hits a Texas Leaguer to left center. Knowing Jack's speed, Roberts waves him around to head home.

Crowns left fielder Nunn cuts off the two-hopper and displays his own gun, rifling the ball home. Jack spots Crowns player/manager Jeremy Whitley crowding the plate, so he chugs full speed ahead, his shoulder dipped for the inevitable collision. At the same time, Whitley retrieves the ball, and Jack blasts him like a linebacker, making the ball spit out of his mitt and sends his goalie-style catcher's mask flying into oblivion. Jack rolls on top of the plate for the score. Lou takes this opportunity to leg out an extra base, stopping on second while Crowns brooding mid-30s pitcher Terry Rozner retrieves the loose ball. Jack and Whitley lie on the ground, each visibly hurt.

"Shake it off, Zoom," next batter Nick tells him as he helps him to his feet.

Meanwhile, Rozner helps his manager. Both catch their breath and separate. While the manager limps back behind the plate, Jack limps to his dugout to take on team-created hand slaps and ass pats.

When the power-hitting Nick gets into his batting stance, the first pitch comes directly at his head in retaliation for Jack's hit on Whitley. Nick ducks to a fall on his ass in the dirt, just missing getting beaned.

"What the fuck was that?!" Nick rises, screaming at Rozner.

He walks towards the pitcher, pointing his bat and scolding him. Rozner jaws back and gives him the bird, escalating the conflict further. Whitley hops in between the two, but it's no help as the infuriated players are too strong for him. The field becomes a heated riot of orange and black and the Crowns colors of dark green and gold.

"Get your fucking asses back to the dugout!" Roberts screams to his team, while he rips players from one another.

MacIntyre and Sarah do the same. Jack, Charlie, and the Crowns coaching staff also separate players before any blows are traded or ejections given.

After several minutes, the umpires clear the field of both teams. They let the coaches of each club talk to their players alone to prevent any further clashes.

"Is this how you want your tournament to end?!" MacIntyre yells at them in the dugout. "They're getting in your heads! They did this last week to Delta too, and it worked!"

"Coach, he threw at my head!" Nick yells back.

"Then knock the cover off the next pitch!" MacIntyre says, practically bumping chests with his much larger player. "We worked too goddamn hard, and have been through too goddamn much to let something like this destroy us!"

"Let's finish what we started," Jack adds from the bench.

"Exactly!" MacIntyre says. "What do you say?"

The rest of the team puts their anger aside and claps. With each clap, the team is getting their heads back in the game.

Minutes later, they're right back where they started; Nick at the plate, staring down Rozner's barrel of a 1-0 count. Still rattled from the confrontation, Rozner keeps the ball away from Nick by trying to paint the corners instead. It's a plan that backfires when he can't find the zone and walks him.

Much of the same happens with Landon, who only takes one strike before four balls give him his free bag to load the bases. Whitley calls time-out to talk to his pitcher, while Shoestring waits to take his turn against Rozner. It's no secret the switch hitter hits better left, and with Rozner being a right-hander, he's going to continue on that side. When the catcher/pitcher meeting ends, Rozner attacks Shoestring with a couple of tight-breaking pitches that Shoestring gets good wood on for fouls. Rozner continues to miss his target, tossing three in the dirt to give Shoestring a full count. The pitcher is so rattled at this point that he paces around the mound before getting the ball back. He wipes his forehead and finally sets and comes from the windup again to try to deliver an inside pitch. The ball gets away from him, and he drills Shoestring's right hand, also giving him a free base and scoring Lou for the tying run. Benches rise in anticipation of another bench-clearing incident, but the Hawks maintain their composure.

"Damnit!" screams Rozner to himself as he sees Whitley making his way to the mound and signaling the young relief pitcher/outfielder, Chad Beaumont, to take his place.

Six-spot hitter Torres digs in after Beaumont warms. The first pitch from him is a wicked upstairs fastball that Torres doesn't bite on, letting it go by for ball one. Torres takes the same sign from Roberts at third again and tomahawks the next pitch right down Main Street, high and deep to the opposite side of the field for a sacrifice fly. Right fielder Christopher Grant catches the ball. Nick then tags up and scores to give his team their first lead of the game 3-2.

Bottom of the 9th. Two outs. Hawks still lead by the same score. Closer Trevor Huff is on the bump, trying to secure Moore's win. Meers left the game after surrendering two hits to the runners that are now on first and second. The lead runner on second is Minoso. And seeing how close the game is with his team in scoring position, he won't chance a steal. Rowdy Crockerty fans have their rally caps on every which way, cheering on the aching Whitley at the plate with rally cries of "We're Not Gonna Take it" by Twisted Sister. Whitley is ready to become the hero for them and his club. Even though he throws right-handed, he's a left-handed hitter, which torments Huff, who was dreadful against left-handed hitting last season.

Huff goes right to work and pitches two split-finger fastballs low and away that Whitley takes the bait on, missing both. The thirty-eight-year-old is ahead of his hitter 0-2. Jack signs him for a finishing knuckleball that he gladly agrees to. Huff's knuckleball is no joke. It's one of the nastiest in the league. Even if someone gets a piece of it, the ball isn't going anywhere. On the other end, Whitley is a seasoned thirty-five-year-old, who has been in the league about as long as Huff has. He's familiar with him and what's about to come. Both hitter and pitcher refuse to fail in this potentially deciding matchup. Huff goes into his windup and releases that masterful knuckler, and it wobbles without spin towards the zone. Whitley is aggressive going after the ball, but it falls just short of his bat, making him miss to retire him and the game.

The Hawks fielders and bench clears to crowd Huff as they have just upset the Crowns. Huff does the run and bump with a few teammates that get to him first. Fans are booming, whether that be from excitement or hate for the Hawks. When Jack leaves the field, his limp has worsened from the earlier collision at the plate.

The next night would see the #3 Hillsdale Wolves face #6 Gamme Grays to wrap up this week's quarterfinal round. The Wolves wasted no time in jumping ahead to a 6-0 lead in the first inning against Gamme's electric left-hand pitcher Jermaine Easter. Gamme tried to cut the lead in half with a three-run third inning, led by shortstop/pitcher Carson Haynes, but after the fourth, the Wolves pulled away by scoring one run every inning for a final result of 11-3. Hillsdale's Grayson Westerman went 4-for-4 with two doubles and four RBIs, while his teammate, second baseman Cortland Briggs, went 3-for-5 with five RBIs and two home runs.

The final four is set: #1 Black Sox versus #13 Wild, and #3 Wolves versus #7 Hawks.

☞   ☞   ☞

The gentle sounds of water washing against docks and piers provide most of the area's sound. Seagulls drift overhead, preying on anything that appears tasty below. These birds aren't timid like most; they are scavengers, willing to eat out of someone's hand. Up the channels that pour into the Gulf of Mexico beyond some nameless distance, small fishing and shrimp trawlers glide across the marvelous vast blue with ease.

The backdrop is rectangular houses lined next to one another, elevated by wood pilings to prevent flood damage. The batture between the inlet and the levees that surround these is completely submerged. Colors of the houses are either gray, green, yellow, or red. Saltwater in the air has eaten away at their paint and buckled any non-treated wood left after the construction of new pilings. Most of the houses have sundries of boats that anchor under them like carports.

Bordering the houses is the rest of the waterfront village of Cocodrie, Louisiana. It's constructed on an inlet of a bay blocked by several barrier islands along the Gulf. Every building here elevates above the ground after last year's disastrous Hurricane Katrina that nearly obliterated the entire community.

Steering into port after a successful day in the Gulf waters that netted 500 pounds of shrimp and bycatch is a grimy white trawler with red trim. On the side of the trawler reads the name in red: *St. Peter*.

When it docks, a bushy blonde-bearded Cain appears from it. He's unrecognizable. Grease and fish guts stain his American flag tank top, and he wears dark gray cargo shorts and a frayed-brim Hawks cap. Standing on the edge of the dock with one foot on it and the other on the bow, the setting sun has never appeared so big to him as it sparkles above the water.

Sometime later in the night, he and his Uncle Jerry dine aboard the *St. Peter*. They share stories about the women they've slept with, and legends of fish caught in the Gulf among competitors. His uncle isn't a sports fan, so baseball and Cain's success in Rupland rarely, if ever, come up.

The first few months in Cocodrie have been everything he had hoped for and more. Enamored with the life of a fisherman, this new adventure is an unexpected breath of fresh air. The quaint village is simple, and few things remind him of back home. The women are not much different, and everyone seems obsessed with LSU football. Baseball isn't the lead sport down here, but all the same, he thinks it's pleasant. His meals are primarily seafood, and no one has ever heard of a pasty in their life. And the preferred beer is Corona instead of Labatt.

Cain's nights end before eleven, and he awakes early to journey the waters with his uncle. Every other weekend the two take a trip to the French Quarter in New Orleans. During the weekdays, they stay in town to drink and dance the night away at their favorite hot spot, Misty's Tavern. Misty's is a smoky, cramped bar next to one of many bait and tackle shops in the same oasis. During the day, it's mostly empty, with the occasional leather-faced bar fly or two at happy hour. During the summer, the place is crawling with college students returned home from school.

On this night, around ten o'clock, Cain and his uncle return to the *St. Peter* separately with women they met at the bar. Cain's performance in bed is off tonight. He loves his big-bottom girls, and tonight he's brought home a pretty brunette with a shapely one. His concentration drifts though. It's not because of the moaning coming from below deck, where his uncle and the owner of Misty's Tavern—Misty herself—are fucking. Rather, his mind is roving elsewhere, other than what's sucking him off at the moment. An hour or so goes by before Cain stops trying to get hard and sends the beauty home. Not before getting a slap across the face, of course.

On the deck, he cracks open a Corona and watches ESPN from a twelve-inch Roadster television, and the only television his uncle owns. By the third or fourth month he's lived here, the newness and excitable unpredictably has worn some. Being on the water, Cain has learned that there is a lot of waiting involved. Time stands still. For someone as impatient as him, this is grueling. The reality is that he is literally a fish out of water. Down here, he's not the best fisherman, and not even a good one. No one knows who he is, or even cares for that matter; just another face in the crowd trying to make an honest buck.

There's a competitive fire in him that still burns. While his former team is basking in baseball glory, he thinks about them each and every day. News of the league's tournament has reached Cocodrie. ESPN, FOX SPORTS, and other sports media outlets have mentioned it regularly. This is the most publicity it's ever achieved, and Cain isn't a part of it. He yearns for that stare-down with the opposing pitcher. Again, again, and again, battling with the arm that vies for a chance to strikeout the star. That feeling of hitting the ball on the sweet spot stills gives him goosebumps.

Moaning below continues as Cain finishes his beer, and figuring it will be a long night, he grabs another brew and gets cozy. Before long, he falls asleep while watching *SportsCenter*.

☞   ☞   ☞

Round 3: July 23rd, 2006
#3 HILLSDALE WOLVES VS. #7 RUPLAND HAWKS

HAWKS	B/T #	WOLVES	B/T #
Jack Dalton	R/R #12 (C)	Clayton Harris	S/R #1 (SS)
Lou Webb	R/R #3 (SS)	Cortland Briggs	R/R #15 (2B)
Nick Kosko	R/R #40 (1B)	Grayson Westerman	L/L #30 (CF)
Landon Steele	L/L #11 (3B)	Rashard Engles	R/R #6 (1B)
Billy Hobbs	S/L #6 (CF)	Garrett Theus	R/R #35 (RF)
JoJo Torres	S/R #17 (2B)	Liam O'Shannon	L/R #4 (C)
Shawn Joski	L/L #27 (LF)	Keith Merrifield	L/L #10 (P)
Bucky Hogan	R/R #44 (RF)	Early Boone	R/R #12 (3B)
Finn Hood	R/R #35 (P)	Eddie Mathis	R/R #32 (LF)

The last semifinal game of the tournament is just a few hours away on a windy Sunday. Yesterday, the #1 Black Sox put on a slugfest for their fans, tromping the #13 Wild 13-6. Once again, Sox's Tim Kanter lit the latest victim up, going 4-for-5 with a home run and five RBIs. Michael Harrow Jr. also put his hitting on display with a 3-for-5, three RBI performance.

There was a late rally by the Wild, led by team leaders Link Weathers and second baseman Hunter Buxton. The duo launched back-to-back home runs in the ninth, scoring a team-high for the tournament—five runs in one inning. However, it came too late when Sox reliever Victor Kent entered the game and silenced them for good to advance his team to the title game for the second year in a row.

In the Rupland locker room, the Hawks ready themselves. The place is in need of many repairs and compares to most high school locker rooms. Nicked black and orange paint on the metal is an eyesore, the smell of body odor and wet shower floors will always remain in the air, and the old wooden benches are on their last legs.

Mostly, this place is for reflection and odd superstitions, such as wearing dirty socks or underwear every game or touching an odd number of lockers before exiting to the dugout. There are some even as crazy as keeping a bat's temperature warm prior to using it, which Shoestring actually does. Today is different. The Hawks are flying high after their latest win against Crockerty a week ago, and now they're just a win away from the biggest game of their lives.

The locker room this afternoon is a young man's den, full of cranked hip-hop and heavy metal music. The jokesters of the team dance to it. Some sing along to it. Others are just spectators to the antics. It's definitely a lighter and looser mood than usual because they're doing what every boy first learns in baseball—having fun.

In front of his locker, Jack ices then wraps his discolored and swollen ankle. It's still very sore from the collision at the plate last game.

Across the room in a tiny office that has ugly 1980s furniture, sit coaches MacIntyre, Roberts, and Sarah. They study today's matchup, talking strategy. A marked-up Hillsdale scorecard from last week's win lies in front of MacIntyre. He's circled players and religiously scribbles stats in his chicken scratch writing next to them. He reads this repeatedly. Taped to the outside of the office door is Rupland's starting lineup card for today. MacIntyre decides to stick with the same order he's had since the start.

His office is the coach's war room. Before any season, game, practice, or tryout, every thought and strategy starts right here. The room has been occupied by many former great managers, each molding understudies to replace them when their time came. MacIntyre is no exception. He's kept the office pretty much the same as his predecessor. One of the earliest things he's learned and passed on is to always keep a coach's mind busy. So on-hand, crossword puzzles, a barely-working Nintendo, and board games add to the decor of his outdated haven.

Sitting on a side chair against the wall, in front of MacIntyre's desk, Roberts uses a pair of scissors to clip his nails. Lifting his head, he does a double take when glancing through the blinds of the only window in the office. Cain strolls into the locker room. With his bat bag in hand, he stands back to admire the team's antics.

"Whoa," Roberts says, forcing his comrades to take a gander at what he's looking at.

Almost instinctively, each stand from their seats and join the rest of the team that's staring at Cain.

"Good timing, huh?" Cain says to everyone, smiling.

"What are you doing here?" MacIntyre asks.

"When your relative is your boss, extended vacations are a perk." He walks forward in between a few players to his former locker, that Joe currently uses. "Am I batting my usual, Fred? Or are you thinking somewhere different?"

No one says anything. The room just watches him awkwardly. Cain acts as if he's never left. Opening the locker, he finds Joe's gear inside and says turning around, "All right, which greenhorn's shit is—" He stops himself when noticing the eyes that never left him. "What?"

"McCloud, what are you doing here?" MacIntyre asks again. "We got a game to prepare for."

"I'm here to play."

MacIntyre gestures Cain to follow him into his office.

"What are you looking at?" Roberts asks his team. "Get ready! And turn down that shit music. Anyone got any country?"

The team continues to prepare. In the office, MacIntyre returns to his chair.

"Close the door. Take a seat," he tells Cain, who does. "Little late to join us."

"I know," Cain says. "I've been living on the Gulf. Word about the tourney traveled down there. Can you believe it? People know, Fred. I can't miss this."

"Sorry, McCloud. I can't add you. We've built good chemistry and momentum with this roster, and I don't want to break that. How would bringing you back on suddenly affect these boys? They've worked hard to get us this far."

Cain's eyes narrow. "We go pretty far back, you and I. I've won you a shit ton of games—a title even. This is what I get?"

"See, that's where you're lost, McCloud. It was never about me, you, or the rest of the team. It's about our town. We won those games for them. For every miner that worked their ass for twelve hours a day. For that child who waited the entire week for a ticket, just to see us play for two to three hours. No matter the result, the fans stuck with us. We give them something to be proud of their town about."

Cain remains silent.

"You never got that," MacIntyre says. "You fell into glory; I get it. Living here being a star, getting treated like you were. But think for a second . . . Did you ever appreciate them like they did you? Did you ever think about them?"

Slouched in his seat like a teenager being scolded, Cain's eyes glaze over. He refuses to let his manager's words sink in.

"Shut the door when you leave," MacIntyre coldly says, having enough of the one-sided conversation.

Cain scoffs with disinterest and heads to the door.

"Good luck on the Gulf," MacIntyre adds, not looking up from the scorecard he writes on again.

When Cain touches the door knob, it becomes too real. This is it. He's officially done being a Hawk. He's done playing baseball forever. A wave of sadness washes over him. His pride crumbling away, the former star humbles himself and turns to face his coach. "Fred . . . I-I gotta play. I don't know anything else."

MacIntyre looks at him.

"If it's a problem with the team, I'll manage the equipment. I can even help you coach these guys. Fred . . . I miss it. I'm a ball player. Please?"

MacIntyre weighs the decision. Realizing the anguish, he remembers that twenty-year-old kid that flop sweat from nervousness when having to speak to the veterans of the team during his rookie campaign of 1995. He remembers Cain's first slump that he fought to shed, and his struggles to work with pitchers, until Charlie took him under his wing to learn pitcher habits and understanding hitters. Memories of his breakout season in 1996 that catapulted him to instant fame seems like yesterday. The manager knows the two have grown together, good times and bad. Players have come and gone, but he always enjoyed watching their progress as ball players and men. Taking this into consideration his eyes soften on Cain.

"You'll sit the bench," MacIntyre says. "I'll platoon you if I can."

"Thank you," Cain humbly says.

"But no pouting. No giving your teammates shit and—"

"Promise I won't," Cain interrupts. "I just want to be part of it again, Fred."

MacIntyre nods him away. Walking back into the locker room, Cain hugs Landon, and a few former teammates greet him. He then moseys on to Joe, who begins to empty his belongings from Cain's locker.

"Don't," Cain says, stepping to a different locker. "It's okay, I'll use this one." He opens the new locker and puts his bag inside, then shakes Joe's hand. "You're the baby Dalton, right? Joe?"

"Yeah," Joe replies.

"Stay ready. Fred could call you at any time."

At a loss for words because he's talking to a great, the rookie simply nods.

Two hours later, the game is in full progress. The scoreboard shows goose eggs in extra innings in the top of the 12th against Hillsdale. It's been a back and forth affair that's turned into a heck of a pitchers' duel between Hillsdale's slick left-handed hurler, twenty-eight-year-old league phenom Keith Merrifield, and Rupland's Finn Hood. Inward wind from center has also been a huge factor, yanking well-hit balls to foul or fly out.

Today, the two teams are on the brink of a title game appearance. In the dugout, Cain continues to support his teammates, helping them correct kinks in their batting stances and cheering on Hood's performance.

Hood has been lights out, punching out 11, while only walking one. If he holds strong and the bats give him support, he could be on his way to a complete game shutout.

With two outs and no runners on, Hillsdale's star hitter Grayson Westerman takes to the dish. He's the only one to have Hood's number this afternoon, going 3-for-3 with two singles and a double. The center fielder has been on scouts' radar since his team's first round victory against Ippling. He's twenty-three, six feet two inches, 190 pounds, bats left and throws left and can absolutely fly in the outfield and in the base paths. His superb plate discipline draws many walks, and he has plus power to go along with a solid glove. Westerman is the ultimate five-tool player.

Hood sends some high and away heat that Westerman lets go by for the first strike. The next pitch Hood tries to squeeze inside, but Westerman takes it deep to right field. Hogan flips down his sunglasses to block the sun as he gets on his horse and runs a good route to get to the soaring fly ball that's steaming towards the warning track.

"Wall!" Shoestring shouts, running to back him up.

Hogan catches the ball over his shoulder just in time, cradling it like a wide receiver. He collides hard into the right center wall and bounces to the ground, and the ball remains in his glove for the last out of the inning.

Hogan doesn't get up from the ground. Shoestring tries to help him with Nick and Jaws, who have since run to aid their fallen teammate. When they bring him into the dugout, Sarah and Cain tend to him. Hogan lies on the bench and holds his head.

"He might have a concussion," Sarah says.

MacIntyre leans next to his injured player, and in hopes of forcing some life into him, asks, "What do you say Bucky, ready to get back out there?"

"Just need a few, Coach," Hogan responds. "I'm a little dizzy."

Cain douses a batting towel in cold bottle water and places it on Hogan's forehead.

"Bucky is on deck, Coach," Jaws reminds him while he puts his own batting helmet on to lead off the bottom half of the inning.

"Can't afford a man down, Fred," Roberts says.

MacIntyre contemplates the situation. With a spit and a grunt, he says, "McCloud. Get on deck."

Cain goes right to it, grabbing his favorite war stick: a Louisville Slugger. It's made of maple and is 34 inches, 33 ounces and black with gold trim. Burnt on his pine tar-ridden handle is his #5 jersey number. He then places his black pine tar-crusted two earhole batting helmet on his head. From the back pocket of his baggy pants, he brandishes his orange batting gloves that carry his last name in black lettering and Velcros them on. The slugger is ready to take his first atbat. His team chants support.

Charlie slaps Cain's ass on his way out. "Go get 'em, rook."

Cain politely takes on the teasing that Charlie and his teammates dish and steps into the on-deck circle. He puts on a weighted-doughnut around the barrel of his bat to take practice cuts with. While doing so, he watches Merrifield smoke Jaws on three zig-zagging pitches that skin each side of the plate.

"Pinch-hitting. Number five. Mr. Hawk himself, Cain McCloud!" the announcer calls over the P.A. speakers to a wave of applause for their longtime fan favorite.

"Cain McCloud enters the game," Frank broadcasts. "When the teams released updated rosters today, many were surprised McCloud was on it, since moving away months prior."

"Big bat replacing Hogan here," Grainger adds.

Cain takes a low pitch for ball one.

"No word yet how serious Hogan's injury is," Reese says.

After pulling his wristbands further down his forearm, Cain takes another pitch for ball two. Merrifield then hurls his third pitch in that the star connects on with an uppercut and a frozen long shot. The crack off his bat is loud and fierce, echoing throughout. It's a towering majestic shot that soars to deep, deep center. The entire park sits in suspense as Cain waves his arms forward, hoping for it to carry just enough. Westerman figures the play is at the center field wall and he sprints to the fly.

"My goodness, what a shot!" Reese stands in the box, holding his mic to his lips. "Does it have enough?!"

Westerman gropes the air behind him with his free hand as he has the ball in his sights. Springing from his feet into flight, he puts out his leather. The ball sails just over the wall, a foot out of reach of Westerman's glove to prevent the robbery and giving Cain a clutch, walk-off home run.

"Gone!" Reese screams. "McCloud advances Rupland! McCloud advances Rupland! Oh, my God, McCloud advances Rupland!"

Rupland's dugout clears. Not one home team fan is left sitting as everyone has risen to their feet. Cain's elation transforms his moment into one of incredible humility as he removes his helmet and holds it to the Rupland crowd for a long overdue thank you while rounding the bases. For a brief moment he's once again a hero, and now, maybe forever.

The stadium erupts in unison, singing "Thunderstruck." Their chants are heard for miles away. When Cain reaches home, he stomps on the plate with both feet and howls a joyous scream as he's pounced on by his congratulatory teammates. In the midst of the celebration, MacIntyre meets him in the middle, and the two share a tight hug to bury the hatchet for good.

Kilo Company branches a unit of twenty Marines that sweep through an urban sprawl between Fallujah and Ramadi. A steady flow of MARPAT combat utility fatigues hover through streets and alleyways with M16 rifles at the ready. They are on a special operation code-named Rubicon. Insurgents have joined by the numbers, taking control of the town of Husaybah. The town lies on the Euphrates River in the Al-Anbar province near the Syrian border, which is on the outskirts of Ramadi.

Nearly 100 civilians have already lost their lives in the past week since its start. For Kilo Company the mission is simple: eliminate the enemy threat to take back the town. Drones have detected an estimated 300 insurgents in control of the area.

The unit snakes in between buildings and slowly walks down mazes of endless alleyways. A few radios among them produce a low humming sound. They approach a tight line of three M1 Abrams battle tanks neatly parked next to a hollow alley. These monstrous war machines gather sand on all horizontal surfaces. Lieutenant Matthews inspects them to find any sign of life. Tracks on the outside tanks are completely removed, and no one is in sight.

"Let's move," Matthews says.

With an M40A3 sniper rifle held in front of him and a wrist cuff shell holder full of bullets, Johnny peers at every corner, every shadow, and every object that moves.

"I don't like this sound," Rusty says to Johnny.

"What sound?" Johnny asks.

"Silence . . . "

Kilo scurries from house to house. Like a chain gang, they're at each other's heels when entering these cement structures. Matthews motions some flankers upstairs to do perimeter checks before advancing levels. Every house searched turns up empty. The only movement on the ghostly streets are the rows of rugs, sheets, clothes, and shoes that dangle from clothing lines out windows, connecting to the other houses on the other side of the street. There are so many of them that they resemble telephone lines. One advantage of the laundry that hangs above is the shade it provides for Kilo.

When the company checks the last house on a dirt intersection, Matthews motions for Johnny and Rusty from the flanks. He points to the tallest building in the square that stands four stories high and is bright pink. "Cushing, I need you to get the boot to that point to give us eyes above. They're ground-hogging around here. Somewhere. We need to flush 'em out."

"Yes, sir," Rusty replies.

"Take Burke, Tate, and Gilly with you."

Rusty motions his group forward to join him. Gilly's hazel eyes are wide on him. This is his first tour. He's been here barely a week.

"Boot," Matthews says to Johnny, "when the bullets start to fly, drop every Hadji you see. Don't think. Just shoot."

"You got it, sir," Johnny replies, ready for the challenge.

After Rusty has gathered his men, they sally forth towards the pink building in the center square. They move past two smaller buildings on the side of it. In the middle of the three buildings is a courtyard that separates them.

The rest of Kilo aim their weapons at every direction, ready to give cover fire if necessary. Rusty and his team enter the building, clearing every room on every level similar to ants in and out of holes on an anthill. Each Marine confirms, *"Clear!" "Clear!" "Clear!" "Clear!" "Clear!"* after every room. Working their way up the levels, they reach the roof, where they find two old Arabic men in gigantic black robes, lying on each other. Both riddled with bullets.

Rusty points to them. "Check. Check."

Burke and Gilly each feel their pulses and give them a light kick. They're gone. They seem to have been dead for a while. Flies buzz above the corpses, and the smell is putrid.

Rusty speaks to Matthews from the BAE system radio in his helmet, "Two deceased males on the roof."

"Are they enemies?" Matthews asks.

"Not sure, sir. No weapons were found."

After a handful of seconds, Matthews replies with, "Continue to the perch."

"Roger that."

Rusty positions his men at each of the four corners of the roof. Near the south end, facing their unit, Johnny mounts his rifle, bolts a handful of .50 caliber rounds in the chamber while keeping the safety on, and kneels behind his scope. He is the eagle eye from this perch. When he's ready, he lets Rusty know, and Rusty relays to Matthews that they're set. Matthews and Kilo then move on to sweep more houses on the next block.

The sun from atop the building's roof is brutal. Johnny has the toughest job of his team here. He can rarely blink. Swiveling his rifle's scope to every angle possible, he remains alert and ready.

"Good God, it's hot," Tate says.

"Quit crying," Rusty says.

Johnny watches Kilo remove two teenage Arabic civilians from the first house on the block that's on the same side of the street as the pink building. Over their radios, each can hear what's happening. Two Marines zip tie and sit the civilians in a corner of the house to interrogate them. A Middle Eastern translator from Kilo tries to force answers from each of them to the whereabouts of the enemy activity. It's useless, the two teenagers stay mute.

Johnny swivels his rifle beyond Kilo to check the windows of the three-story houses across the street. A light's reflection catches his eye. Peering closer at its location, he detects a hint of black hair from a window.

"Think I got something," Johnny informs Rusty.

Rusty kneels next to him asking, "Where?"

"Third level, four clicks from the left."

He and Rusty witness the head rise from his spot, a stone-cold killer face shows on what seems a middle-aged man. They wait a second to see whether he's a civilian or not. The man suddenly spots them before hurriedly ducking back down.

"What are you doing?" Johnny mutters to himself about the man.

A long, charcoal black barrel of a rifle sneaks through the window across the way. Johnny and Rusty's eyes grow. Before Rusty can say anything, a tracer round fires at them, entering the left armhole of Rusty's flak jacket, exiting his body out the other armhole. He falls to the ground.

Kilo company responds to the threat, crouching and moving to cover. Johnny stays locked on his scope. He locates some skin in another window and fires a round, hitting the enemy in the shoulder. Blood blooms across the enemy's uniform, and he drops from the window.

"Rust!" Burke yells, running to his aid with Tate.

Rusty fights through the pain, "I'm all right! I'm all right! It went through!"

"Get a bandage on him!" Johnny yells to his team while checking every window on the enemy's side.

Gilly remains at his post. His eyes flutter for any sort of activity on his end.

"Talk to me, someone!" Matthews says on the radio.

"Rusty took a bullet," Burke responds. "He's okay—"

"Sniper is down across the way," Johnny tells Burke.

"Sniper down in the building directly in front of you, sir," Burke relays to Matthews. "Twelve o'clock."

Matthews orders the rest of his unit to fall back into the building they're in to shield them from the street. He doesn't trust what may be lurking in the building across the way.

"Anything else?" Matthews asks Burke and his team.

Johnny trains his eye on the enemy's building. There isn't a soul in sight. Directing his rifle back on the hideout Kilo takes cover in, he spots activity on the roof suddenly. Four men with semi-automatics, faces wrapped in scarves, rise from their bellies and make their way down the building. Johnny observes two of them holding small propane tanks.

"Four targets approaching, sir," Johnny tells Matthews.

"Our way?" Matthews asks.

"From the roof. I spot two with some propane tanks or something."

Matthews and three of his men maneuver up the stairs of the house. A metallic clunking sound is heard in front of them. Matthews notices two propane tanks with bombs attached, tumbling directly towards them.

"Back! Back!" Matthews screams.

They try to dive into side rooms. Enemy rounds from upstairs fire upon the tanks. Each hit them and create a massive explosion that annihilates a trailing Marine.

From Johnny's periphery, he catches some movements in the building again during the explosion. Insurgents fill three windows, two to a window, and hail gunfire upon Kilo across the street. The two zip-tied captives take on the rain of bullets, flat-out killing them. The explosion was their signal to make the move.

"Ambush!" Johnny shouts. "Ambush!" He picks off one of the insurgents in the windows and scours for more.

Kilo returns gunfire across the street, while Matthews and his two men focus on the four enemies upstairs, sending return fire their way.

"Help me up!" Rusty says to Burke and Tate, who tend to his wounds.

Gilly shuffles towards his group next to Johnny. The bodies on the roof mysteriously begin to shake. An al-Qaeda child soldier, no more than eight or nine-years-old, slithers out from underneath them, where he was hiding. He tries to hold an Ak-47 in his mitts but can't quite firmly keep it in his grasp as his own body is stuck under the corpses. Gilly catches a glimpse of the boy and freezes in his tracks. The boy pulls the trigger, spraying bullets at him and the others, eventually losing grip of the rifle, and it slips from his hands.

Gilly drops against the two-foot lip that surrounds the roof, before being able to even squeeze a single shot. Tate has taken several rounds to the stomach, and Burke has taken one to his heel. Rusty returns gunfire from his M16 at the boy, who has cleverly tucked himself back under the corpses.

Johnny lifts himself from the ground after taking cover from the boy's fire and helps Rusty to his feet. Each crouch, hidden from any sniper scopes. A heavy gun battle can be heard from the ambush occurring between Kilo and insurgents.

"Get him?" Johnny asks Rusty and doubles back to his perch.

"Don't know . . . "

Meanwhile, Tate presses his hands against the blood that gushes from his stomach. With a close eye on the corpses, Rusty and Burke tend to him. Burke lifts Tate's arm from his stomach to see just how bad the wound is. His life pours from him. It's critical. Burke then makes his way to Gilly and checks his pulse. He shakes his head to Rusty. Dead.

POW!

Johnny snipes another insurgent who falls out of the window after he revealed himself too long. He racks his bolt-action for some more.

Matthews takes another handful of Marines up the stairs. Pinned back in the only room at the top, two insurgents appear. Matthews eliminates one with two shots to the chest. The other insurgent lunges at Matthews before he can reload his rifle. They roll on the steps, while the last two enemies force themselves back on the roof. Matthews delivers punch after punch, almost caving in the insurgent's face before ending him with a bullet to the head from his sidearm.

"They're fleeing to the roof!" a member of Kilo is heard on the radio.

Johnny swings his rifle back to Kilo's house. Both insurgents pour on to the roof once again.

POW!

Johnny executes the first with an incredible shot, exploding the enemy's head like a water balloon. Avoiding being winged by deadeye Johnny, the second insurgent lies on his stomach. Johnny goes back and forth from Kilo's roof to the enemy building across the street.

"Talk to me, Rust!" Johnny demands, not being able leave his post.

Rusty and Burke have since stopped working on Tate and now hold his hand, seeing him to his final living moments.

"Gilly and Tate are gone," Rusty reveals to Johnny.

Having had enough of their backs against the wall, Rusty checks his rifle, partly rises and fires at the corpses, pelting them with bullets. Blood splatters from them. When Rusty finishes his clip, he waits for any sound or movement from under the corpses.

Johnny sees Kilo Company has taken the last insurgent in the house as prisoner on the other roof. Gunfire has ceased between the enemies and Kilo.

Matthews radios base for support. "Raf-Hab, this is Kilo Company . . . " Rusty informs his lieutenant of the two Marines lost from their position.

Rusty and Burke can do nothing but stare at the corpses. After several minutes, Rusty decides to check them. He moves towards the pile with caution. Seeing the child soldier's AK-47 has been lost to the side, he's not sure if there is another gun under there. His foot crunches the debris around bullet holes left from the shots. Stopping in front of the corpses, he pokes at them. There isn't a movement or sound. Burke keeps his rifle on the pile to cover Rusty.

Click . . . Click . . . Click . . . Rusty hears from under the corpses. It doesn't sound like a gun though. It sounds different to him.

The spaced clicks become rapid: *CLICK, CLICK, CLICK.*

Rusty's eyes grow wide with panic, realizing exactly what the sound is. He turns around and makes a mad dash towards Burke and Johnny and dives on them. The corpses explode in a massive blast that clears the roof, forcing the three Marines to fall onto the clotheslines. Johnny and Rusty become tangled in them, which softens their descent some. The rest of Kilo helplessly watch as they collapse on the street below. The roof above has completely vanished. Various body parts rain on roofs and hoods of abandoned vehicles parked along the street.

"Cushing?" Matthews calls on his radio. " . . . Dalton? Burke?"

Tangled in heaps of laundry and lines, Rusty lies on top of Johnny. They're submerged in brick dust. Matthews keeps trying to radio them to no avail. Kilo can't break their position because they're pinned in from the ambush. Insurgents from the enemy building have since gone quiet, but unknown danger continues to lurk.

Johnny coughs first, coming too. He spits strands of dirt and blood from his nearly bit through tongue. Rusty awakens not long after.

"You okay?" Johnny asks.

"Okay-ish . . . " Rusty says, coughing as well.

"Get your fat ass off me," Johnny says. "I think . . . I broke my ribs."

Kilo notices their movement.

"Cushing?" Matthews radios.

"Dalton and I are fine, sir," Rusty responds.

They stand to search for Burke. Their eyes set on him, hanging by his neck from a couple of lines that didn't snap. Half his body remains from the blast, leaving his bloody meat hanging.

"Damnit," Rusty says before radioing back to Kilo. "Burke's gone."

Both dust themselves off and check their weapons. Johnny can't find his rifle near them. Rusty crumbles to a knee, seriously injured from the fall. A faint noise is heard in an alley across the street from Kilo. Louder and louder, the sound closes in, becoming more distinct. It's voices chanting.

The Marines on the roof with the captured insurgent, radio in what they observe from above, "Twenty. Christ, maybe thirty Hadjis coming towards the street from the east!"

Matthews realizes that the ambush party fell back to inform their friends. Their echoed chants become more comprehensible to his translator.

"What are they saying?" Matthews asks, concerned.

"They're chanting some sort of death song," the translator says.

Matthews prepares his men to fight, positioning them and doing ammo checks. Without warning, the insurgents are on top of them immediately. Legions of men and children cloaked and clothed with rags torn from the dead they've murdered pour from every dark alley and doorway. Twenty or thirty soldiers is a joke. From ground level, it seems like a hundred. They carry soldiers' heads on make-shift spears, guns pump in the air, and rounds and rounds of ammo pass through them into yonder. Their faces are scarfed, with only the whites of their large eyes visible, just glaring at the Americans in hatred.

Gunfire and grenades suddenly devastate the area, turning it into a war zone in a matter of seconds. The first wave of horribles are eliminated, but their numbers keep increasing. The terror won't stop.

Johnny grabs an increasingly weak Rusty. "Does it hurt to walk on?"

"I don't recommend it," Rusty jokes.

"Come on," Johnny says, and they retreat into the courtyard of the pink building they were previously on.

Three insurgents tail them, leaving their al-Qaeda brothers to battle on the street.

Making their way into the courtyard, Johnny practically carries Rusty as best he can. A heavy attack from the chasing insurgents begins. Sounds of helicopters are heard flying overhead. The five in the courtyard look to the skies to see two CH-53E Super Stallions with an arsenal of Marines filled in them for support.

While this distraction keeps the insurgents occupied, Johnny draws his sidearm from his belt and empties his clip on two of them with fatal shots to the chest and head. The two Marines retreat from the returned gunfire by the remaining insurgent. Johnny pushes Rusty behind a lone date palm tree that stands in the center of the yard and then heaves himself into bushes several feet from him.

Left in the open, the teenage insurgent takes refuge behind one of his dead friends' bodies. As the gunfire subsides, Johnny realizes he has no more ammo clips left. They're lost on the street. From his vantage point, he sees Rusty dipping into unconsciousness.

He tries whispering loud enough to keep him awake, "Hey! Keep your fucking eyes open, Marine!"

The insurgent fires at them again. No return fire occurs. Testing the waters, the insurgent fires once more without returned fire and realizes what Johnny dreads he would—he knows they're out of ammo. Being closest to the tree, the insurgent stands cautiously and sneaks closer to it. Spotting hints of Rusty's right arm and leg protruding, the insurgent jackhammers the thin tree in hopes he can break through.

Johnny helplessly watches. Rusty starts to come to but is too weak to defend himself.

"Fear nothing," Johnny whispers to himself under his breath.

Rising from his cover, he rocks on his heels and boldly makes a choice to bolt to the tree to save his friend. Instead of going for Rusty, Johnny heads straight for the insurgent. The enemy turns and fires two rounds into him. Johnny desperately throws his empty sidearm, hitting the insurgent in the face. His momentum carries him, and he tackles the enemy, sending the rifle and himself skidding in unison feet apart.

Johnny lies still, bleeding heavily on top of the rifle. Rusty leaves his cover and struggles to crawl his way to him. Dazed from the sidearm throw and tackle, the insurgent comes to and spots Rusty inching towards Johnny. He grabs his backup piece—a Glock 18—and aims it at him. Knowing he will most certainly die, Rusty makes a last-ditch effort to shield Johnny by lying on top of him.

The enemy steps to Rusty, his vicious eyes ablaze with delight for the impending American trophy kill. Johnny recovers. Without hesitation and in one motion, he grasps the rifle by his side, barrel rolls over and tucks Rusty underneath and fires at the enemy at the same time the enemy shoots. Bullets hit flesh on both men. The insurgent slumps back dead. Rusty rolls Johnny off himself and tends to the fallen Marine.

Bullet holes smoke from Johnny's Kevlar. Blood pools. Rusty realizes that Johnny has died from his injuries. He lifts him on his shoulders and exits the courtyard to the street, where Kilo and reinforcements have neutralized the threat. He limps to the helicopter, stepping over the bodies of dead al-Qaeda littering the street. The dog tags hanging from Johnny's neck drip blood onto Rusty's back.

☞   ☞   ☞

Jack performs a barbell bench press in the barn while Joe spots him. In between his repetition of eight, Jack abruptly finishes, and Joe helps him rack the 175-pound barbell.

"Everything okay?" Joe asks.

Jack loses his footing and stumbles. Joe catches him.

"Yeah," Jack says and sits on a hay bale in the corner, wiping his shiny and sweaty face with his cutoff. "Just kinda dizzy. Think I held my breath too long . . . Give me a sec."

Joe adjusts the bench for his height. He grabs two fifty-pound dumbbells on the side, then lies on his stomach and does ten prone single-arm raises per arm.

Near the end of the driveway, James works on a buddy's rusted white F150 truck. Behind it, several other beaters sit. He intends on fixing these for some extra cash. His head lifts from the hood when he hears a vehicle approaching from their road. The car is a slick, black 2004 BMW 3-series. It's not the sort of car that someone expects to see rolling around these parts.

Jack and Joe leave the barn, and Sandy also curiously steps onto the porch. Two young Marines in their Service C uniforms exit the BMW. A visceral sensation of panic engulfs James, paralyzing him. He doesn't move an inch from the truck, instead giving the men a thousand-yard stare.

"James?" Sandy asks.

James breaks focus and takes his time, wiping his hands with a rag and senselessly organizing his tools, stalling and thinking that if he drags this out the dreadful news won't come. *Or maybe,* he thinks, *it's not real.*

When the Marines remove their Barracks Covers, Sandy falls to her knees—the wind taken from her. Witnessing this, Joe runs to her, not fully understanding what has happened. Jack doesn't move, however. He knows exactly what has happened.

☞   ☞   ☞

Skies of gray provide the backdrop to the Rupland cemetery. Sorrow fills the hearts of family members, teammates, friends, former classmates, and other locals. Dozens of flowers and an American flag decorate Johnny's closed casket.

Rupland praises its veterans. They've seen their fair share of bodies of their loved ones brought back from wars. Death has rocked the community every decade since its existence. Much like baseball, soldier war stories go hand in hand and are the very foundation this town was built on. First and foremost, this is an American town, and when one of their own has died fighting for it, there is no greater honor.

Seated in the front row in a cluster of chairs, under an awning that extends beyond the casket, is the Dalton family with Katie. Though profoundly sad, they're overwhelmingly grateful for the outpouring of support for Johnny. Behind them, Nick stands beside many players in support of the family. When he glances back, he notices his own father standing near the rear of the gathering. There's a sway to George's stance. Nick inconspicuously disappears into the crowd to reach him. He stands close enough to him, using his own body to help keep him upright.

"Seriously?" Nick whispers. "You get loaded? Today?"

"I can't handle . . . these sorta things, Nicky-boy," George says. "You should know that."

"Then you shouldn't have come, Dad. . . . You just shouldn't have come."

Jack becomes more anxious as the funeral service continues. He takes several heavy breaths and undoes his tie. Watching his mother and Katie cry and Joe wiping tears, the tragedy is too surreal.

Before the funeral, Rusty and two other Kilo Company Marines spoke of Johnny in a light that the family only saw for a short time. They talked about his playful ways and how he enjoyed a good practical joke on his fellow Marines in the morning. They said he always fought for the underdog, a trait James and Sandy instilled in their boys at a young age. They expressed Johnny's fortitude and drive, and his heroic acts during the deadly battle that saved Rusty's life. And they mentioned how he couldn't stop talking about his son Jake and Katie and where they would go and what they would do after his tour. One Marine said Johnny would've been a lifer in the Corps. Rusty disagreed and said Johnny wanted to buy land to raise his own family on, just as his parents did. The only story Rusty did keep to himself is that he added Johnny's name to the memorial tattoos on his back with the other souls that were lost in battle.

Johnny just scratched the surface of life, and now Jack and his family are left wondering what his future could've held for him, Katie and Jacob. He was nineteen when he died, and he will stay nineteen forever to anyone who knew him.

A three honorary guard Marine rifle party raises their M14 rifles to the sky and fire a three-volley salute. The ceremonial shots echo as a lone bugler brings the bugle to her lips and plays "Taps."

Reduced to walking with a cane from the wounds he suffered that fateful day, Rusty takes the casket's flag that's folded into a triangle and presents it to Sandy.

"Mrs. Dalton," Rusty addresses her, "on behalf of the President of the United States, the United States Marine Corps, and a grateful nation, please accept this flag as a symbol of our appreciation for your loved one's honorable and faithful service."

She tearfully accepts the flag with both hands and clutches it tightly against her chest. Jack and Joe witness their father in tears himself. They've never seen him cry until this moment. They realize what every child does when they reach a certain age, that their father isn't Superman.

Jack and Joe remain at the gravesite, long after the service. They stand next to the plot and watch a roughneck county worker in a backhoe pour dirt on their brother's vault. When the hole is nearly filled, Joe says to Jack, "I'll drive us home."

Turning around, they see Savannah in a black dress, sitting quietly in an empty chair in the middle row. Joe greets her with a hug and tells Jack he'll wait for him in the car. Even though her eyes are puffy from crying, she's still as angelic as Jack can remember. Her hair is much longer with blonde highlights, and that high school youthfulness has vanished from her. She's blossomed into a woman.

"Jack . . . " she says, standing to hug him.

Jack holds her tight before he steps back and slides his hands into his pockets to not over-emphasize the moment.

"When did you get in?" he asks.

"Yesterday," she says. "Jack, I'm so sorry about Johnny."

"Doesn't seem real, you know? I can't even cry. I want to, but I can't."

"That's normal. Everybody handles things differently. Don't be hard on yourself."

The awkwardness of seeing each other sinks in.

Savannah says, "There were a lot of people that came. Just . . . so great to see."

"Yeah," Jack says with a slight smile before grasping for a change in topic. "So how have you been? Your folks come in the store every once in a while. They told me you don't play softball anymore?"

"After my freshman year, I just wanted to focus on my studies."

"They said you changed your major? Broadcast Journalism, right?"

She politely nods, not really wanting to talk about herself. "You cut your hair."

"Oh yeah," Jack says, touching his head. "Kinda got tired of it getting in my eyes under my mask. Sweat burned them." He laughs cheerfully.

Savannah chuckles before saying, "I heard the league returned. You must be excited. You guys made it to the championship, too. That's amazing!"

"It has been a blast. Are you staying for the game?"

"I wish I could. I've been taking summer classes so I can take the fall semester off."

"Oh, all right. Going somewhere?"

Savannah cautiously reveals her left hand that sports a white gold, halo sculpted diamond ring.

"You're engaged?"

Savannah nods, "I'm engaged . . . "

" . . . Wow . . . Savannah. Wow. Congratulations!" He hugs her.

"Thanks." She weakly smiles.

"When's the big day?"

"September 22nd."

"That's . . . that's coming soon. Good for you," he says with some pain behind his facade.

"He—my fiancé. We went to the same school. Met him there a couple years ago. He just graduated this past semester."

Bland smiles shared between them end any further small talk. Both understand they've gone in separate directions with their lives, and couldn't be more different. They aren't the same naive high-schoolers that clung to young love.

"Joe is waiting for me," Jack says. "I should probably get going."

"Of course," Savannah responds, almost too fast. "Me too."

Jack and Savannah hug goodbye. He gazes admiringly at her one last time. "God, look at you. I'm really proud of you, Savannah."

Her radiant smile disappears as quickly as it came, knowing there is nothing left to say.

Jack leaves her side.

Driving home from the funeral, James and Sandy don't speak. Rain finally shows itself and pours with a mixture of tiny hail that pelts the truck.

Sandy holds the flag given to her family on her lap. Pressed between her thumb and index finger, she rubs it. Nausea suddenly overwhelms her, and she pleads with her husband to pull to the side of the road. He does, and she hastily exits, falling to her knees and pukes in a ditch. James slaps the truck in park and rushes to help her. She is too weak to stand, so he embraces her, and she collapses in his arms.

"My baby . . . " Sandy cries. "My baby is gone . . . No, no, no . . . "

James gives in and cries himself.

"How do we tell his son about his father?" Sandy asks. "I don't want to talk about Johnny in the past tense. I don't want to have to tell Jake the great things his father did or what he was like . . . Johnny should himself . . . "

James is too upset to answer her. Soaked, they hold each other in the drenching storm, not knowing where to go from here.

Jack buys a fifth of Jack Daniels from the liquor store and runs back into the rain to his car, where Joe sits, keeping the engine running. They drive to the Little League field and park in the lot, facing it. Jack tosses his wet suit jacket in the backseat. Joe does the same. The bottle passes back and forth, each taking pulls from it.

"I can't believe our fuckin' brother's gone, dude," Joe says.

"Pretty shitty hand we've been dealt," Jack says.

"Jake and Katie now . . . The whole thing's a mess . . . "

Jack snags the bottle from Joe, who's held it too long, and takes a generous drink. He runs his sleeve across his lips to wipe them and points to the field. "Remember that?"

"What?" Joe asks with some droop in his eyes.

"Little League, man. Just fucking simple, not a care in the world. Go and have fun with your friends, that was it. Those were the good ol' days."

Joe steals the bottle back from Jack. "When . . . when did shit get all complicated?"

"No clue."

"Johnny's dead, Eli, your shit, baseball is almost done . . . Everyone moving outta here . . . "

Jack pauses, reflecting on what he heard, "My shit?"

Joe has the liquid courage pumping, so he reveals, "Those pills and vials you hide—I've seen them before, dude."

"What?" Jack asks, taking the bottle back from Joe.

"Look, it's none of my business," Joe says.

"Damn right it's none of your business! Are you going through my things now?"

"No man, I just know something is going on, that's all."

"You don't know shit!"

Joe isn't in the mood to have Jack attack him this way and retaliates, "Jack, I don't even want to know what the hell is going on with you! If you're cheating, that's your thing, but that shit you're taking is dangerous. Last thing our family needs is to have this hanging over our heads."

"Get the fuck out of my car," Jack says coldly and calmly.

"You're not serious," Joe says, pointing at the storm.

Jack swipes the keys from the ignition and whips them out of his window into the dark, "Get the fuck out of my car! Walk to a buddy's to give you a ride!"

Joe glares at his brother with outrage before he exits and starts his trek. Jack leaves the car and teeters to the field's fence, the bottle of whiskey clenched in his hand.

"Bastard," Jack mutters. "You're a selfish bastard."

After taking another long swig from the bottle, he chucks it deep into the parking lot where it smashes into a shallow puddle. He then grabs the fence and shakes it madly. His shaking intensifies, and he stumbles to the ground. Rain pelts on his face as he looks up at the stormy skies. His eyes brim with tears. He tries to fight the urge of letting go by wiping them away but eventually gives in, and he cries, cries, cries . . .

☞　　☞　　☞

A phone call awakens Nick in the wee hours of the night. When he gets to the phone, he answers it with a groggy, "Hello?"

On the other end is a bartender at The Pickaxe, "Nick. Sorry to call you late, but your dad is here."

"What now?"

"I've got him in the back," she says. "He's passed out. I didn't give him a drink, I swear, Nick. He was pretty loaded when he came in tonight. He puked in a stall, and I had to clean his mess too."

Nick sighs, "All right. I'll be there in ten minutes."

"Okay," she says, seemingly reluctant to reveal more. " . . . Nick . . . When I helped him to a table some things fell outta his pocket. Just thought you'd want to know."

Nick knows what "things" she's referring to. Before long he arrives at The Pickaxe, that's been closed for a couple of hours. After a brief exchange with his coworker, he loads his father into the truck. George slumps in the bench seat, slurring his words. Nick grabs the meth pipe and any dime bags from his jacket pocket to examine them. He brings back his arm to heave the paraphernalia but stops himself and tucks them back into George's pocket. He then walks around to his door and picks his father's head off his side of the seat, placing his motionless body against the passenger door.

Driving back home, Nick doesn't flinch other than his right hand that shifts through the gears and his intermittent spitting of tobacco on his floorboards. His whole reaction during this process is business as usual. Since his father's release from prison, he's picked him up from random locations because he was either too drunk or too high to get himself home. When they moved into a trailer park a year ago, because they couldn't afford Nick's childhood home anymore, George promised to help with the finances. When they had to sell their hunting cottage because they couldn't afford the property taxes anymore, George promised to get sober and do anything to help his son more. These were false promises due to the fact the drunk has never held a job longer than a month.

It's an understatement to say that Nick has come from the school of hard knocks. The gentle soul has always taken care of himself, including other people. From his father to when he even lived with his grandmother, he was constantly taking care of somebody. But no one has taken care of Nick since his mother died. On this night he's had enough. His tough past suffocates him.

"Okie from Muskogee" comes on the radio and complicates the young man's emotions further. Memories of his mother rush through his mind and break the wall he built around his heart until it completely crumbles. He whips a hard left on the steering wheel and the truck squeals to a stop. He clutches his unconscious father and shakes and slams him repeatedly against his own door screaming, "Wake up! Wake up you son of a bitch!"

Once he gets control of himself, he leans back against his door, tormented with anguish. It takes him some time to calm down. His father is still out cold, snoring without a care.

"I remember when I was six, maybe seven," Nick says. "It was during one of my tee ball games. You were there cheering for me. Mom too. The entire afternoon, I just couldn't hit the ball hard enough. I kept trying and trying and the kids there were laughing at me and my little dribblers I'd knock off that damn tee. I remember it clearly. You came from the bleachers and showed me how to hit that ball good and hard." Nick mimics with his hands, lost in the pleasant memory.

"Shifting my hands in the correct spot. Choking up. Bat off the shoulder and back," Nick continues. "Next chance I got, I smacked the shit outta that thing, went past everyone's head. Shut 'em all up. They started cheering me on, and . . . and you . . . you hugged me and took me and mom out for ice cream after . . . Hell, I think that was the last time you saw me play. Dad, if you would've watched me in the last sixteen years, you'd see that I've been hitting the ball hard ever since . . . "

Nick positions himself in front of the steering wheel again. He looks ahead, "I wanted to be exactly like you. Everything you did I thought was cool . . . But that man I knew is gone now . . . " He takes a moment to compose himself and puts his hand on the door to open it.

Looking at his father again, he says, "Not a day goes by where I don't see her cross on the side of that highway. I remember how good she smelled. Always smiled . . . She was the only person always there for me, my mother . . . " He exits the truck and goes to his father's side to help him out, "I'll never apologize for this."

Beyond them, Nick's truck sits in front of a building. The sign ahead reads: Rupland Sheriff's Office and Detention Center.

A hinder no longer, Nick makes the decision to turn George in for a parole violation. A violation that indeed carries a heavy sentence.

☞ ☞ ☞

A group of eight and nine-year-olds play a pickup game on the Rupland Little League field. Lying on the bench in the Little Hawks dugout, Jack is sound asleep with his suit jacket draped over him.

The morning's sun becomes shaded on his face. A recognizable smell of Marlboro-laden sweat from his father jolts him awake. He sees James standing before him with a blank stare at the dugout wall. Over 100 more names have been added to it in the nine years since Jack last played here.

Jack sits up, wiping his eyes and straightens his clothes so his father doesn't dwell on his hungover state.

"Sitting in that house is driving me crazy," James says, before taking a seat next to his son.

"How's Mom doing?" Jack asks with a yawn.

"She's—you know . . . " James says. "She left early this morning to sit in front of Johnny's grave. I just came from bringing her a chair. Figured she'll be there a while."

Jack nods.

"She's not coming to your game either this weekend, Jack. She'd rather listen to it on the radio at the gravesite with Katie, because she believes it doesn't feel right not to have him be a part of it somehow."

"Can't blame her," Jack says. "The championship just doesn't seem important anymore."

The two Dalton men watch the kids play. There isn't much to talk about since Johnny's passing, so after some thought, James says, " . . . Did I ever tell you I was at game seven of the '68 series?"

This grabs Jack's immediate attention, "The Lolich-Gibson duel?"

"Well . . . I saw it on TV," James jokes, which strikes some light laughter between them.

"Good one."

"Watching it though . . . I mean, you should have seen Mickey Lolich. He was the real deal. The whole—"

"Series. Yeah."

"Exactly. A thrill to watch. It might've been Denny McClain's season, but it was Lolich's series."

The conversation stops for reflection. Jack hesitates but asks a question he's always wondered, "Why'd you stop playing ball, Dad?"

"There was a time when I thought baseball was it for me. And you know, I believed I would've been okay with that. Your uncle was damn good also."

"That's what Mom said."

"Played catcher, just like you. We had these dreams that took us far beyond Minor League ball. Reality set in when we faced actual Major League talent. That's when we realized what our hopes actually were—dreams. The Marine Corps became a life we knew we could succeed in. I missed playing ball, sure, but when I think back on it, you kids gave me a life far more satisfying than any dream. That's what I was always meant to be—a father and a coach. That's what made sense."

Both notice a dark-haired boy in the field. He's wearing a homemade #12 Dalton jersey, resembling Jack. He tries to mimic his play.

"There's a good chance Saturday might be the last time I ever step foot on a field," Jack concedes. "What am I, if I can't play anymore?"

"Jack, when I began teaching you this game I put a lot of pressure on you," James says, gripping his son's shoulder. "Sure enough, you always gave me everything I've asked of you and more. You're it, boy. You're far better than I was. But make no mistake, there's more to you than baseball. My sons have so much potential and so many more options than your mother and I ever had. I pushed and pushed and pointed you in just one direction . . . Maybe now I'm thinking I shouldn't have. I should've told you all that I'll be proud of you, regardless. Your mother and I raised fine young men . . . I'm sorry, Jack . . ."

"Dad . . . " Jack says.

James stands and faces the wall of carved names again, this time focusing on Johnny's faded signature.

"Johnny was most like me," James says. "And it kills me that I can't regret not steering him another way. Fact is, he made his choice to become a Marine. To fight. Your mom wouldn't understand, but Johnny died a warrior's death. I refuse to take that away from him. He died doing something he believed in. Not everyone can understand something like that."

He traces Johnny's name with his finger and then says to Jack, "The only thing I regret was how I raised him. Was I too hard on him? Am I too hard on you and Joe?"

Jack pauses before answering. "Sometimes, yeah. We understood though. We respected the bigger picture."

James clears the lump in his throat and raises his crumpled fist to Jack. From it he spills Johnny's dog tags onto Jack's palm.

"Rusty gave me these. I want you to keep them," James says. "On Saturday you're Mickey Lolich; make the game yours."

Jack humbly embraces his brother's tags.

☞   ☞   ☞

Championship Game: August 5th, 2006
#1 CLARKSTON BLACK SOX VS. #7 RUPLAND HAWKS

Summer's embers slowly burn out the final weeks of the season. One final parade celebration pours in the streets this evening and ends at the field just before sunset.

The entire Hawks locker room is empty. Jack is the last player remaining behind. He slides his wristband on his left arm, straps his shin guards on his legs, and finally, puts on his chest protector. His ensemble is not complete without the smearing of eye black in that famous Apache warrior style. Lastly, he tucks Johnny's dog tags that he wears around his neck under his jersey and then takes the opportunity to kneel next to the wooden bench in the middle of the floor to pray. When done, he signs the cross and rises to find Joe standing close by, staring at him.

"Ready?" Joe asks.

"Yes," Jack says. He grabs his mask and begins to exit with his little brother by his side.

On the way, Joe asks him, "We good?"

"We're always good," Jack says.

From the quiet of the locker room, the two transcend into an entirely different atmosphere when they reach the top of the dugout stairs. An atmosphere of celebration, happiness, and competition—this makes the most sense to them; always has.

"You know I still have questions," Joe reminds Jack about their argument on the day of Johnny's funeral.

Jack smirks when replying, "I guess I've got a lot of explaining to do."

Crowd noise rises, and Jack, followed by Joe, walks onto the field. They join the tail end of their teammates' line. They reach into the bleachers to hug, shake, grab and slap the hands of the town that has supported them through thick and thin. On the opposite side of the field, Clarkston does the same. The warmth of these fans is felt with every fiber of their being. No town has loved their teams more. Player and fan, each life has touched one another. They're one family.

At home plate, MacIntyre and Black Sox manager Hoyt Perkins shake hands and pass their final tournament lineup cards to the umpire.

HAWKS	B/T #	BLACK SOX	B/T #
Jack Dalton	R/R #12 (C)	Cole Clancy	R/R #10 (CF)
Lou Webb	R/R #3 (SS)	Mark Jones	S/R #51 (2B)
Cain McCloud	R/R #5 (3B)	Tim Kanter	R/R #20 (RF)
Nick Kosko	R/R #40 (1B)	Michael Harrow, Jr	L/L #4 (C)
Landon Steele	L/L #11 (RF)	Kyle Kennedy	R/R #5 (LF)
Billy Hobbs	S/L #6 (CF)	Richie Leigh	S/R #33 (3B)
JoJo Torres	S/R #17 (2B)	Brody Nolan	R/R #18 (SS)
Shawn Joski	L/L #27 (LF)	Jordan Steinberg	L/L #43 (1B)
Charlie Hylman	R/R #1 (P)	Tommy Rizzo	R/R #29 (P)

James joins the fans for a standing ovation after the Hawks leave the stands. Before he arrived, he stopped by Johnny's gravesite to give Sandy and Katie with baby Jake a radio and some leftovers for dinner. The women chose to stay there next to Johnny's grave, sharing stories of him and listening to the game as a family.

When James scopes the crowd, he spots clusters of scouts in attendance—the most since the first round. Aside from scouts, the park has about as many Clarkston fans as it does Rupland fans this evening, making the place louder than it's ever been. Rupland versus Clarkston is a heated and traditional rivalry; even when most of these players were still in Little League and high school, they've had fierce matches.

In honor of Johnny, both clubs sport black bands with a white #8 stitched around the left sleeves of their uniforms. Tournament sponsors donated them. While the Black Sox stand on the foul line for the national anthem, the Hawks form a circle around the mound. They each touch the dirt out of respect for Johnny. Rupland's marching band begins the anthem, and each player and coach leaves their hand in dirt for the entire song.

Frank Reese and Mel Grainger dress in their weekend best to say farewell to the league in style; a first for them.

"Well, well, I'd never thought I'd be saying this," Reese broadcasts. "Today we are here for the last game ever of the Summer League. We will see the number one-seeded Clarkston Black Sox face the seven-seeded Hawks of Rupland."

"Get ready for a showdown," Grainger adds.

The best seeded team bats first, so the Hawks take the field. Starting pitcher Charlie stops to stretch his shoulder after throwing some warm-up pitches.

"Both teams have been through so much this past year," Grainger somberly comments. "In the midst of the mine closing, the Dalton family suffered the loss of their son, former Hawk, Johnny Dalton. The late Marine is being honored by both teams today."

The home plate umpire signals to start, and the Black Sox's leadoff batter Cole Clancy takes to the box. Charlie hurls in some fire for a strike to start the title game.

"Brought the goods!" Reese says. "A 92-mile per hour fastball."

"Come to think of it, I don't believe he's hit 90 in a couple years," Grainger says.

The second and third pitches are strong off-speed throws that hit the edges beautifully for swinging strikes. Jack throws the ball around the horn, while Charlie shrugs away his first strikeout of the game.

Black Sox second baseman Mark Jones doesn't have any better luck. Charlie goes to work quickly and tosses two breaking balls that Jones' timing is behind on—the last one he watches go by for the backwards "K." Jones' small, punched-in face taunts the umpire about the strike call he feels was questionable. The umpire dismisses him and gives him a warning before he can continue his tantrum. The second baseman jeers him and Charlie that he'll "be back later," and returns to the bench.

Clarkston star Tim Kanter struts to the plate next. "Sox Pride" is branded on the knob of his stick. He's become one of the deadliest hitters in the entire Summer League.

Charlie takes a breather to think of how he'll throw Kanter while he slaps some rosin on his hand. He wipes the excess on his rosin-covered cap that's usually a mess of chalky white by game's end. When he tries to work the plate, Kanter sits back in the box and pulls every one of them for deep fouls; animatedly holding his long, one-handed swing before him after each. Kanter adjusts his stance some to Charlie's pitches so he can straighten these and battles him through four more pitches. By the seventh pitch, Kanter all but shrieks with joy, watching it hang just inside. He stabs a hard line-drive back to the mound that Charlie snags from the air to retire the side. He surprises everyone, including himself. Kanter's bat lies in splinters on the field.

Charlie hurries to the dugout, clenching his teeth. When removed from fan sight and opponents, he rips off his glove and shakes the sting from his left hand. He wants to scream in pain but holds it in.

Bottom of the 1st inning. Black Sox's number one ace, Tommy Rizzo starts on the hill. His teammates call him Rubber Rizzo because he's an absolute innings eater that seems to never tire. They joke his arm is probably made of rubber.

After getting Jack to ground out to second and striking out Lou on lookers, Rizzo gets his turn to face Cain for the first time. He throws his first pitch high and in, brushing him back from the plate to show him his boldness early. Both benches rise in anticipation of another Crockerty incident.

Cain points his bat at the lip-snarled Rizzo and warns him, "Try that shit again."

Rizzo delivers a second pitch in again but not as high or inside, figuring he scared Cain with the last throw. If anything, it's made Cain angry, and he slams the pitch for a deep one-run blast to put his boys up 1-0, in the first.

Cain stares down Rizzo as he rounds the bags. In the midst of celebration in the stands, a fan fight erupts between two middle-aged male diehards. Police security breaks them apart.

Top of the 3rd inning. Clancy leads off second after a single and a pop-up by Jones that moves him over. Kanter is back at the plate, and Charlie gets ahead of him in the count. Infielders position themselves deep enough to where they're standing on the outfield grass.

Charlie places one in that just misses the zone for his first ball. Jack returns it and sees exhaustion start to take its effect on the aging veteran. Charlie works his pitch clock down to the last second between throws. He's taking deeper breaths and pumping his fingers on his throwing hand to get feeling back in them.

Jack signs for an off-speed throw for a change of pace, but Charlie declines. Jack then signs him for a fastball that Charlie then accepts. He pauses, then goes from the stretch and wings it low. Jack chomps his mitt to snag the ball but jolts when Kanter tees off on it with a golf swing, for a two-run shot to put his Sox up 2-1. Watching the ball fly over the wall, Kanter flips his bat high in the air and begins his slow home run trot around the diamond. After some serious hang time, the big stick hits the ground for the bat boy to retrieve. His teammates stand and lightly clap the palms of their hands at the golf chip shot Kanter hit. He laughs as he rounds the bases.

The old ace shows his disgust, removing his glove and squeezing it with both hands as if he wants to tear it in half. Jack goes to the mound to check on him.

"Char?" he asks, concerned.

"There's still some gas left," Charlie tells him, his glove over his mouth.

"You gotta tell me when it's enough."

"I'll shoot ya straight, Zoom."

Jack plants the new baseball given to him by a field umpire in Charlie's glove and returns to the plate.

Bottom of the 4th inning. Tower lights slowly fade on, becoming brighter as day turns to night. Jack walks to the dish after nine-spot hitter Hylman was K'd on three Rizzo curves. On a 2-0 count, Jack hits a liner into the right field gap. He rounds first on a dime and then second just as Kanter gets to the ball.

The Black Sox dugout lunges from the bench when they notice Jack isn't slowing down. Realizing what they see, Kanter ignores his cutoff and tests his cannon arm, throwing a frozen rope to home. Roberts tries to hold Jack at third, holding his hands out, but the kid's ferocity puts his wheels into another gear as he rounds this bag as well, looking to score in a blaze of determination. Catcher Michael Harrow Jr. receives the ball that's off target to the side of the plate, then awkwardly twists his body back around to make the tag. Jack flattens himself for a feet-first slide. When the dust settles the umpire signals the safe call.

"Inside the park home run!" Reese broadcasts. "Zoom-Zoom flashes in to take the score at two-a-piece. Now that's heads-up base running!"

Winded, Jack stands and garners applause from his team and fans. Angry Clarkston fans, however, clamoring for respect, rain trash on him. They consider Jack legging the four-bagger as an insult. For a second time today the game halts so the grounds crew can clear the field of garbage. Meanwhile, Harrow remains on the ground in pain from the impossible acrobatic twist his body had to make to catch the ball. Rizzo helps him to his feet.

Top of the 7th inning. Black Sox shortstop Brody Nolan takes a small lead on first with one out, after squeezing a hot shot through the infield. Charlie stands on the mound. His pitch count is up to 90 at this point, and his arm hurts to high hell. Jack can see the last chapter of pain in the story of the veteran's eyes.

Charlie's next pitch is a mighty thrown sinker that's hit by first baseman Jordan Steinberg towards the shortstop. Jack rapidly bolts to back up first. This is a lesson James has taught him since the day he handed him a catcher's mitt. Lou gobbles up the ball and makes a wild throw that sails behind Nick. Reacting instinctively, Jack catches the baseball on the run, then sidearms it to Nick for the out. Nick then guns the ball to Lou to put the oncoming Nolan in a pickle. The ball flips back and forth between Lou and Nick until it's tossed to Jack covering first, who runs Nolan down for the double play, effectively ending the inning.

"Dalton turns two!" Reese announces.

"His iron will is really leading the team tonight, Frank," Grainger says.

On their way to the dugout, Lou comments to Jack, who's about as exhausted as one would be after doing as much running as he did this evening, "What is that, a 2-3-2 double play? Um, highlight reel, bruh."

Top of the 8th inning. After a scoreless bottom inning, the Hawks take the field again. Charlie rises from the bench to grab the ball from the umpire. As soon as he leaves the dugout, the ball oddly falls from his hand. Charlie reaches to grab it and feels the surface of it as if he were blind. He then squeezes his hand to get the feeling back. He can't. When he locks eyes with MacIntyre, the realization is clear. His career is done. It's the end of the road. Roberts goes right to work and begins to wrap Charlie's cradled arm in ice.

Meers and Huff haven't fared well in late innings when the team is behind; the only pitcher left with a full tank and a fresh face that Clarkston doesn't have any knowledge of is the unproven Joe Dalton. With the number nine batter Rizzo up and the fact that he's a right-handed hitter, this could be a good situation for Joe. MacIntyre isn't overly concerned about righty/lefty matchups in some cases, but here and for the next few batters, it could help the rookie.

As soon as Charlie gets word that Joe is relieving him, the vet softly calls to the rookie from bench purgatory, "Little Dalton—" Head lowered and his thick-framed glasses removed, he hands the ball to Joe, saying, "Finish my win, kid."

Joe takes these words to heart. This is the first action he's seen in the tournament, and he's quite excited. He's neither naive nor ignorant of this important torch-passing moment between veteran and rookie.

"I'll do you proud," he says, trying to mask his excitement.

Charlie lifts his head and replies, "Shut up."

Joe swallows hard and heads to the mound to warm up, almost forgetting his glove in the process. When he looks up, he notices James is delighted to see him hustling to the mound in relief.

Joe takes his first sign from Jack and delivers some serious smoke that scouts clock at 93 MPH for an impressive strike. Jack then returns the ball to Joe and signs for a curve, figuring Rizzo will be looking for another fastball. That's what Rizzo would pitch, anyway. Unfortunately, this throw gets away from Joe, and Rizzo takes advantage of it, slugging the poorly placed ball deep to right field, past Landon's head. Rizzo pours on the juice and turns his hit into a triple, sliding into third. He calls time-out to empty the dirt from his cleats.

Top of the order, Cole Clancy walks to the plate next with no outs and a runner in scoring position. Jack calls time and hustles to the mound to have words with his brother.

"Got away from you there, huh?" Jack says.

"It was supposed to be a curve," Joe explains.

"Didn't curve much."

Joe drops his head in disgust.

"Now, you know these guys can hit," Jack says. "No pitcher should ever let a hitter feel comfortable. Bury the nerves and prove you belong here. Don't let them take that from you."

Heading back to the plate, Jack's encouragement helps Joe's focus. He throws three flawless pitches with good framing from Jack to get ahead of his hitter 1-2. On the fourth throw, Clancy hits a soaring fly to shallow center. Shoestring makes an incredible diving catch and rolls to a stand. Rizzo tags and is off to the races. Shoestring takes his chances and guns it home off one foot. Jack squares himself, blocking the plate. Rizzo realizes the ball is about to beat him and flies through the air spikes high in a drop kick motion. Jack catches the ball and Rizzo's steel digs into his thigh. Jack punches him in the mouth with the tag for the out, and both drop back in pain.

Blood begins to seep through Jack's pants. He stands from the ground swiftly to show it doesn't affect him. Rizzo rises too, holding his gashed-mouth and spitting his front tooth into his palm.

Cain charges Rizzo from third base incensed, "Come here, asshole! Steeling up my catcher?!" He pushes Rizzo to the ground.

Joe tries to hold his irate teammate back. Both benches are ready to run from their foxholes, but Cain composes himself quickly.

"Are you okay?" Cain asks Jack.

Fighting through the searing pain, Jack nods. His eye black is a mess and partially wiped away by the sweat. MacIntyre exits the dugout to check on his player. When Jack spots this, he straightens his posture even more in anticipation of MacIntyre replacing him.

"I'm good to go, Coach," Jack tells him flat-out.

"You're not good to go," MacIntyre says. "You're bleeding. Get outta that gear, and we'll move you to third. Cain, suit up."

Jack refuses, placing his hands on his hips and glaring at his coach dead in the eye, he says, "Coach, no. I'm fine."

Cain stops his stride when hearing this, unsure whether to put on his gear or not.

"We need your bat next inning," MacIntyre says. "Let's wrap the leg, and switch positions to lighten your load."

Jack retrieves his mask from the ground, then urges to MacIntyre, "I know best how Joe throws. Really, I'm fine."

After some reluctance, MacIntyre agrees to it and returns back to lean on Roy's Fault, knowing there isn't a chance he can pry Jack from behind the plate.

Roberts stands next to his friend, "Didn't think you were gonna win that one anyway."

"Hardheaded son of a bitch," MacIntyre says.

Joe returns to the mound. Still concerned, Cain stays behind.

"If you're gonna ask if I'm okay again, I'm gonna knock you in the fucking mouth," Jack says, sensing Cain's presence without even looking at him.

"Nah," Cain responds with sarcasm. "I was actually gonna tell you to quit whining about a little scratch and buck the fuck up."

Jack turns to Cain, and the two share a grin before hitting gloves and returning to their positions. Mark Jones digs in again on the left side of the box, vowing to make good on his jeer from earlier. So far he hasn't been successful tonight, going 0-for-3.

With the bases empty and two outs, Joe feels a tad more comfortable about the situation. He comes from the windup each time and throws a nice mix of tight pitches that Jones' flailing swings can't touch, before punching him out with a 12-6 curveball for the first strikeout of his career. Jones returns to the bench, his head hanging in shame.

Bottom of the 8th inning. Jack drops his pants in the dugout, and Roberts treats the wound by wrapping it with gauze and bandages. After which, Jack pulls up and buckles his pants, grabs a bat and helmet and goes to the plate. He has a small limp but refuses to let it bother him. Right away, he notices the first and third basemen each playing deep. When he steps into the box, he spots Harrow grunting in some pain, still hurting from his fourth inning twist. Even the catcher's knee savers can't help the hurt he endures. Jack also perceives that Rizzo is starting to wear, so he figures the ace's throws are more about command than velocity at this stage.

Stepping on the rubber, Rizzo's composure he had at the beginning of the game is gone. He spits a sizable wad of spit through the hole where his front tooth was and tosses a weak inside pitch that he expects the hitter to watch. But Jack surprises everyone with a smooth bunt along the third baseline. He jets to first. Sox third baseman Richie Leigh sprints in for the ball, snags it bareheaded, and lasers it to first, off-balanced. Jack beats the throw by a mile. The park erupts with applause, stomping, and cheers.

Next batter Lou takes a breaking ball for a three-hopper to left, advancing Jack to second to put his team in scoring position. Cain is in a good spot, taking to the box now. He digs in and keeps his intimidating squint on Rizzo. A couple chopped fouls later, Cain finds himself in the hole. He knows he has to be aggressive on anything close. Rizzo slings in a tight two-seamer that Cain rides deep to center field.

"A deep drive . . . " Reese announces, watching and holding his breath with the rest of the park.

Clancy darts up Prevo's Peak with speed and grace, leaping to rob the slugger of a home run that could've sealed the win.

"What an insane catch!" Grainger shrieks. "That could've been the one!"

Gasps of *almost* give heart attacks and fast-fading goosebumps to Rupland. Jack and Lou scramble to tag up before each advances a base on the sacrifice. Cain kicks the dirt in disappointment as he rounds the foul line returning to the dugout. Up next, Nick fist bumps Cain on his way to the batter's box.

Manager Perkins has seen enough from Rizzo's dead arm. With the Hawks threatening here in the bottom half of the inning, he decides to do the complete opposite of MacIntyre and go right to one of his rotation starters to pitch to Kosko. Long time Sox veteran Harry Bloom has had the most rest and is no stranger to these kinds of situations.

Nick situates himself in, once Bloom is ready. Jack does what Jack does best and tries to intimidate the new pitcher by hopping back and forth along the third baseline to get in his head. As Bloom goes into his windup, Jack sprints down the baseline and casually heads back to the bag. The ball hits the dirt, and Harrow scoops it to a stand to force Jack back to third faster. Bloom figures he won't steal, but a hit-and-run is likely. However, Jack did take a chance earlier in the game by stretching that destined triple to a home run.

Jack knows he's in Bloom's head, wondering if he's going to steal. When the pitcher winds up, Jack starts to sprint again, leaving the bag at a considerable distance.

"Is he going?!" Grainger yells.

The ball sails with accidental and serious hang, which Nick doesn't sit on and ropes along the left field line. The field judge waves his arms to his left to show it fair. Jack easily scores and Lou tries to do the same, but Sox left fielder Kyle Kennedy is quick to the ball and relays it in to force the Hawks shortstop in a running error that costs his team a second out. But the damage has already been done. The Hawks have taken the lead 3-2.

After a third out, Rupland fans and teammates that leave the dugout to take the field, each hold three fingers high in the air, indicating the number of outs they need to win the game.

"Rupland is three outs away from greatness!" Reese says.

Jack's limp has worsened the last half inning. He breathes harder than normal now too. The amount of effort and drive the fearless catcher has displayed is the stuff of legends.

Top of the 9th inning. Joe faces Sox star, Kanter, to start. After he misses a nasty cut-fastball, Kanter takes Joe's following circle changeup for a base hit to right field.

Joe gets the baseball back. He's quite upset with himself, knowing he shouldn't have thrown that changeup. Now he's put a runner on with no outs. Jack motions him to calm himself and extends his right leg and crouches very low. Joe exhales deep and works his next batter, Harrow, much better, getting him to bite on two low-inside throws. With his next pitch, Joe comes from the stretch and out-classes him with a tight slider that the Sox catcher couldn't resist swinging at for an out.

Five and six hitters Kennedy and Leigh don't let Joe fool them, each poke base hits into the outfield to load the bases with just one out. Joe knows he might be yanked after this. MacIntyre has since sent rotation starter Mack Moore to warm in the event he has to enter to relieve.

"Trouble brewing with bases loaded," Reese broadcasts.

Jack starts to make a move for the mound, but when he sees that expression of determination in the rookie's face, he stops himself. In Jack's experience, these are the moments that define greatness. Some rise to the occasion and others accept defeat. It's players like Charlie and Cain that when their back is against the wall, they don't succumb to the pressure, they embrace it. The look Joe is giving him is wonderfully telling he thinks.

Jack squats and signs for nothing but breaking balls. The more Joe can force grounders for a double play the better. Jack's wound begins to bleed through his bandages.

Nolan has good odds here, hoping the momentum of Joe's bad luck continues with his atbat. Joe sizes him up and doesn't cower from the challenge. He fires three devilish pitches that Nolan must take a hack at. Each are whiffs, the last spinning him like a top.

The left-handed hitting Steinberg walks to the plate. Jack can let Joe loose a bit now with a few high-and-insides or low-and-aways since they have two outs. These are spots Jack knows that Steinberg notoriously can't hit for shit. The pitch Joe throws is high and in, but not enough to touch the zone, for a ball. Jack frames low for the next pitch and Steinberg misses it for strike one. Jack urges Joe to try high again. He does, but the rookie misses again for another ball. Jack figures a change in placement could work since Joe isn't hitting his spots well, and Steinberg isn't biting anyway. Out and in might do the trick, and he signals and frames as such. Joe throws a wild back door slider that goes front door instead, bouncing in the dirt and flies out of the reach of Jack. It's far enough for Kanter to make a move for home, however.

"Runners are off . . . " Reese announces.

Jack gets to and retrieves the ball at the farthest end of the backstop, then flees back towards the plate. Joe is running in from the mound but is slow and won't be able to make it in time for the tag. Kanter glides into a feet-first slide. Jack lunges forward in the air like Superman, extending his mitt as far as he can to tag him. Kanter's right foot touches the back corner of the plate, but not in time as Jack has since tagged the star on his thigh.

"Out!" The umpire dramatically calls and signals. "Out!"

Pandemonium explodes in the park. Jack's teammates from the field and the dugout pile on top of him at home.

"Rupland wins it!" Reese announces.

The Rupland crowd is a mixed bowl of emotions. Some cry, some scream with joy, and others just watch the celebration in silent contentment.

Amidst his celebration with fans, James detects Jack squeeze from the mob of players, his mask, and glove left behind in the pile. He just stands there grinning and staring ahead at nothing in somewhat of a euphoric state. Without his team noticing, he collapses to the ground.

What was bliss turns into sheer horror. James scurries down the stands, pushing through celebrating fans to make his way on the field. Nick eventually sees his friend lying on the ground and rushes to his side. Flipping over his lifeless body to cradle him, he realizes there is something very wrong and immediately waves teammates to him for help.

CHAPTER 8 — FALL OF '06

"Baseball died on August 5th, 2006."
—Unknown Rupland Fan

COLORFUL TREES OF RUPLAND begin to lose their leaves. It is deep into fall, and winter is right around the corner. Baseball has disappeared, and the sense of football looms.

Most rooms in the Dalton house are dark, and packed boxes clutter just about every corner. Gathered around the dejected dinner table are James, Joe, Sandy, and Katie who is feeding baby Jake in his high chair.

Boisterous laughter and conversation filled this table not long ago. The boys would compliment Sandy's delicious cooking, and there wouldn't be any leftovers to speak of. Every so often, someone will glance at the two empty chairs that Jack and Johnny used to sit in. Family dinners will never be the same again.

Jack was put in the ground on a Thursday. The coroner explained to his family that his heart simply gave out due to a congenital heart disease. With age, the disease worsened. Not only did this go undetected by others, but Jack managed to keep it a secret from everyone upon discovering it. A secret that if revealed, would've prevented him from ever playing baseball.

Everything came to light from the revealing of his secret. The heart medication that was found in his apartment. A doctor in Dixon who first diagnosed Jack, and remained his physician for three years after. Not a fan of sports himself, the doctor didn't even know Jack was playing baseball. There was Kelly, the drug dealer who worked at the pharmacy that Jack paid to provide him with under the table medication he couldn't afford without decent insurance. Jack kept his secret from everyone—family, friends, teammates, and coaches. No one knew. While it was frustrating to discover it this way, they could understand his actions.

Later this afternoon, the family closes Rupland Family Foods for good. While media exposure from the tournament brings a hearty cash flow to keep the town afloat, including the store, it's seasonal at best. Steady decline throughout the years takes its toll, and the death of their sons is far too great for James and Sandy to continue living in Rupland.

James strips the flag from the store's front, while Sandy places a *For Sale* sign in the window. With Joe's help, they finish any last-minute cleaning, including dusting the empty shelves, sweeping the floors that never seemed quite clean enough, and wiping the coolers down. Joe wraps a chain around the front doors and locks them. They leave the store a shell of what it once was. A few businesses would later take over the space: a bait shop, a feed store, and even a gas station, but those too succumb to the bad economy of the area. A decade later, the building was left abandoned.

Leaving the farm is even harder on the Daltons. For James and Sandy, they raised their children here. Memories of everything that made them a family and the closeness they shared here seems like the end of an era—an era they don't want to see end but know they must.

Joe remembers every inch of these eighty acres he and his brothers used to roam. The tree forts they played war games in feels like yesterday. He remembers the steep sledding hills behind their house and the ones with groups of birch trees in the middle of them that they'd bet each other to sled down, knowing an injury awaited them before reaching the bottom. He remembers the many camping spots his father took them to, fishing in the ponds and lakes and shooting an arsenal of guns from their father's impressive collection at the dilapidated shacks surrounding the property. He remembers the many deer and small game hunting seasons that graced their dinner table with plenty of meat. And the endless hiking trails that wrapped around the property and showed just how gorgeous their land truly was.

Joe remembers a time when a thirteen-year-old Johnny stole his dad's truck and went mudding on the trails in the back forty. He was able to return it before James could discover it missing. Unfortunately, the lie didn't last long when James found his truck a mess and the bumper practically hanging from its hinges the following day.

Joe remembers Jack dragging him and Johnny, rain or shine, to not only play baseball but just about every sport imaginable. Or the times Jack was left in charge while both parents were at work. Those were opportunities for his older brothers to antagonize him. There was a time Joe thinks of where he and his brothers were left alone, and a tornado touched down. Jack put a then five-year-old Joe in a wagon tied to his bike, and the brothers foolishly rode to a distant neighbor's house for fear their house would blow away.

A week later, the day came. Moving day. Katie buckles baby Jake in a car seat in James' truck that Joe drives. James cradles Daggett with both hands and places him in the backseat of the truck as well. The last time he even carried the dog was when he was a puppy.

Katie's father moved across the country for work, and the Daltons, wanting to stay close with Jake and Katie, were able to find her a job downstate near where they bought a new house. Sandy loves having Katie around. Her hard-working attitude and maturity that developed after Jake was born fits right in with the Daltons. She's become the daughter Sandy never had.

James does a last check of the property to make sure they haven't forgotten anything. He then locks the full U-Haul that's parked in front of Joe and steps inside it, where his wife sits on the passenger side. Both vehicles drive down the road, away from the farm. James takes a final glimpse back at it through his side mirror. *This place was supposed to be perfect,* he thinks to himself. The cruelness of the hand the family has been dealt is far beyond his comprehension.

Though James and Sandy will never speak aloud of Rupland, to Joe it wasn't entirely bad. It remains a place he always holds close in his thoughts. Maybe it's the unique people. Maybe the old-fashioned bucolic setting or the nostalgia it brings—he'll never be sure. But it's there he knows that his family truly became close. Of course, their end there was tragic, yet he knows those years were something else. Those years were the best of their lives.

EPILOGUE

July 15th, 2011

THE CRISP AIR OF SUMMER, the eye-pinching, slightly metallic and burnt-flesh smell of cheap hot dogs in soggy buns, and leather, dirt, freshly cut grass and discount beer—lots of beer. It was baseball season. My season.

Down a dark tunnel, a flash of white uniforms with navy blue lettering ran toward a bright light that beamed from the afternoon sun. I remained in the tunnel long after they left. Me, a husky six-foot four-inch, broad shouldered rookie. My nerves were laughable to anyone that saw me. Let's not sugar coat it, they were pathetic. And I was one of those finicky bastards with a tic, so I kept fidgeting with the belt to my baggy pants, not giving a thought to what I would do if they dropped from my ass. Whatever. The humiliation wouldn't nearly be as bad if I played poorly on that day.

When I reached the light at the end of the tunnel, I stopped. Mostly because I dropped my glove out of nervousness. If not for the hint of orange on it, I would've surely lost it in the dark crevasses of the tunnel. Come to think of it, I played every game with that glove. Never once did I change it for another, even after the laces needed to be replaced. Maybe it was my egotistical youth, but I always thought Nokona surely made that glove for me. Like it was meant to be.

Looking out of that tunnel, a dream of a field awaited me. God, it was gorgeous. The chalked lines were pearl white and stretched to their 345 foot left and 330 foot right sides of the field. A sea of Kentucky Bluegrass in the outfield and the golden brown dirt in the infield was almost too perfect, even for this shit-kicker. Must've been a crowd of 38,000 surrounding that masterpiece. There were familiar sounds of anticipation and maybe even glory to some. My Major League Baseball debut. I made the show. My road to get there was long and bumpy but well worth the journey.

From what would go down as 'the legendary tournament of 2006,' college and pro scouts were able to sign a record-breaking 24 players from the Summer League. Having showed, what one scout told me, superior arm strength and solid command, I was able to garner a few scholarship offers of my own, mostly from the Big Ten. Michigan State had my commitment from day one though. Being closer to my family was of the upmost importance. They needed me.

After two losing seasons with no real accolades, a position switch to third base, and a favorable scouting report that set my draft-ability within the first 10 rounds, I decided to officially enter the 2009 MLB First-Year Player Draft. To my pleasant surprise, the Detroit Tigers selected me in the 5th round. I was so damn humbled.

I played well enough to rise through their Minors, and the time finally came on my mom's birthday when the big club called me up from Toledo to be the first person in my family to become a Major Leaguer. My parents attended almost every home game from that point forward.

I remember my debut vividly. Even the tiniest of details. Before I exited the tunnel that day, I took a moment to observe my brother Johnny's dog tags that proudly hung around my neck, and what it meant to wear Jack's number 12 on my back. Although my brothers stayed in my thoughts, it was my time to shine for once, and I never took that for granted. When I finally left that tunnel, the next chapter of my life began.

Now, I'd like to say that I had a Hall of Fame career, but my time as a pro was short-lived. In the last game of the 2012 season against the Kansas City Royals, a devastating knee injury on a shallow infield fly not only effectively ended my chances of helping the team in their great World Series run but ended my career as well. Still, great memories remained. After baseball, I became a skilled welder, like my dad. The trade landed me in a shipyard, where I worked on Great Lakes freighters. Not a bad gig at all.

Although my life moved on, Rupland was never far from my thoughts. I never forgot those years we lived there. For the next decade after 2006, the town became a summer tourist destination, reminiscent of the Baseball Hall of Fame in Cooperstown. Much like surrounding county parks, Oren P. Rollins Field remained intact as a monument and baseball museum of sorts.

Visitors would come from miles away to ogle over the once-secret league's heroes, the chronicled timeline, and the storied moments that gave baseball's history further admiration. Thinking back, my hometown was never more alive than during the summer. Those precious moments became frozen in their history.

As years passed, the interstate grew through the county, and the town was completely bypassed, or at most, a gas-filling destination for travelers. With the population's decline, the school system lost enrollment too and then decisively closed its doors for good. The appealing baseball allure Rupland had maintained was gone, and nature claimed it, leaving it an abandoned, overgrown ghost town.

Friends, teammates, and coaches stayed in contact with my family and me for a few years after my brothers' deaths, but over time, they too, would lose touch as life goes. Manager MacIntyre retired after the tournament and stayed in Rupland for the rest of his life. His daughter, Coach Sarah, left a year after the tourney and followed in her father's footsteps of coaching when she took an offer to manage a D1 college softball program. Coach Roberts moved westward to Colorado, where he became a long haul trucker.

I heard Charlie Hylman went on to coach a D2 college ball team in his home state of Texas. He even brought Cain onboard as part of his staff. The hire proved successful, as the duo accumulated many wins together. Cain stayed on the staff for three seasons. During these years he shed his playboy ways and settled down with a ball-busting English professor, almost eighteen years his senior. After the birth of his first child, he and his family migrated to the east coast, and no one really heard from him again.

Following the tournament, the Milwaukee Brewers offered Lou a professional contract. After spending a season with the Double-A affiliate Huntsville Stars, he hung his cleats up for good and took his parents' advice to pursue employment in the medical field. By the time he graduated medical school and officially became a doctor, he was in his early 30s. He eventually started his own practice, which was very successful.

Nick Kosko was one of a few teammates to remain in Rupland. He opened his own auto shop there before opening a second in Clarkston a decade later. He'd never speak or hear from his father again until 2016 when he got news of George's passing of a heroin overdose in prison.

My parents didn't speak of the deaths of their sons ever again. I could recall just twice when they would even come close. A while before his own passing, during one of our many fishing excursions that became tradition between us and my nephew Jake, Dad explained to me how he felt responsible for the tragedies in our family. He spoke of a deal made with God in Vietnam, and how he had to pay that debt, he thought. That deal he said was "fucked from the start." To him, it was a curse. His curse. And our family suffered greatly because of it. He revealed to me the constant dream that terrorized him for so many years, and how it played differently one night, shortly after Jack's funeral. Uncle Jacob let him try to save those soldiers that were being dragged away from the blast hole. What seemed like forever, Dad eventually reached the Marines, but it was too late. They had perished. When he flipped the bodies, their identities were finally shown to him after trying to discover who they were and why they were important for so long. The bodies were Jack and Johnny's. That was the last time Dad ever had that dream. I never forgot that grave conversation with him. His words haunted me every day after.

Mom mentioned something about my brothers a while after Dad was gone. This day was particularly important. It was the 16th birthday of my first born; a beautiful girl my wife and I named June. Her birthday was of significance, as it was the date of Jack's death, which would forever coincide with the Hawks' championship victory. While Mom and I stood back and admired June blowing out the candles on her cake, Mom whispered to me, asking if I ever thought of my brothers much. I said, "Of course."

She went on to say, "Always remember them, Joe, because they were the truth . . . They were beautiful."

The older I got, I came to the conclusion that maybe what happened was meant to be. Maybe Jack and Johnny's purposes were greater than our family could ever imagine. There are other times I wondered if I was just competing against ghosts.

When my nephew Jake turned thirty, I brought him back to where everything began. There we saw the gravesites. It was the first time I had returned to my hometown since moving away, and it was the first time Jake had even seen his father's final resting place. My brothers' tombstones sat next to one another, each with a thin film of moss covering them. I should've brought something to clean them up. Wherever they are, I could hear Jack and Johnny bitching at me to get my shit together. But I made good. I made sure to tell Jake every single story of them that I could remember.

As the day went on, we visited Oren P. Rollins Field. To my surprise, there was nothing left but ruins around patchy, colorless grass at the end of a stretch of uneven asphalt that was once the parking lot. Weeds had crept into the cracks of it. Looking at the pitiful site, it was hard to imagine a ballfield ever being there, if not for the graffiti-marked statue of Oren P. Rollins that still stood in front of the ruins. That commemorative piece that fans used to touch before they entered was left to the birds, who perched and shit all over it. Such a travesty. Certainly, I thought, this was the site of baseball's death.

When Jake and I drove to the Little League field, we found the dugouts were the only structures still standing. I don't like to admit it, but I had a good cry when we came across the wall full of carved-names that miraculously was still intact. The names were mostly faded, but I could still make out my own, my brothers, and people I remembered.

By day's end, we drove through the rundown neighborhoods and vacant streets of the destitute town's limits. It was dingy and forsaken. Whatever twinkle and competitive excitement there once was had vanished.

I couldn't help but humbly smile when every elderly local we spoke to when walking downtown or eating at Karen's diner—yes, it was still in business—each fondly remembered the league and the tournament that they still held dear in their hearts. These were memories and stories that were passed on to their own families. Each conversation they would constantly rave about three things that they and even former locals proudly took claim to, like their own badge of honor. They'd say during the league's heyday that they "lived in God's country." That they "lived in the times of pure baseball." That they "lived in the times of the Dalton boys."

The End

About the Author

 Michael Dault was born in Norfolk, Virginia, and raised in the beauty of Michigan's Upper Peninsula in a small town called Republic. A former sports writer and one-time professional baseball prospect, he currently owns and operates his own film/television production company—TipToe Pictures.

CPSIA information can be obtained
at www.ICGtesting.com
Printed in the USA
BVHW041826050521
606581BV00022B/344